The Empress and the Bishop

The Triumphs and Tragedy of John Chrysostom

— PATRICK WHITWORTH —

Sacristy Press

Sacristy Press
PO Box 612, Durham, DH1 9HT

www.sacristy.co.uk

First published in 2024 by Sacristy Press, Durham

Copyright © Patrick Whitworth 2024
The moral rights of the author have been asserted.

Maps copyright ©Kevin Sheehan 2024

All rights reserved, no part of this publication may be reproduced or transmitted in any form or by any means, electronic, mechanical photocopying, documentary, film or in any other format without prior written permission of the publisher.

All Scripture quotations, unless otherwise indicated, are taken from the Holy Bible, New International Version®, NIV®. Copyright ©1973, 1978, 1984, 2011 by Biblica, Inc.™ Used by permission of Zondervan. All rights reserved worldwide. www.zondervan.com The "NIV" and "New International Version" are trademarks registered in the United States Patent and Trademark Office by Biblica, Inc.™

Every reasonable effort has been made to trace the copyright holders of material reproduced in this book, but if any have been inadvertently overlooked the publisher would be glad to hear from them.

Sacristy Limited, registered in England & Wales, number 7565667

British Library Cataloguing-in-Publication Data
A catalogue record for the book is available from the British Library

Paperback ISBN 978-1-78959-370-9
Hardback ISBN 978-1-78959-385-3

To the Ecumenical Patriarch Bartholomew

Archbishop of Constantinople–New Rome

Successor of St John Chrysostom

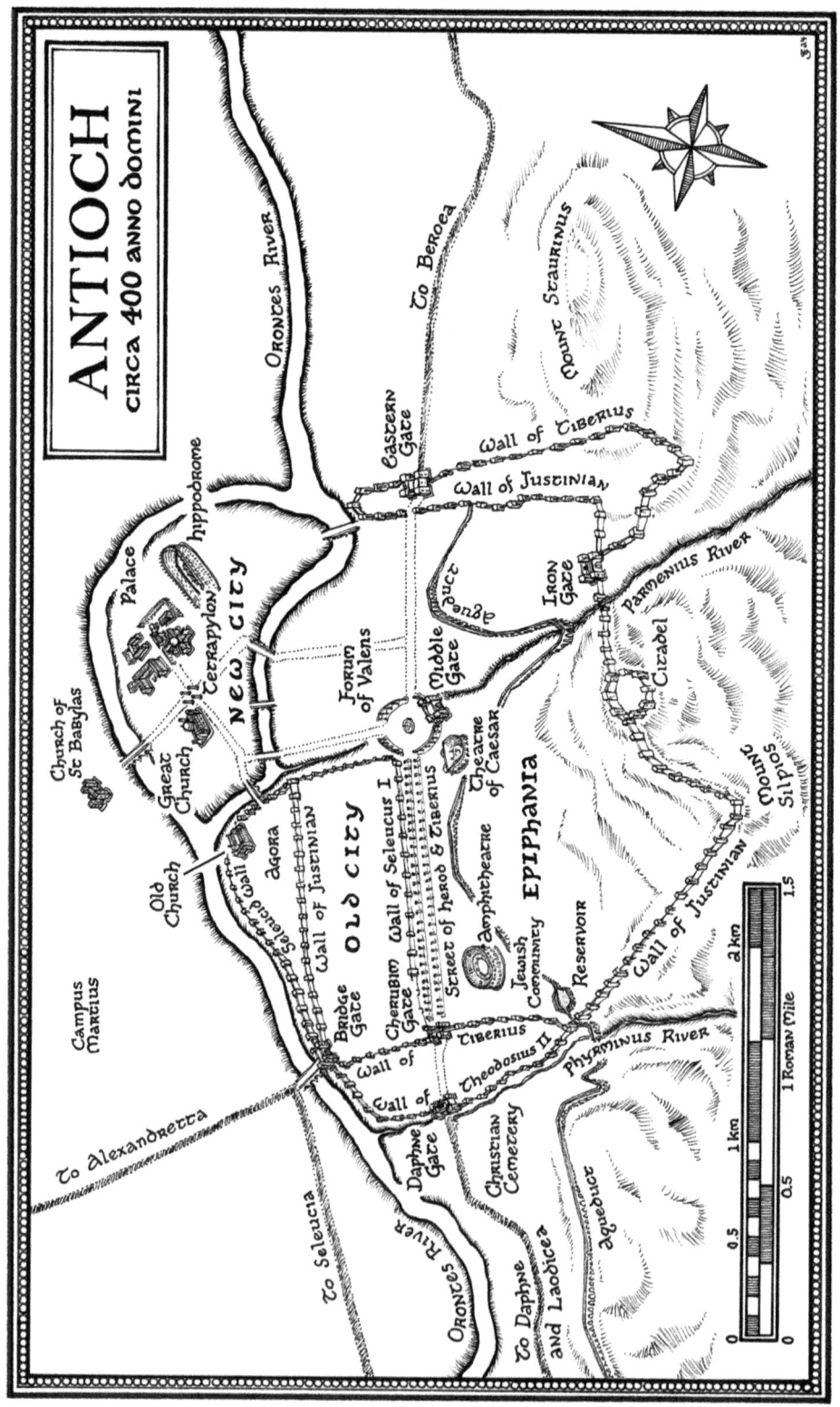

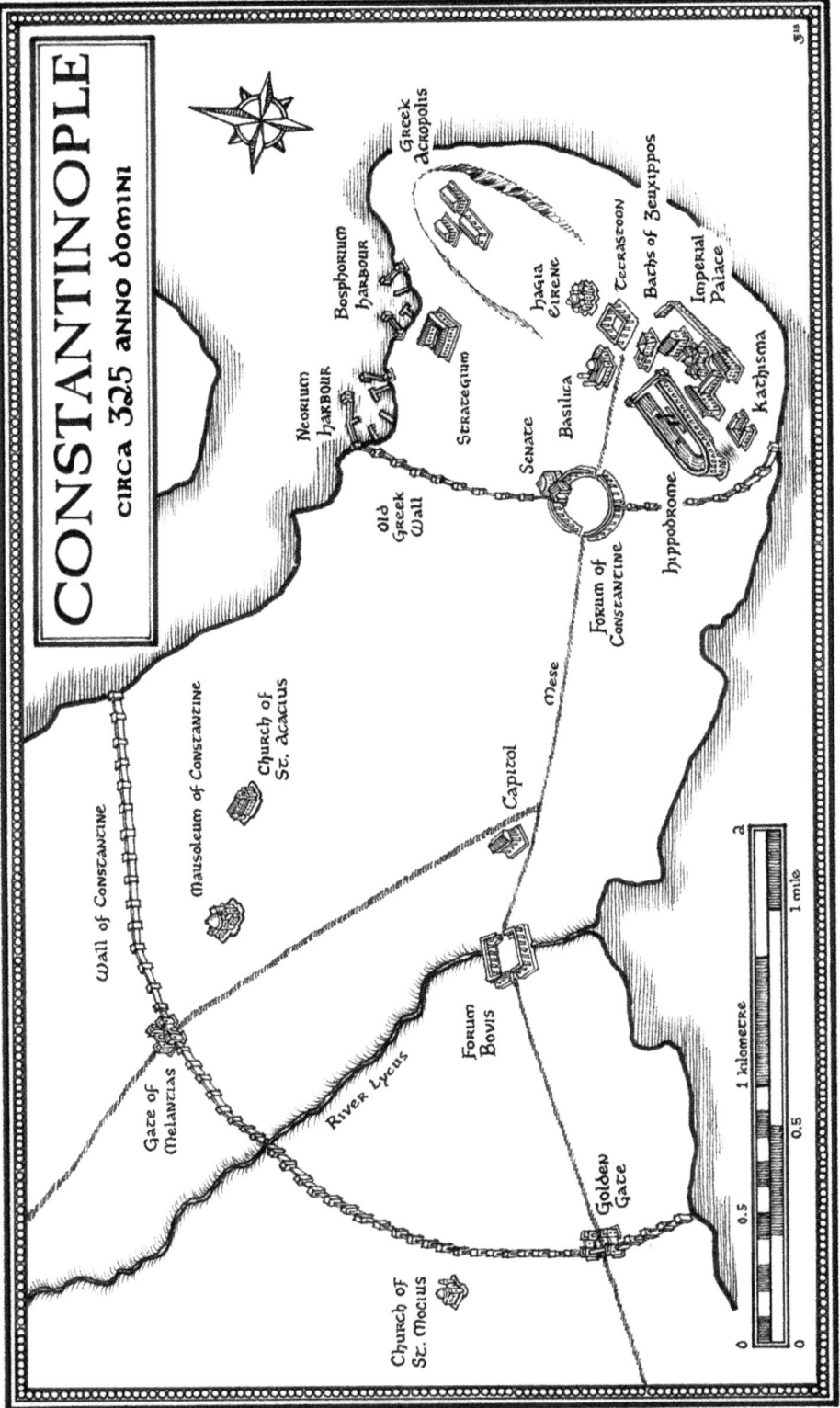

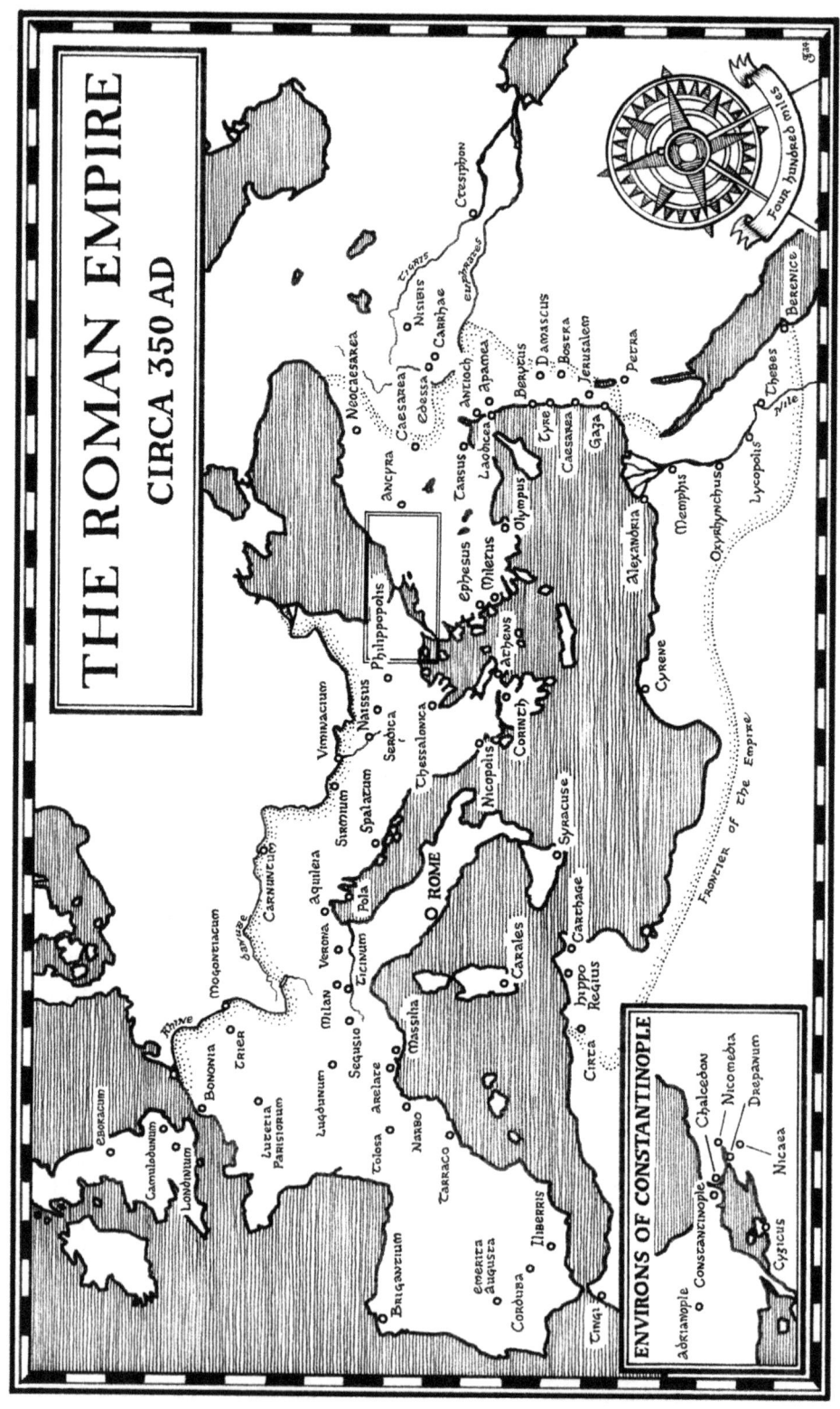

Contents

Foreword .... **viii**
Preface... **x**

Chapter 1. The empire after Constantine the Great 1
Chapter 2. The Church in the fourth century 19
Chapter 3. A tale of four cities: Antioch, Constantinople,
    Alexandria and Rome 41
Chapter 4. John Chrysostom: Early years and vocation 61
Chapter 5. Pastor, polemicist and preacher 81
Chapter 6. Church and State 103
Chapter 7. A new broom in Constantinople...................... 115
Chapter 8. A city of God 133
Chapter 9. A eunuch, a Gothic commander and the empress 167
Chapter 10. Ecclesiastical politics............................. 185
Chapter 11. The gathering storm 195
Chapter 12. The last exile 213
Chapter 13. The final journey 231

Timeline **246**
Dramatis personae **249**
Glossary of terms **257**
Abbreviations **258**
Primary sources **259**
Bibliography **264**
Index **267**

Foreword

It is with joyful appreciation that we welcome *The Empress and The Bishop: The Triumphs and Tragedy of John Chrysostom*, a biographical work authored by Canon Patrick Whitworth, in honor of our venerated predecessor in the Most Holy Archepiscopal See of Constantine's City.

John Chrysostom, a colossally eloquent and erudite luminary of the Early Church, assumed the weighty mantle of Archbishop of Constantinople from AD 397 to 407, during a period marked by tumultuous upheaval within the Roman Empire. Elevated to the Episcopacy toward the waning years of the fourth century, John's tenure did not bear witness to the fall of the Roman Empire's Western domain and the lamentable sack of Rome in AD 410, an event transpiring merely three years following his passing. Concurrently, in the East, the Empire endured for another millennium, until the fateful conquest of Constantinople–New Rome on 29 May 1453, by the Ottoman Sultanate.

John Chrysostom's era was beset by strife and discord. Born in the great city of Antioch, where his influential ministry as a presbyter and preacher resonated deeply, he was summoned by Emperor Arcadius to Constantinople–New Rome, the capital of the Eastern Empire. Arcadius, son of Emperor Theodosius I the Great, was wedded to Aelia Eudoxia, an empress consort who exerted significant influence over the Eastern Empire due to her husband's susceptibility and inexperience.

The narrative of John Chrysostom reminds us that Christian martyria is often marked by strength of spirit in light of tribulation, even amidst the most unforeseen adversities. Upon his arrival in Constantinople in AD 397, John brought with him a formidable reputation as a preacher, pastor, writer, and ascetic. Yet, against the workings of Constantinopolitan affairs, encompassing the imperial court, governmental institutions, and military echelons, his archpastoral ministry encountered formidable barriers, and his eminent oratory prowess, which earned him the epithet "Golden Mouth," often fueled the very flames of his own suffering.

The machinations of the court, the aspirations of the empress, the specter of Gothic incursions, and, gravely, opposition from the See of Alexandria, transformed his hope-bearing tenure into a harrowing and martyric ordeal. Falsely accused and subsequently exiled, John found himself estranged, separated from intimate confidants, including the venerable Abbess Olympias the Deaconess, whose moving correspondence with Chrysostom is preserved to this day. His life culminated in exile along the borders of Georgia and Armenia, solitary and drained, yet bestowing an enduring legacy to posterity.

This legacy reverberates emphatically within the sacred halls of the Holy and Great Church of Christ, located in Constantinople—present-day Istanbul—to this day. His liturgical compositions, immortalized in symphonic melodies by preeminent composers, continue to ignite the fervor of our worship. His exegetical elucidations of the New Testament invigorate and fortify our spirits. His life's example instills jubilation and unswerving conviction in the face of endless and furious affliction.

In presenting this seminal biography written by Canon Patrick Whitworth, which offers a fresh perspective on John Chrysostom's remarkable life, we ardently anticipate its contribution towards a deeper understanding of our eminent predecessor and extend our paternal and Patriarchal blessings to you, the reader, as you immerse yourself in its pages.

At the Ecumenical Patriarchate, on 30 March 2024
    Your fervent supplicant before God,

+Bartholomew
Archbishop of Constantinople–New Rome and Ecumenical Patriarch

Preface

Every so often a city resonates with a single voice. In Athens, in the fourth century BC, it was Demosthenes. But in the Christian era other voices came to resonate and reverberate through other cities: none more so than John Chrysostom, first in Antioch and then later in Constantinople. In other eras, Savonarola's preaching (1452–98) came to dominate Florence in the late fifteenth century, and likewise the Reformer John Calvin in Geneva in the sixteenth century. In London, in the nineteenth century, the preaching of Charles Haddon Spurgeon held thousands transfixed, and when he died an unknown number lined the streets of London, with 800 extra police on duty.

Chrysostom bestrode first Antioch and then Constantinople. Chrysostom means "Golden Mouth" in Greek, and the epithet was truly deserved by a man educated in the Greek and Roman classics but then immersed in the Bible. His pagan teacher Libanius considered him the finest orator of his age, speaking in impeccable Attic Greek but able skilfully, vividly and compellingly to engage with his audience in an everyday and almost informal way, although he was also no stranger to theatricality; and his life would give him his fair share of dramatic moments whilst preaching. His themes were the need to help the poor, the right use of power, the necessity of leading a moral life and the majesty of Christ as the resurrected, redeeming, eternal Lord summoning all from death to life. What John gave the Church more than any other Church Father was the example of preaching through Scripture in a sequential verse-by-verse way. If others did this, none did it so comprehensively as he did, although events, especially in Constantinople, would interrupt this attempt at what became known as expositional preaching, in which the preacher let loose the Word.

If John was a preacher, he was also a monk. Before he was ordained, like so many of the very serious Christians of his age, he sought prayerful isolation, and drastic asceticism, and struggled to overcome sexual desire. A life of chastity, in both spirit and body, and of poverty, in terms of simplicity and renunciation, was the tenor of his whole life; and he would commend it passionately to others. The result was that he could be both severe and soft: severe in the sense that he had little time for warm hospitality and for social life, soft in that he forgave quickly without imposing the tariff of penances which had become well established by the late fourth century. He regarded women too often as a threat to male holiness; and when it came to handling the mercurial and exotic empress, half his age, he started by flattering her but then regarded her as a latter-day Jezebel. A more temperate approach would have been more fruitful. In alienating the court, he opened the way for his enemies, who were, for the most part, his ecclesial opponents, and in particular the Patriarch Theophilus of Alexandria. Theophilus was resentful of a new ecclesiastical centre emerging in the recently founded Rome of the east, Constantinople. He was determined to bring John down, which he did through trumped-up charges and through people whom John had upset.

John would die in exile. His chief correspondent was the Abbess Olympias, with whom he had a moving correspondence as she shared his painful fate, and he shared her unremitting depression, responding with advice that failed to shift it. In Constantinople the ordinary people remained true to him, even if the court sought to denigrate his memory. But a campaign in Rome and Antioch, and the death of his opponents, would lead to his eventual posthumous rehabilitation as one of the great bishops of Constantinople.

John was undoubtedly one of the great preachers of the first 400 years of the Early Church. He also had a vision of transforming a city not only through preaching but also through prayer and liturgy. He would give his name to the great Eucharistic liturgy of the Orthodox Church, much later set to music by the greatest composers like Rachmaninov. These were occasions of worship when earth touched heaven and were filled with the numinous and the transcendent power of Christ. It was on such an occasion some centuries later that the ambassadors from Rus experienced this heavenly vision not knowing "whether they were on earth or in heaven" and commended the faith to their ruler in Kyiv.

Alongside these means of grace was a vision of myriad Christian households in the city which would be like "little churches", where the head of the house would be as much pastor as ruler, where the scriptures would be honoured and discussed, where slavery would be all but commuted into household service, where the poor would be remembered and chastity observed. It was a transforming vision fed by the teaching from the scriptures and the worship of the Church. It remained an enduring vision too.

The story of Chrysostom has been faithfully told previously, notably by J. N. D. Kelly in 1995 and much earlier by the German Benedictine monk Chrysostomus Baur in 1910. My own researches were much enlivened by a meeting with the community of the Ecumenical Orthodox Patriarchate in Istanbul in 2022. I was given an icon of John Chrysostom, and I am very grateful to His All Holiness Bartholomew, The Ecumenical Patriarch of Constantinople, for writing the foreword to the current book. Once again, I am grateful to Sacristy Press and my editor Dr Natalie K. Watson, to Professor Mark Edwards for his help with this period, to Marian Aird for the index, and to Olivia, my wife, for her support in tackling yet another of the Early Church Fathers.

Patrick Whitworth
27 January 2024
Feast of John Chrysostom, Teacher of the Faith
and Bishop of Constantinople

1

The empire after Constantine the Great

Constantine the Great, the first Christian Roman emperor, died on the Feast of Pentecost, 22 May 337. Chrysostom was born some 14 years later in 351. Eusebius, Bishop of Caesarea and Constantine's biographer, tells us that as soon as Constantine expired

> the assembled spearman and bodyguard rent their garments, and prostrated themselves on the ground, striking their heads, and uttering lamentations and cries of sorrow, calling on their imperial lord and master, or rather like true children, on their father, while the tribunes and centurions addressed him as their preserver, protector and benefactor.[1]

It was a fitting demonstration of mourning for an emperor who had ruled for more than 30 years from the time he was first declared *augustus* in the West, in 306 in York.

Having fallen ill some weeks before and sensing that his end was near, Constantine had requested baptism, casting aside the outward vesture of an emperor, the gold and purple tunic, to become a simple candidate for baptism. He was baptized like all neophytes, in a white shroud, "seeking purification from sins of his past career".[2] Baptized in Nicomedia by a group of bishops, Constantine became "a partaker of the mystic ordinance". As Eusebius wrote, he was

> the first of all sovereigns who was regenerated and perfected in a church dedicated to the martyrs of Christ; thus, gifted with the divine seal of baptism, he rejoiced in spirit, was renewed, and filled with heavenly light: his soul was gladdened by reason of the

fervency of his faith, and he was astonished at the manifestation of the power of God.[3]

In fact, he was regarded by some as another apostle, and was to be buried in the Church of the Apostles in his city, Constantinople.

Constantine's reign had ushered in a new era, but not in the way that governments often say they will be doing, and in effect seldom do. Constantine had indeed begun a new epoch, which lasted until the twentieth century in various forms, undergirding as it did the very notion of Christendom. His body, which was now the preserve of his successors, was taken with due solemnity from the palace at Nicomedia across the Sea of Marmara to the new Rome, now called Constantinople: the emperor's new eponymous capital. He was laid in a golden coffin on a catafalque surrounded by candles and upon it the symbols of sovereignty: the diadem and a purple robe. There he was watched day and night by attendants. Surely this was the pattern of obsequies set for monarchs throughout Europe, not least in Britain, as was witnessed after the death of Queen Elizabeth II. Counts, magistrates, senators and officers of all kinds came to pay their respects, and then "multitudes of every rank" attended his lying-in-state. Pointedly, he was buried in Constantinople's newly built Church of the Apostles.

Constantine had a large family. From 307, he had been happily married to Fausta, who had given him three sons: Constantine II (*b*.316), Constantius II (*b*.317), and Constans (*b*.323), all of whom would become *augusti* in succession from 337, as planned. However, Fausta had been mysteriously removed from all public records in 326, when Crispus, Constantine's son from an earlier marriage, was executed.[4] His hitherto beloved wife Fausta appears to have been ostracized at the same time. Some think the two may have had an affair and that Constantine, in a fit of overwhelming temper, punished them both, but we shall never truly know. What we do know is that Constantius, the second son and the one who would rule longest following Constantine the Great, handled the funeral arrangements.

Shortly after Constantine's death, in August 337, there was bloodletting in part of the imperial family. In fact, all the children and grandchildren of Constantine's stepmother Theodora were massacred, except for Julian and one other. Julian was then only six years old and would eventually become emperor himself, whereupon he would attempt to restore paganism. In his *Decline and Fall*, Gibbon called this purge a "promiscuous massacre",[5] and it is quite probable that Constantius was involved.[6]

Constantine's successors

Constantine's family would rule until 363, and it would be during this period, during the reign of Constantius II, that John Chrysostom would be born in the East in 349. Many of the events to shape the empire in this post-Constantine era would become familiar to John. In the imperial centre of Antioch, he would have heard stories about Constantine the Great, about the scramble for power between the emperor's three sons, and the emergence of Constantius in the East. Constantine II, the oldest of Constantine's heirs, had begun positioning himself in June, scarcely days after the burial of his father. It was he who ordered the restoration of exiled bishops such as Athanasius to their sees, and who, for a while, sought to exert control over his youngest brother, Constans. Still in his teens yet ambitious, Constans was keen to secure the western part of the empire in Gaul and Italy. Constantine II, however, wanted greater control and so led an army across the Alps from Gaul to invade northern Italy. Constans sent troops to confront him and managed to ambush Constantine's army near Aquileia, resulting in the death of his brother, whose reign was thus very short. This left Constans in control of the West and Constantius in charge in the East.

After the defeat of Constantine, Constans assumed control of the provinces of the West in Gaul, Italy and North Africa. He created bases both at Trier on the Moselle and at Milan, making just occasional trips to Rome. Nevertheless, the city prefect of Rome, Fabius Titianus, gave his loyalty to Constans in 340, when the latter was still only 17 years old. Constans's youthful reign was marked by vigorous campaigns against old foes like the Franks and Alamanni across the Rhine, and, according to Libanius, in 343 he crossed the Channel in winter with just a hundred soldiers to visit Britain,[7] most probably on an administrative rather than a military visit. There was no shortage of energy in his reign.

For most of the 340s, Constans's rule in the West was stable and effective. He proved a bulwark against the barbarians to the east of the Rhine, maintained the support of Italy, and was influential in North Africa in *Africa Proconsularis*. Following in the footsteps of his father, Constans sought also to strengthen the Christian legacy in both Italy and North Africa. He legislated against paganism, condemning pagan cults in Italy. Later this measure was adopted fully in the *Theodosian Code*, a codification of Roman law enacted in 438 by Theodosius II. Pagan rites and sacrifices were now debarred at temples beyond as well as within Rome's walls.[8] Paganism was on the retreat, vanquished by law. Furthermore, Constans sent a delegation to North Africa in 347, in which two imperial officials, Paul and Macarius, arrived in Carthage to distribute imperial funds to the Church. There they faced the Donatist split in the North African Church, which had so dogged Constantine the Great, and division followed. After the delegation was actively opposed by the Donatist bishop of Bagai, the imperial embassy sent in the troops and the bishop and other Donatists were martyred, further fuelling the controversy. It was one of the first examples of force being used by civic power on behalf of the Church in order to impose either doctrine or church discipline, and was to be a bloody thread in the Church's history thereafter. The Proconsul of Africa issued a decree that henceforth all churches should be controlled by the Catholic (i.e., non-Donatist) bishop of Carthage, but such strong-arm tactics only strengthened the determined resistance of their religious opponents. In fact, the Donatists saw Constans as nothing more than the reincarnation of his imperial pagan predecessors.[9]

If Constans was the principal enemy of the Donatists, to those further east, in Alexandria, he was the principal friend. Athanasius was to side closely with him in opposing his older brother, Constantius II, who had sided with the anti-Nicene party, backing their attempt to water down the doctrine of *homoousios* in the Nicene Creed (in which the Son was declared as being of the same substance as the Father). We thus have the ironic situation of Constans being bitterly opposed by the puritan Donatists in *Africa Proconsularis* and championed by the Nicene party in Alexandria and in Rome. For his part, Constans, who sought to weaken his brother's rule, supported those who, like Athanasius, were thorns in Constantius II's side. Such was the intermingling of political and ecclesiastical disputes in the fourth century.

Although Constans supported Athanasius's campaign against Constantius, either from Christian conviction or realpolitik, the latter was not prepared to stand idly by when a usurper threatened the Western empire, and indeed destroyed Constans. The usurper, Flavius Magnus Magnentius, whom one tradition gives a Frankish mother and a Breton father, represented a new breed of barbarian-commander in the Roman army. He sought permanent power in the Constantinian family by marrying Justina, great-granddaughter of Constantine the Great, and later the wife of Valentinian I.[10] Because of widespread disaffection with Constans, possibly due to his unruly court with its reputation for licentiousness, Magnentius was able to obtain the support of the Gallic prefecture, which included Gaul and Spain. Furthermore, he was able to gain support in Italy and North Africa, even though Rome itself was subject to its own microclimate of politics and rebellion, centring on one Julius Nepotianus, a descendant of Constantine's half-sister Eutropia, who briefly held sway in Rome.

By January 350, Magnentius had been proclaimed *augustus* of the West by the army that had deserted Constans (himself killed in the same year). Magnentius was to govern the Western empire between 350 and 353, although another usurper, Vetranio, came to the fore in Lower Pannonia (present-day Croatia). As a former *magister peditum* (Master of the Foot), Vetranio was popular with his troops and used by Constantius as a buttress against the encroaching power of Magnentius.

While all this was going on, as so often with Eastern emperors, Constantius was engaged in restricting Persian power on the Tigris at Nisibis (present-day Nusaybin in eastern Turkey). As soon as he could, he extracted himself from that campaign and marched to the Balkans to face down Magnentius in the last weeks of 350. Vetranio swiftly supported Constantius but was divested of his command and went into retirement. Gallus, a cousin of the childless Constantius, was created heir and Caesar (in effect Constantius's deputy). And amazingly, with so much at stake, Constantius still had time to call a church council at Sirmium in 351, where Bishop Photinus of Sirmium was condemned for his heretical views on the nature of Christ. Like Marcellus of Ancyra, Photinus maintained that Jesus had an entirely divine mind. Less orthodox, Sirmium also held that the *ousia* language of Nicaea should not be further promulgated.

By September 351, the military campaign was fully underway, and on 28 September of that year one of the great—and costliest—battles of the period took place at Mursa in present-day Croatia. Magnentius lost about 20,000 soldiers, nearly half his men, and Constantius a third of his. Magnentius was driven back from northern Italy to Gaul. North Africa was repossessed and Magnentius was finally defeated at Mons Seleuchus in August 353. By 10 August, he had committed suicide in Lugdunum, now Lyon. It is said by the chronicler Ammianus that at this point Constantius became increasingly suspicious, vindictive and punitive towards any potential rival. Given his unopposed tenure of imperial office, it was now time to enforce his will on the Church.

At this point, around 350, Constantius saw Athanasius as the main obstacle in reaching the settlement Nicaea had not been able to achieve. Too many Eastern bishops opposed the Nicene definition of the Son being of the same substance as the Father (*homoousios*). Constantius therefore advocated that the Son should be described as "like in substance" to the Father (*homoiousios*), a position actively maintained by Bishop Basil of Ancyra. Athanasius would have none of it, and was supported in this by the papacy and most of the Western bishops, as the church historian Sozomen records:

> Those who were opposed to the doctrines of the Nicene Council thought this a favourable opportunity to calumniate the bishops whom they deposed, and to procure their ejection from the church as the abettors of false doctrine, and as disturbers of the public peace; and to accuse them of having sought, during the life of Constans, to excite misunderstanding between the emperors; and it was true, as we related above, that Constans menaced his brother with war unless he would consent to receive the orthodox bishops. Their efforts were principally directed against Athanasius, towards whom they entertained so great an aversion that, even when he was protected by Constans, and enjoyed the friendship of Constantius, they could not conceal their enmity.[11]

In fact, Athanasius had the most fleeting friendship with Constantius. It is not surprising that when Athanasius was accused of consorting with Constans, and of accepting a delegation from Magnentius, an Eastern synod at Antioch (351/2) saw it as an opportunity to depose him and replace him with George of Cappadocia.[12] In 356, an arrest party was sent to Alexandria to detain Athanasius, but he slipped away into his third exile, which lasted until the death of Constantius in 361. Despite Constantius's brief hegemony, the empire was never secure.

Threats to the empire (356–79)

While the 20 years following Constantine the Great's death in 337 were marked by rivalry between his sons, division in the Church and, as ever, threats from outside the borders of the empire, these tensions would only increase in the next 20 years until one of the greatest defeats of Roman arms occurred at Adrianople (present-day Edirne) in 378. Although the rivalries between Constantine's heirs ended with their deaths, the rivals were then replaced by emperors who were weaker, and consequently more vulnerable to attack from outside.

Constantius's reign, although at times fragile, was nonetheless enduring. He had appointed Gallus as his Caesar or deputy in the East, but this did not prove successful. By 354, Gallus had been deposed. By 355, there appeared another potential usurper in Gaul, the *magister peditum* in that province, called Silvanus.[13] Furthermore, there were repeated incursions by the Alamanni and others across the borders of Gaul. Up to 45 towns were lost to these cross-border raids. Despite this, Constantius was sufficiently confident of his power to move his court from Milan to Rome in 357, in part to celebrate the reunification of the empire under his leadership and the 20 years of his reign, or *vicennalia*. In so doing, he was following his august emperor forebears: Diocletian, who had created the new *tetrarchic* system with four rulers (two *augusti* and two *caesars*) and Constantine the Great. Both had ruled for 20 years and more.

The celebrations were manifestly Christian, since Constantius's father had abolished the long-standing worship of Jupiter in the

Capitol, and Constantius himself had issued a raft of decrees from Milan curtailing pagan worship.[14] Nor were the celebrations short of theatrical magnificence and ceremony. Accompanied by his wife Eusebia and his sister Helena, who was married to Julian, Constantius rode into Rome in a golden carriage surrounded by a military guard in gleaming armour. The historian Ammianus, a soldier of Greek stock in the tradition of Livy and Tacitus, records the event fully, writing with heavy irony:

> He had never been seen fighting at the head of his men or even in the front rank in moments. [Nevertheless] his object was simply to display his gold-inlaid standards and his brilliant retinue in procession of inordinate length before the eyes of the populace that was living in peace and neither expected nor wished to see any such show.[15]

Constantius's time in Rome was short-lived and, in the opinion of Ammianus, he was short in stature, shallow in substance and deficient in personal courage. Although a stranger to his historic capital, in deference to the past Constantius followed some of the traditions of Rome, such as paying court to the senators, attending the games and submitting himself to the populace. He nevertheless remained something of "a stranger to his heritage".[16]

If the senators and the political establishment of Rome were eager to give Constantius their allegiance after flirting, or worse, with the usurper Magnentius, who in the end had been defeated, the church in Rome was much more ambivalent about welcoming their emperor. They recognized him as a Christian emperor who had completed the church at the Vatican over the site of Peter's martyrdom, but also as the one who had exiled their bishop, Pope Liberius, for his support of Athanasius in the dispute over the formulation of the Trinity. Indeed, Liberius and his messenger had been faced down at the Council of Arles for his support of the Nicene definition of the Son's status as being of the same substance (*homoousios*) with the Father. Such were the pressures on the emperor, however, that he had only spent a month in Rome before hearing news of incursions by tribes across the Danube, such as the Suebi, the Quadi and the Sarmatians, which needed his attention..[17] He left quickly for

Pannonia (in modern-day Croatia) and, while he was there, Constantius would not only direct operations against invading tribes, but also, from 357–9 would seek a further settlement for the Church while Athanasius was in exile in Egypt. This would be attempted, as we shall see, at the joint Councils of Ariminum and Seleucia in 359–61.

In 359, Constantius moved from Sirmium to Constantinople, still in pursuit of a settlement for the Church, which now looked more and more unlikely as he was increasingly reliant on imperial power to force a solution. Although he did not spend much time in Constantinople, his father's new capital, Constantius did have special ties with the place. It was here at the founding of the city in 324 that he had been titled *caesar* by his father when only a seven-year-old boy. Constantius now completed the first Hagia Sophia, which would have its third great rebuild by Justinian in the sixth century. (Constantius's Hagia Sophia would be partially destroyed and rebuilt, as we shall see, by a fire during John Chrysostom's life at the time of his enforced exile.) While he was in Constantinople, Constantius increased the ruling establishment. The number of senators or *clarissimi* grew to 2,000, a governor was appointed with prefect status and the praetorships increased from three to five. Despite this enhancement of the city's hierarchy, Constantius could not stay long. The Persian leader Sapor, who had been earlier quelled at Nisibis, was on the move once again, seeking territory in Armenia and Mesopotamia. Summoning troops from Gaul under the leadership of his cousin and Caesar Julian, who himself now had ambitions to be emperor, Constantius set off for the East and to Amida on the Tigris where he expected to join forces with Arsaces, the king of Armenia, and an ally of Rome.[18] However, the campaign around the Tigris was unsuccessful, and Constantius was unable to dislodge Sapor. He then wintered in Antioch before heading west to Thrace, where he met Julian, his relative and Caesar from 355, with his troops from the West. In the foothills of the Taurus Mountains in present-day southern Turkey, Constantius caught a high fever and on 3 November 361 died aged 44 and childless, with Julian now the sole heir of the house of Constantine.

Julian was to prove a tempestuous and unconventional emperor: a rare nephew of Constantine the Great who had not been killed in "the promiscuous massacre" of relatives in 337. He was now a fine military commander, an intellectual and a convinced pagan. He had briefly attended Athens University along with Basil of Caesarea (c.330–379) and Gregory of Nazianzus (c.326–90), and there he had imbibed Greek philosophy and with it the worship of the gods. Previously, he had been taught grammar and rhetoric in Nicomedia by the pagan scholar Libanius (who would also teach John Chrysostom).[19] His older brother, Gallus, had been made *caesar* to Constantius, but his rule had ended prematurely in disloyalty in 354. Julian was increasingly drawn into a heady mix of philosophy, magic and paganism, all of which turned him strongly against Christianity. In the later years of Constantius's rule, Julian had begun an effective campaign against the Alamanni in Gaul by retaking cities like Cologne and later Strasbourg in 357. When Constantius demanded more troops to serve with him in the East, Julian's soldiers effectively corralled Julian and declared him emperor or *augustus* in 360. Julian was hardly an unwilling partner in this rebellion and was soon marching with his troops to Illyricum, present-day Slovenia. It was while he was at Naissus (present-day Niš in Serbia), that *comites* came from Cilicia to inform him of Constantius's death, and to tell him that with his dying breaths Constantius had named his cousin, Julian, as his successor and the sole *augustus* of the empire. He was emperor from 361 to 363, barely two years.

If the plus side of Julian's accession was the return of exiled bishops such as Athanasius to their sees, as was the custom, the downside was that wherever he could, Julian pursued active pagan policies in worship, education and civic ceremonies. Although like other consuls or emperors before him, such as Marcus Crassus in 53 BC and Valerian in AD 264, he would fall foul of the Persians, he managed to promote his pagan agenda erratically in both Constantinople and Antioch.

Although pagan in outlook, Julian was puritan in the exercise of power. Not for him the luxuries of the previous court of Constantius; instead he favoured a hard simplicity which was reminiscent of the days of the Republic. To this end he cleared out many of the cronies and office holders of Constantius and sought also to eject large numbers of palace servants and minor officials.[20] As Socrates the historian tells us, "He [Julian] expelled the eunuchs, barbers and cooks from the palace."[21] For these actions, he was lauded by Libanius and Mamertinus in panegyrics.

Furthermore, in the style of a Cicero or a Cato from the days of the golden age of the Republic, Julian attended the Senate in Constantinople and actively took part in debates there. Not everyone was impressed by the emperor's devotion to philosophy and debate, however. Ammianus criticized him for rushing out of the Senate like a student at news of the arrival of his favourite philosopher from Ephesus, Maximus, whom he greeted "in an undignified and ostentatious display of affection".[22] For Julian, support of classical philosophy came at the expense of Christian teaching. Nowhere was this more clearly evident than in his edict of 17 June 362, in which he called for the appointment of suitably qualified teachers in the cities. He was looking for men of character and morality with clear knowledge of and love for the classics, "who showed piety towards the gods [who should otherwise] withdraw to the churches of the Galileans to expound Matthew or Luke".[23] There was thus no place for Christian teachers in the public sphere.

If Julian's stay in Constantinople enabled him to partially remake the city culture in his own image—in particular within his own court, where he encouraged pagan worship—in Antioch he did not have the same latitude. Even more than Constantinople, Antioch had a long tradition of Christianity going back to Barnabas and Paul, Ignatius, and the saints and martyrs who resisted the Great Persecution. The blood of the martyrs did indeed speak from the ground. It was always going to be more difficult to replace Christian worship with pagan worship. This issue came to a head when Julian sought to remove the remains of a local saint and martyr, Babylas, installed by his brother and Caesar Gallus, in order to revive the great Temple of Apollo at Daphne. Desecrating a Christian shrine by reimposing pagan worship of Apollo was never going to be popular imperial policy, especially in Antioch, and indeed it provoked much popular resistance. Furthermore, Julian's habit of drenching pagan altars with blood from the extravagant slaughter of animals—giving him the nickname *victimarius* or slaughterer—in a time of food shortages and even famine did not recommend him to the citizens of Antioch.[24] When a fire occurred on 22 October 362, damaging the roof of the Temple of Apollo at Daphne, Christians were quick to see God's judgement against Julian. For his part, Julian saw it as arson by his opponents, seeking to thwart his policy of paganization. Perhaps it was with some relief that in early 363 the citizens of Antioch saw Julian leave to resume the ill-considered war against the Persians, from which he would not return.

Julian's campaign against the Persians followed on from his cousin Constantius, but it more grandly conjured up the spirit of Alexander the Great and of Trajan, whom he now sought to emulate. Many thought the campaign was foolhardy, born more from romantic echoes of the past rather than from any military necessity. Julian conveyed his army of 65,000 soldiers by a fleet of transport vessels down the Euphrates in April 363, making for Ctesiphon on the lower Tigris (35 miles south of Baghdad and the ancient capital of the Sasanian empire from 236 to 637). Bogged down in the waterways between the Tigris and Euphrates, forced to abandon their fleet of boats which were burnt, separated from the other Roman force under Procopius, and denied food by the Persian scorched earth policy, Julian's army became demoralized and isolated. When the battle came, Julian was dragged from his horse, felled by a spear and died later that night in his tent. Rumours about his last hours abounded. Christians saw his death as the judgement of God on his apostate life and believed that he had been killed by his own side for his apostasy. Others said he spent his last hours discoursing with his mentors, Maximus and Priscus, on the nobility of the soul. In any event, Julian's ill-fated classical zeal had ensnared the Roman army once again in the East, and it was only with great difficulty that it was extricated from its predicament. Jovian, a fairly undistinguished but Christian officer, was elected emperor, and through negotiation with the Persian leader Sapor, five provinces and several towns, including Nisibis, were handed back to the Persians in return for the Romans' safe retreat. Jovian now marched back to Antioch, while Procopius took the body of Julian to Tarsus. Once in Antioch, Jovian met the reinstated Athanasius, who had written a letter to Jovian laying down the Nicene Creed.[25] Furthermore, Jovian officially returned the empire to Christianity, although by January 364, while journeying from Antioch to Constantinople near Ancyra (modern-day Ankara), he had been found dead in his tent, either from asphyxiation from a charcoal burner or from strangulation.

Once again Roman soldiery needed to choose an emperor and, in this case, they decided to follow the Diocletian system of the tetrarchy and choose two *augusti*. In the first instance, on 25 February 364, they chose Valentinian, the commander of the second division of *scutarii* (heavy infantry), and then asked him to nominate a colleague as the fellow *augustus*. Valentinian chose his brother Valens who was to rule in the East, while Valentinian would rule in the West. The two brothers were theologically on different sides: Valentinian (321–375) was a Nicene Christian supported by Athanasius, while Valens subscribed to the recent Council of Sirmium (357) which supported the Arian position.

Leaving aside their religious differences for a moment, an emperor's lot in the very late stages of the Roman Empire was to be in an almost permanent battle of extinguishing fires. The fires in this case were the unceasing incursions over the empire's borders to the north and east from migrating, warlike tribes, whether Alamanni, Quadi, Sarmatians, Huns, Goths, Parthians or Persians. These regular and powerful incursions in turn led to unrelieved pressure on the army, in both its border force and field army form, and also on the provincial administrations. Valentinian, much more a soldier than an administrator, was a born commander. In 367, he oversaw the campaign against the Alamanni; later he sent Flavius Theodosius, *magister equitum*, the father of the later emperor Theodosius the Great, to retake London from a rogue Roman general. In 375, Valentinian fought the Quadi in present-day Hungary, suppressed rebellions in North Africa, and presented his son Gratian to the troops as the future *augustus* in 367, when the boy was only eight. Valentinian remained emperor in the West until 375, when his son Gratian succeeded, aged 16, whereas his brother Valens would continue for another four years until the fateful battle of Adrianople in 378, when Roman forces were devastatingly defeated, and Valens himself was killed by the Goths.

Valens's main opponents were the Persians and the Goths. The Persians once again sought to invade Armenia, which had been a client state of Rome and which then occupied most of present-day eastern Turkey, east of Cappadocia. The campaign came to an unsatisfactory halt, however, when Valens heard of a greater threat in the West in Thrace. The Huns, who lived a nomadic life in the steppes beyond the Sea of Azov (the Maeotic Sea), were pushing southwest into the lands of the Tanais River (the present-day River Don in Russia) and thereby, in turn, pushing the Goths southwest towards Thrace. These Goths were the Thervingi led by Alavivus and were given access to the empire on the basis that they would provide much-needed recruits for the Roman army. At the same time, the Greuthungi led by Fritigern were not warmly welcomed into the lands of the empire. Inept handling of the Greuthungi's desire for living space and pasture led to the kidnapping of the Goths' leaders, Fritigern and Alavivus, and a confrontation in 376 from which war ensued. Having made yet another peace with Sapor and having moved his court back to Constantinople, in 378 Valens was now free of his Persian commitments. From there, in July, he moved west to Naissus, where the Goths had gathered.[26] Gratian was coming to meet him with a Western army, and so Valens took his forces to Adrianople. On 9 August and in blazing heat, despite attempts at negotiation by Fritigern with a suspicious and overconfident Valens, the battle commenced. Two thirds of Valens's forces were killed, Roman standards were captured, and Valens himself, wounded by an arrow, died in a peasant's cottage near the battlefield. It was one of the worst defeats for Roman arms since Crassus lost legions in Persia and the Emperor Augustus lost legions in Teutoburg Forest under Publius Varus's command in AD 9.

Surprisingly, in pauses during these campaigns, Valens found time to pursue a settlement for the Church. Still riven by the Arian controversy and its effects, the Church—now restored to its previous position under Constantine after the apostasy of Julian—found itself deeply divided. The Western Church and Rome were almost entirely Nicene, with Western emperors, such as Constans and now Gratian, supportive of the Nicene definition of orthodoxy. The Eastern Church, with its emperors Constantius and then Valens, were supportive of the more Arian position, although not its most extreme rendering, but rather the more moderate idea that the Son was like the Father (*homoiousios*), although not of the same substance (*homoousios*). If the period from 337 (the death of Constantine) to 361 (the death of Constantius II) was marked by almost incessant councils and creed making, the period from 361–78 was marked more by the appointment of Arian-leaning bishops in the East. Here Alexandria, and the long tenure of Athanasius—who died in 373—as its bishop, was the great exception.

The defeat and death of Valens at Adrianople provided an opportunity for a change of direction. As Western emperor, Gratian moved quickly to appoint a capable commander to deal with the Goths and the crisis in the East. He chose Theodosius, the son of a very effective Roman general mysteriously executed in Egypt in 374. Theodosius was Spanish in origin and committed to Nicene orthodoxy, and everything was about to change.

The Theodosian revolution

On 19 January 379, the 19-year-old Emperor Gratian, the nephew of Valens, crowned Theodosius emperor or *augustus* at Sirmium in the Balkans. Having campaigned with his father (who had quelled rebellions against Valentinian I in Britain, Gaul and North Africa), Theodosius came with proven military experience. He needed to act quickly as the Roman legions in the East had been decimated by the defeat at Adrianople. Non-Romans were thus now admitted to the Roman army in unprecedented numbers.[27] Making Thessalonica his campaign base in 379, Theodosius began the painful process of reclaiming land and assets from Gothic power. Led by Fritigern and Allotheus, the Goths had occupied Thrace, Macedonia and Thessaly, but were persuaded to settle in Pannonia II, Savia and Valeria, present-day Croatia.[28] Theodosius had fallen ill in 380–1 but had recovered. He now astutely reconciled the Thervingi, who had been so successful at Adrianople, by burying their leader King Athanaric with full honours in Constantinople.[29]

Having prevented further destabilization of the empire by the Goths through a mixture of warfare and diplomacy, Theodosius was able to turn his attention to settling some of the abiding controversies in the Church. Coming from the western part of the empire, where Nicene orthodoxy was widely accepted, he now sought to either impose or enable a fresh direction for the Church in the East. He first declared his own faith by saying in a blunt and soldierly way that orthodoxy was "the form of religion handed down by the apostle Peter to the Romans and now followed by Bishop Damasus of Rome and Peter of Alexandria".[30] At the same time, he deposed the Arian bishop of Constantinople, Demophilus, and empowered the Council at Constantinople, now led by Gregory of Nazianzus after the premature death of the previous president, Meletius of Antioch, in 381. The Council endorsed and somewhat extended the Nicene Creed, including the belief that the Son was of the same substance as the Father and that the Spirit equally shared the Godhead. Gregory of Nazianzus found chairing the proceedings of the Council a great strain however (see *Oration* 42). He requested to be allowed to return to his home as it became clear that Theodosius wanted to appoint someone more capable of reconciling differences among the bishops as Archbishop of Constantinople. Gregory had found it difficult to introduce the necessary nuances or compromises to keep the bishops of the East together and had backed the wrong candidate as Bishop of Antioch (to which we shall return). And so Theodosius appointed Nectarius, a consummate diplomat, to be the next Archbishop of Constantinople.

It was this new Theodosian dynasty that would shape the future of the empire, and to some extent the Church. In fact, Theodosius would be the last emperor to rule both East and West, and soon after his death the empire in the West would finally unravel. Theodosius was able to establish hegemony in the East, with Gratian and then Gratian's brother Valentinian II becoming increasingly dependent on him in the West. The usurper Magnus Maximus arose in Britain in 381 and pursued Gratian to his death in Lugdunum (Lyon) in 383, but he was eventually defeated by Theodosius at Poetovio (now Ptuj in Slovenia) in 388 and subsequently executed at Aquileia. Theodosius's older son Arcadius was made *augustus* in Constantinople in 383, and it was his wife, Empress Aelia Eudoxia, who was to become the imperial opponent of John Chrysostom. She was the empress; he was her bishop. But we must first trace their respective development before coming to their historic confrontation.

Notes

1. Eusebius, *Vita Constantini* IV (Limovia Net, 2013), p. 209.
2. Eusebius, *Vita Constantini* IV, p. 206.
3. Eusebius, *Vita Constantini* IV, p. 207.
4. David Potter, *Constantine the Emperor* (Oxford: Oxford University Press, 2013), pp. 298–9.
5. David Hunt, "The Successors of Constantine", in Averil Cameron and Peter Garnsey (eds), *The Cambridge Ancient History, Vol. XIII, The Late Empire, AD 337–425* (Cambridge: Cambridge University Press, 1998), p. 3.
6. Hunt, "The Successors of Constantine", p. 3.
7. Hunt, "The Successors of Constantine", p. 6. See Libanius, *Oration* 49:137ff.
8. Hunt, "The Successors of Constantine", p. 7.
9. Hunt, "The Successors of Constantine", p. 9.
10. Hunt, "The Successors of Constantine", p. 14.
11. Sozomen, *Ecclesiastical History* IV and VIII.
12. Hunt, "The Successors of Constantine", p. 23.
13. Hunt, "The Successors of Constantine", p. 27.
14. Hunt, "The Successors of Constantine", p. 30.
15. Ammianus, Book 16, §9, in *The Later Roman Empire (A.D. 354–378)/ Ammianus Marcellinus*; selected and translated by Walter Hamilton with an introduction and notes by Andrew Wallace-Hadrill (Harmondsworth: Penguin, 1986), p. 99.
16. Hunt, "The Successors of Constantine", p. 30.
17. See Ammianus Marcellinus XVI.10.20.
18. Hunt, "The Successors of Constantine", p. 41.
19. Hunt, "The Successors of Constantine", p. 45.
20. Hunt, "The Successors of Constantine", p. 63.
21. Socrates, *Ecclesiastical History* III:1, in *Nicene and Post-Nicene Fathers: Second Series, Vol. II: Socrates, Sozomenus: Church Histories*, ed. Philip Schaff (Grand Rapids, MI: Eerdmans, 1987), p. 78.
22. Ammianus Marcellinus XXII.7.3; Hunt, "The Successors of Constantine", p. 63.
23. Hunt, "The Successors of Constantine", p. 67.
24. Hunt, "The Successors of Constantine", p. 69.
25. Athanasius, Letter LVI.

26 Hunt, "The Successors of Constantine", p. 99.
27 Hunt, "The Successors of Constantine", p. 102.
28 Hunt, "The Successors of Constantine", p. 102.
29 See Ammianus Marcellinus, Book 31, XXVII.5.4, in *The Later Roman Empire (A.D. 354–378)/Ammianus Marcellinus*; selected and translated by Walter Hamilton with an introduction and notes by Andrew Wallace-Hadrill (Harmondsworth: Penguin, 1986), p. 337.
30 Hunt, "The Successors of Constantine", p. 103.

2

The Church in the fourth century

In 351, the year John Chrysostom was probably born, the Church had already been 50 years in the grip of what came to be known as the Arian controversy. It would continue for another 30 years, and even longer in some eastern parts of the empire, despite the seeming settlement at the Council of Nicaea in 325. For nearly 300 years, since the Pauline missions recorded in the Acts of the Apostles, the Church had both struggled and flourished, suffered and grown, with pressures from both without and within. Chrysostom inherited a history of persecution and controversy that nevertheless now presented much opportunity.

By 351, the Church had been well established in the Roman West, as well as in the East, for up to 300 years. The Apostolic mission of the mid-first century had founded Christian communities in most of the principal cities of the empire, including Rome, Corinth, Ephesus, Alexandria, Antioch, Jerusalem and Thessalonica. Other centres would follow, as the compassion of Christians in times of famine and distress became manifest as an alternative to the harsh realities of empire, and the hope of the Resurrection was made known. Teaching around a dying and risen Christ as the true *divi filius*, the Son of God, was both attractive and powerful. The Gospel writers had made this clear in their narratives. Mark quite possibly wrote his Gospel from Imperial Rome in the days of Nero. Luke, himself a Gentile and a doctor, wrote his Gospel from the great missionary church at Antioch which had spawned the early missions of Paul and Barnabas (Acts 13:1–3). Matthew wrote from Judea, where he especially sought to persuade the Jewish Church to embrace and follow the Messiah who had come in Jesus of Nazareth. Finally, and latterly, John, most probably writing in Ephesus in *c.*90, reflected in a different way on the ministry of Jesus in a Gospel that uniquely describes

Jesus as the eternal Word made flesh, whose glory was revealed in his lifting up on the cross and in his resurrection from the dead. By 100 and the turn of the second century, many Christian communities had been established and the writings of the New Testament completed, so as to guide the Church in its life and future. And despite waves of persecution from particular emperors, such as Decius, Severus and latterly Diocletian, the Church survived and indeed often thrived in the storm.

The way the Church was formed by the early second century followed a definite pattern. Manuscript copies of parts of the New Testament, notably the Gospels and the Pauline epistles, were widely copied and read in communities. Indeed, the so-called Muratorian Canon (*c.*170) indicates that a list of commonly accepted New Testament books, including the Gospels and epistles, was established by the late second century. It is clear from the writings of Ignatius in the works of the Apostolic Fathers that the churches in most urban communities were formed around bishops who were often not so much regional spiritual rulers of a diocese, as local overseers of distinct Christian communities in sometimes quite small towns.[1] The leaders of churches in great metropolitan centres, such as Antioch, Alexandria and Milan, soon took on greater, even metropolitan, significance, while others, as in Rome, were in time to claim even more authority. Ignatius makes it clear that where the relationship between bishop and community is strong and good, then so too the Church remains fulfilled and healthy. The main challenges to the Church and to its flourishing were, as always, a combination of persecution and heresy.

Without detailing all the waves of persecution from the inception of the Church, from the Apostles to Constantine, it is worth simply stating that persecution ebbed and flowed. The challenges persecution produced were not just the obvious ones of intimidating Christians to leave their faith through a combination of physical punishment, financial cost or martyrdom. Persecution also divided the Church itself, not only in its response, but also in its response to the lapsed. Some were willing to see lapsed Christians restored after penance, while others maintained that the lapsed should have no part to play in any future fellowship. Such were the Novatianists in Rome, the Donatists in North Africa and the Meletians in Egypt.

The other great challenge to the Church in the early centuries was false teaching. In the first and second centuries, this would principally be the Gnostic heresy, which reached its height in Rome and Egypt in the second century. Gnosticism was a ragbag of beliefs and sects that maintained its appeal to the ancient mind because of a number of myths about creation, a notion of redemption being mediated by enlightenment or knowledge (*gnosis*), and initiation ceremonies leading into a specious deliverance and separation from material influences, including sex. *Gnosis* is simply the Greek word for knowledge, a knowledge which transcended the simple faith of the Church in the divine and salvation-giving Christ, and which was based instead on diffuse and grandiose myths about the origin and destiny of the world linked with personal renunciation. One such myth described the creation of the world as the result of a pre-cosmic disaster, which in turn led to the existence of evil and the misery of our current existence.

The Gnostic system held out the possibility of redemption from the effect and grip of this plight. "The content of the Gnostic gospel was an attempt to rouse the soul from its sleep walking condition and to make it aware of the high destiny to which it was called."[2] Indeed, Gnosticism taught a profound dualism with regard to the created order, which it held to be utterly infected by the pre-cosmic disaster. The way out of the consequent misery was linked to secret or semi-secret ceremonies at which individual souls might experience *gnosis*. There were in fact two equal and opposite views circulating among the various Gnostic sects about experiencing this *gnosis*. The majority of the Gnostic sects demanded a form of asceticism that demonstrated freedom from the fallen and evil material world, and that included celibacy and mortification of the flesh. Procreation was rejected as it served only to further populate an evil and fallen world. Through asceticism the divine soul could be liberated from its corrupt and ensnaring bodily appetites and see and experience higher things. Other sects counselled the very reverse, however: a kind of Gnostic antinomianism in which no amount of indulgence was off limits because the soul had already attained a state of freedom and redemption through its *gnosis*.

Gnosticism rang many bells with its half-truths appropriated from Christianity, Judaism and Platonism, all of which made it very appealing to the ancient mind. At certain points, it seemed to resonate with the accounts of the creation and fall in Genesis, hence underlining the corruption of creation. Eve was presented as a pre-cosmic mother who had gone astray and infected creation. The serpent was ascribed great power and influence. It was as if he had encircled creation and out-manoeuvred Jesus. Gnosticism seems to have also appealed to some Jewish myths in which creation was depicted as a bone of contention between rival angelic armies, both good and evil. In Jewish apocalyptic writings, this scenario was seen as the grand finale before the redemption of God's elect. And finally, Gnostic mythology seemed to concur also with an idea of the fallen world in which evil inhabits the created order, as in Plato's *Timaeus*. For all these reasons, Gnosticism became the syncretist's smorgasbord and appealed because humans frequently prefer complexity to simplicity, and the notion that we contribute to our salvation rather than being completely dependent on grace. At the same time, human beings tend to be titillated by secrecy rather than an "open statement of the truth" (2 Corinthians 4:2b, RSV). Gnosticism, in other words, appeals to the vanity of humankind.

The extent of Gnosticism's influence in the second century can quickly be seen from the large cache of Gnostic Gospels found in Nag Hammadi on the Upper Nile in an important discovery in 1945. These Gospels trade on familiar characters, such as Peter and Thomas among others, but in their versions perpetuate the Gnostic worldview that was so prevalent in Egypt. Likewise in Rome, Valentinus (*c.*100–180) taught Gnostic doctrines and came within a whisker of being elected bishop of Rome. A number of Church Fathers, principally Irenaeus, Tertullian, Justin Martyr and Clement of Alexandria, taught against Gnosticism, but even so the false teaching of the Gnostics made substantial inroads into the Church.

If Gnosticism, with its associated ideas concerning liturgy, baptism and the Bible—Marcion, for example, held that the two Testaments proceeded from different gods—was the principal source of false teaching in the second century, by the fourth century, the principal battleground was with Arianism and its views about the Trinity and the full divinity of the Son and the Spirit together with the Father.

The onset and development of Arianism

It appears that one of the by-products of the fight against Gnosticism, also present in the teaching of Justin Martyr, was a renewed emphasis on the ultimate unity and majesty of God.[3] Perhaps it was only to be expected that, in the plethora of demiurges and urges that made up the panoply of semi-divine beings in Gnosticism, there would be a new requirement to express the majesty and unity of the Godhead. However, this in turn led to a challenge about how the Trinity might best be expressed. By the end of the second century, what had been received simply and originally in the writings of the Apostles and in the Gospels as indicating a triune God—in which there coexisted the coeternal Father, Son and Spirit—was now subject to further scrutiny and the demand for greater definition in light of the previous controversies in the Church and the pressure of renewed Platonism.

At its simplest, what became clear was a tendency to raise the status of the Father as the monarch in the Godhead at the expense of the status of the Son and the Spirit. This became an attractive answer for those who wanted to distinguish Christianity from some of these foregoing heresies. This seems to have happened repeatedly in the period towards the end of the second century. Tertullian would write fully and strongly against Praxeas, who, as a Monarchist, exalted the Father at the expense of the Son and the Spirit. In doing this, according to Tertullian, Praxeas did the devil's business, "expelling the Paraclete and crucifying the Father".[4] By contrast, Tertullian gave a crisp definition of the Trinity which became seminal in the West, i.e., "one substance (*substantia*) consisting in three persons (*persona*)". If in time the Eastern Church wanted more precise definitions of terms like substance and person, Tertullian's description offered a memorable and workmanlike definition in the meanwhile.

Praxeas, himself from Asia Minor, was not the only one to seek a redefinition of the Trinity, however. A presbyter in Rome called Sabellius, who was possibly a little earlier than Praxeas, although we have no exact dates for him, also muddied the Trinitarian waters. Sabellius adopted a Modalist view of the Trinity, holding that the Father, Son and Spirit were modes of the same being. While such a view heightens the sense of unity in the Trinity, it does so at the expense of the distinctiveness of each of the members of the Godhead. One principal effect of this teaching was that the Father himself could be said to have suffered in the Son, a notion called Patripassianism, in terms of which, once again, the distinct suffering of the Son was impaired.

Sabellius's views created division in Rome. Zephyrinus, who was by then Bishop of Rome (pope 198–217), appeared to be sympathetic to the Monarchian Trinitarian views, but was opposed by Hippolytus (c.170–235), a principal theologian in Rome, who took the view that the Father and the Son are distinct persons. Hippolytus was further undermined by Callistus, who succeeded Zephyrinus as bishop of Rome, and who publicly denounced Hippolytus as a ditheist (i.e., one who believes in two Gods: Father and Son).

The dispute in Rome drew interest from further afield, and in particular from Alexandria. Alexandria had one of the principal theological schools of the ancient world, led first by Clement of Alexandria (c.150–215) and then by Origen (c.185–254). It is thought that Origen travelled to Rome in c.212, heard first hand the teaching of Hippolytus, and became familiar with Hippolytus's *Logos* theology, which is a rebuttal of Sabellianism. When Origen came to write his own great work on systematic theology, entitled *On First Principles*, he wrote of Christ:

> Let no one think, however, that when we give him the name "wisdom of God" we mean anything without hypostatic existence, that is to take an illustration that we understand him to be not as it were some wise living being, but a certain thing *which makes men wise* by revealing and imparting itself.[5]

Here we can sense Origen searching for a description of the Son in which his individuated and hypostatic existence is distinct in the Godhead, and who bears the power to conform others to his image by imparting to them dynamic wisdom (see Romans 8:29). In the end, Origen appears ambivalent in his definition of the Son's true status, however. Indeed, as Rowan Williams wrote: "Origen presents us with so varied and nuanced a picture that it is easy to see why his relation to Arianism has been the subject of so much dispute."[6] It is as if there are two parts in his writings: the neo-Platonist, sympathetic to the idea of distinct hypostases subordinated to the Great Monad, and the biblicist who follows Hippolytus and the *Logos* theology of John. It is possible to choose either dish from the buffet of Origen's writing.[7]

While Origen, as one of the great teachers in Alexandria in the third century, was searching for a language to describe the Trinity and was himself informed by the monarchical debate in Rome, a little later his pupil, the bishop of Alexandria and Coptic Pope Dionysius the Great (r.233–65) also drew from this controversy. It was thought that Dionysius, like Origen, had so distanced himself from the false teaching of Sabellius—which had become rife in his diocese, the Pentapolis region in particular—that in reaction he overstressed the individuated existence of the Son to the point of ditheism. When Rome caught a whiff of this theological stance, the bishop there, another Dionysius, wrote to his counterpart and namesake in Alexandria reproving him for writing as if the Son were subordinate to the Father, or had in some way been made by him rather than begotten. In response, Dionysius (of Alexandria) wrote a lengthy *Refutation and Defence* which affirmed the co-essentiality of Father and Son and agreed with the use of the word *homoousios* to denote this, adding that he would have preferred something more scriptural. Later, in the midst of the Arian controversy proper, and when the Arians were claiming that Dionysius was an early Arian, reproved for his views by Dionysius of Rome, Athanasius rode to the defence of Dionysius of Alexandria in c.350 in his *De Sententia Dionysii*, making the case that the Arians misunderstood Dionysus in falsely claiming him as one of their own.[8]

What is clear then, is that although the Arian controversy was about to burst upon the Church with new energy, its theological elements had been smouldering in the background for some time. It was, as we shall see, not simply about one man, catalyst though Arius was. It was instead about a deeper dispute over the biblical understanding of the Trinity, and how to find language that would adequately represent the biblical mystery of a triune God who was coeternal and consubstantial. That which lay at the heart of the Christian faith, and had seemingly been easily believed and experienced in the Apostolic age, now needed to be defended and redefined in the face of the Greek philosophical schools and the pressure of Jewish and pagan beliefs.

Arius and Arianism

Arius (*c*.250–336) and his teaching did not burst out of a cloudless sky. As we have seen, some of the issues had already been aired and debated in the Church, causing concern and consternation in Rome, especially nearly a hundred years earlier. New fuel was now added to the fire of the controversy over how to rightly define the Son and the Spirit by a bishop of Antioch, Paul of Samosata (*c*.200–75). Paul was elected bishop of Antioch, one of the principal sees in Christendom, in *c*.260, where he remained until he was deposed for heresy by a council of bishops convened in Antioch in 269. Although it was some time before the direct intervention of imperial power in the affairs of the Church, Emperor Aurelian hoped to restore harmony in the Church where there was growing discord. Until 269, Paul had been principally protected by Queen Zenobia of Palmyra before she in turn was defeated by Emperor Aurelian for defying Rome. Aurelian now hoped that a synod of some 70 bishops at Antioch would settle the matter of the definition of the Godhead.

Following on from the earlier Monarchian controversy in Rome, and influenced also by the so-called Antiochene school, Paul of Samosata appeared to take the view that as a perfect man, Jesus had been adopted into the Godhead by the Father and had not therefore been God from all eternity. It was in Antioch that the North African, probably Libyan, Arius imbibed this theological thinking. It was noted as early as 1683 in Cave's *Ecclesiastici* that Arius (a pupil of the martyr and Platonist Lucian of Antioch and quite probably of Iamblichus of Apamea), who taught in the Antioch area from *c*.304, had been influenced by neo-Platonist teaching. Lucian subscribed to the neo-Platonist theory of a hierarchy of hypostases, a theory that quite probably also formed Arius's thinking on Trinitarian issues.[9] If this is correct, it demonstrates how influential Greek Platonic philosophy was in underscoring Christian theology, especially in relation to the Trinity. For Arius, the second hypostasis (i.e., the Son) "was connected to God's purpose as creator".[10] This is only a step away from calling the Son a created being.

At some point, Arius, by now no longer a young man, returned to his native diocese of Alexandria, where he was ordained a deacon and presbyter by Bishop Peter of Alexandria in 312. Between 312 and 318, the controversy appears to have taken root. If the seeds of Arius's thinking had been sown in the intellectual centre of Antioch, they now developed in Egypt. Armed with the views that he had formed in Antioch, Arius was not content to hold them quietly but began to advertise them, through preaching, writing and catchy songs.

It became clear that his influence was not just in the Platonic schools of the city, but more especially reached ordinary people, among whom he cut an impressive and ascetic figure. He cultivated an immense following, both among the young women of the city, particularly the thousands who had taken a vow of virginity, and the dockers, for whom he wrote theological sea shanties.[11] It was in this way that Arius now infiltrated the Church with his teaching on the Trinity. At root, he believed that "the Son who is tempted, suffers, and dies, however exalted he may be, is not equal to the immutable Father beyond pain and death: if he is other than the Father, he is inferior".[12] Elsewhere, in his work called *Thalia* (literally meaning feast), which now exists only in quotation form in the writings of Athanasius,[13] Arius is reputed to have written the following: "God was not always a Father, but was once alone, and not yet a Father, but afterwards he became a Father".... "The Son was not always"; for whereas all things were made out of nothing, and all existing creatures and works, so the Word of God himself, were "made out of nothing", and "was not before his origination", since, like others, he "had an origin of creation". Here Athanasius quoting Arius's *Thalia* identifies the heart of Arianism.[14]

Arius maintained that the Father alone was immutable, not the Son, and that there was (a time) when the Son was not, and a time when the Father was alone and not a Father. The Son was himself created out of nothing, having an origin and beginning. These were the theological grenades which set the Church on its longest quest to express the truth of the Trinity. It would take the best part of a century, and very many twists and turns, to do so. The process began in Alexandria.

Given the scant records available, it is not possible to be precise about the exact chronology of the controversy, but a generally accepted timeline has emerged. In 319, Bishop Alexander of Alexandria, quite possibly aided by his secretary and later successor, Athanasius, wrote a letter to his clergy along with several other bishops called *henos somatōs*.[15] In this letter, he identified the teaching of Arius and others as heretical and pronounced their apostasy. A Council held in Alexandria confirmed their excommunication. These opening salvos were followed by a lengthy letter called *hē philarchos* written to Bishop Alexander of Byzantium, Alexander's opposite number there, shortly before the founding of Constantinople by Constantine in 324. While Arius was looking for wider ecclesiastical and episcopal support for his cause outside Egypt, by writing this lengthy letter, Bishop Alexander of Alexandria was seeking to staunch any flow of support to Arius. It is clear from this, and from Arius's own efforts to drum up support for his position, that the controversy had quickly spread beyond the borders of Alexandria, Egypt and the Pentapolis (Libya). For his part, Arius was not slow in garnering powerful backers, and, having moved from Alexandria to Palestine,[16] he wrote to the most influential bishops in the area, particularly Eusebius of Nicomedia and the church historian and bishop Eusebius of Caesarea, to gather their support. Meanwhile, soon after his victory over Licinius, Constantine sent his personal ecclesiastical troubleshooter, Bishop Ossius of Cordoba to Alexandria, who was to track the Nicene controversy and all its vicissitudes virtually to his hundredth year in *c*.357, to see if he could bring some resolution to the issues disturbing the Church.

By 325, it was becoming clear that a wider synod of bishops was needed to clear up the controversy that had been sparked by Arius, but which also reflected a much more deep-seated division in the Church over the expression of the Trinity and the status of the Son and, to a lesser extent, the Spirit. It was mooted firstly that a council might be held at Antioch, then at Ancyra, but finally it was decided to convene a great council at Nicaea, which was the emperor's summer palace situated on a pleasant lake south of the new capital, Constantinople.

Nicaea and its aftermath

By 325, Constantine had become used to intervening in the life and councils of the Church. He had intervened in the Donatist controversy in North Africa by calling a Council at Arles in 314, although with only limited success. And now, with the visible panoply of imperial power, he hoped to settle the dispute about the nature of God: Father, Son and Spirit. It proved far harder than he expected.

Although different sources dispute the numbers, the attendance at the Council was probably around 250 bishops, as recorded by Eusebius of Caesarea.[17] They were given safe passage via the imperial travel system, called the *cursus publicus*, and by far the majority came from the East. The agenda was strongly controlled by Alexander and the anti-Arius party, with a credal statement from Eusebius of Caesarea read, repudiated, and torn up in the presence of its advocate. At some point in the proceedings, the seminal word which was to define Nicene theology was introduced: *homoousios*. It was a word which had had some theological use hitherto in the monarchical dispute about the Trinity in Rome, but it did not have uniform acceptance. By maintaining that Father, Son and Spirit were of the *same substance*, the term struck at the heart of Arian theology. Yet what Eusebius of Caesarea took it to mean, and what Alexander of Alexandria took it to mean, seemed to be different things. It was one thing to agree on the use of a word, but another to understand it as meaning the same thing. Thus, in his exposition at the Council, Eusebius of Caesarea explained what it meant in a way that would satisfy both Eusebius of Nicomedia and Alexander of Alexandria, which was no mean achievement, as they were deeply opposed to each other. As Rowan Williams says, in his exposition of the creed Eusebius of Caesarea had achieved a considerable semantic *tour de force*.[18] However, although almost all the bishops signed up to the creed in the presence of the emperor (because who would not do so?), as soon as the Council was over, the meaning was explained in differing ways. Those few who had not signed were exiled. And the controversy was far from over; indeed, it was just beginning. Three distinct periods were to follow: from 325 to the death of Constantine in 337; from 337 to 361, the period during the reign of Constantius II; and from 361 to the advent of Theodosius in 379. These periods form the background to

John Chrysostom's ministry in Antioch, which, like all of the East, had been deeply affected by the Nicene controversy.

The first period immediately following the Council, and during the remaining years of Constantine's life until 337, saw the fight back from the Eusebians. Their position was defined not so much by the definition of *homoousios* as by a new emerging concept and term meaning *like in substance*. Initially, the fightback by the Eusebians focused on discrediting Alexander's successor, Athanasius, who was consecrated bishop of Alexandria in 328. Athanasius's high-handed action against the Meletian schismatics gave the Eusebians and their allies the opportunity they had been looking for to act against the new and campaigning Alexandrian bishop. Following the Council of Tyre in 335, where charges of bullying were laid against Athanasius, and which were re-enforced a year later at Antioch, he was exiled and sent to Trier and then Rome. From there, he sought support from the Western Church, and in particular from Pope Julius I. Furthermore, having submitted a bland confession of faith that convinced the emperor of his retraction, Arius himself was readmitted to communion in Constantinople, if not in Alexandria, although he soon came to an untimely end in Constantinople. For his part, Athanasius continued to govern his diocese from exile, and around this time he completed his greatest theological work, *Contra Gentes: De Incarnatione*, which represented the bedrock of his thinking about the Incarnation and the divine status of the Son, deemed essential for providing redemptive reconciliation and the forgiveness of sins.

Following the death of Constantine during the lifetime of Constantius, his second son and *augustus* in the East, the controversy now entered a second phase (337–61). This was to be the most protracted period of imperial support for Arianism, and it lasted until Constantius's own death in 361. The period was marked by numerous attempts through councils and creeds to find a solution to the Trinitarian controversy that did not include the word *homoousios*. The period was also marked by increasing polarization between Nicene and anti-Nicene parties, although these were not yet neatly defined. During this period, Athanasius would be exiled twice. Once was when he was replaced by Gregory of Cappadocia before his restoration in 346 (which initiated what is called his Golden Decade as bishop of Alexandria). This period was brought to an aggressive conclusion, however, when imperial soldiers were sent to arrest him in his great church of Theonas in Alexandria. Behind this attempt and the start of Athanasius's lengthy third exile from 357–61 was the increased power of Constantius, who had seen off the usurper Magnentius (see above) and whose rival, younger brother and patron of Athanasius, Constans, had died in 350. Constantius was more determined than ever to force a theological settlement on the churches and to crush his main opponent, Athanasius. As Henry II of England would think of his archbishop, Thomas à Becket, Constantius wondered, "Who will rid me of this turbulent priest?"

A theological settlement that united the Church in the empire, East and West, proved elusive. Indeed, such were the theological trajectories and the language of East and West that the hope of unity seemed a chimera. And for a time, the theological tide linked to political realities ran against the Nicene position. While in Rome, Pope Julius and the Western bishops gave Athanasius almost unqualified support, in Antioch, it was a different story. At the Dedication Council at Antioch in 341 (summoned for the dedication of the great church begun by Constantine the Great), influence had already shifted to Eusebius of Constantinople, formerly of Nicomedia. During this council, no less than four creeds were produced, the second of which, known as the *Dedication Creed*, contained a phrase calling the Son "the unchanging and unaltering, exact image of the Godhead and the *ousia* and will and power of the glory of the Father who was in the beginning with God".[19] While this was a refinement of the Nicene/*homoousios* position, it was also anti-Sabellius and anti-Marcellus of Ancyra, both of whom took a more extreme anti-Arian position, questioning the distinctive *ousia* or *hypostasis* of the Son. Then a further council held at Serdica (now Sofia in Bulgaria) in 343 demonstrated the complete impasse between Eastern and Western bishops and was abandoned without achieving anything, or the two sides even meeting.

From 350 until 359, and having seen off his political rivals, whether the usurper Magnentius or his brother Constans, Constantius sought greater control over ecclesiastical policy. It was nevertheless a period marked by ongoing theological turmoil. A council in Sirmium in 351 sought to condemn Photinus, a disciple of Marcellus, and his more extreme Nicene position, but also condemned the use of *ousia* language so prevalent at Nicaea. Further councils followed in Arles (353) and Milan (353). Constantius's aim was to isolate Athanasius and adopt a credal structure around which East and West could join. Yet the sides could not be so easily corralled, even by imperial power: Liberius, the new pope (352–66), supported Athanasius just as his predecessor Julius had done, and likewise the Western theologian Hilary was strongly in favour of the Nicene Creed, earning him the disfavour of the emperor and his officials. A division was emerging in the ranks of the more Arian groupings, and it came from the more irenic and settlement-seeking theology of Basil of Ancyra. The divide represented the *homoiousians* (who held that the Son was *like the Father* both in activity and essence) and the more rationalist and logic-seeking theology of the *homoians* (who held that the Son was only like the Father, but not in essence or in *ousia*). If the former thinking was represented by Basil of Ancyra, and to an extent by Cyril of Jerusalem (bishop from 348 to 387), the latter *homoians* were strongly represented by Aetius and his much younger and able disciple, Eunomius. These two were essentially logicians who argued that by definition, to be a Son meant inferiority to the Father. Anything that is generated, whether by will or essence, cannot have the same status as the ingenerate. Hence the Son could never share the full essence or being (*ousia*) of the Father. This more extreme position was never going to bring reconciliation and was later extensively and comprehensively answered, especially in the writings of the Cappadocian Fathers, and to a lesser extent by John Chrysostom as well.

From 359, there was a concerted effort by Constantius and his close advisers to resolve questions relating to the Trinity, and the status of the Son and Spirit in relation to the Father. Bishops capable of agreeing were summoned firstly to the imperial residence at Sirmium, where the "Dated Creed" (359) was produced. It appeared as a compromise between the *homoian* and *homoiousian* positions and as a basis for future deliberation by the bishops.[20] Constantius's thinking was that if he could exclude Athanasius, who represented to the emperor the unyielding Nicene position, and Eunomius, who represented the extreme rationalist position, a compromise creed might be agreed. The Western bishops were then summoned to Rimini in large numbers in June 359, where the

Sirmium Creed, based on the *homoiousian* compromise that the Son is in all respects like the Father, was put to them. By detaining the near-400 Western bishops until winter was almost upon them and they were faced with the prospect of perilous journeys home, he exerted pressure on them to settle. Eventually an embassy was despatched to Constantius, now in Constantinople, signalling agreement to the Sirmium or Dated Creed of 359. It was, however, a very half-hearted assent procured under pressure. Meanwhile the Eastern bishops met at Seleucia in Cilicia in September 359. However, that council faced an immediate split in the Arian position, which produced only factional in-fighting and dissent. A last-minute embassy to Constantius followed and a creed called the Nice Creed was signed in the final hours of 359.[21] In truth, it was a watering down of the statement that "the Son was like the Father in all respects". No further revisions were possible as Constantius died in 361.

The next 16 years, until the defeat of Valens at Adrianople in the East by the Goths and the advent of Theodosius, were marked by the influence on the Church of the Cappadocians and the formulation of Trinitarian doctrine. Immediately following the death of Constantius, his cousin Julian the Apostate became emperor briefly (361–3), followed by Jovian. With the accession of Julian, an apostate emperor, Athanasius was ironically restored to the See of Alexandria, although only briefly, before another exile, his fourth. He was soon readmitted to his See again, and from 366–73 enjoyed his final years as an esteemed, battle-hardened and revered church leader. By then, Athanasius had established his own narrative of the Arian controversy with important works on the synods (*De Decretis Nicaenae Synodi, De Synodis Arimini et Seleucia* 359, and *Historia Arianorum* 357). More importantly, having latterly adopted the language of Nicaea, Athanasius now sought common ground between the *homoousios* and *homoiousios* parties.[22] Indeed, in the final section of his work *De Synodis*, Athanasius addresses George of Laodicea, a leading proponent of the *homoiousios* position, arguing that "fundamentally they teach the same doctrine".[23] If something of a rapprochement was breaking out in Alexandria from a more secure, and possibly more mellow, Athanasius, in Cappadocia there was developing a creative and prayerful reworking of the Nicene position, which stressed both the individuated existence of the three hypostases of the Trinity and the notion that each might be known in their activity, but also that their *common substance* (*ousia*) might only be explored through contemplative prayer. This coming together of doctrine and prayer brought a welcome spirituality to the exercise of seeking to understand the Trinity. Gregory of Nyssa (c.334–95) would very much make this his position, while Gregory of Nazianzus would bring welcome clarity and depth to his explanation of the Trinity in his *Orations* in Constantinople in 378. And Basil of Caesarea would discern the need to build up the Nicene party, which was prepared to explore new depths of Trinitarian theology and the relationship of Father, Son and Spirit as coeternal and co-operative (i.e., what one does, all do). With the advent of Theodosius, who held to an orthodox and Nicene position, and the beginning of a new council in Constantinople in 381, which affirmed and expanded the Nicene Creed, a new phase in the history of the Church seemed to be opening up. Much damage had nevertheless been done, as we shall see, in Antioch. Before turning to the specific events in Antioch and the birth of John Chrysostom in 349, we must note one other deeply influential development, which, alongside this doctrinal controversy, profoundly influenced the development of the Church from the fourth century onwards.

The ascetic movement

Anyone reading the New Testament might be surprised to see the degree to which asceticism had become part of Christian discipleship by the fourth century. Although the figure of John the Baptist existing on locusts and wild honey in the desert and wearing the simplest of clothing (Matthew 3:1–6; Mark 1:6) and the heroic fasting of Jesus in the wilderness (Matthew 4:1,2; Mark 1:12,13; Luke 4:1,2) are clearly part of the Gospel narrative, asceticism does not play a significant role in the pattern of Christian living held up by Paul or Peter in their teaching in the epistles. It is true that Paul enjoins abstinence from sex and marriage on those who can embrace that (1 Corinthians 7:8ff.,25–8) on all, and a modest lifestyle. Yet he is also wary of making a virtue out of abstinence itself (Colossians 2:16–19), or of people imposing their disciplines of diet or lifestyle on others, thereby curtailing or risking their freedom in Christ (see Galatians 5:1). Nevertheless, by the early fourth century, asceticism was one of the most significant features of Christianity in both East and West. The most popular of Athanasius's writings was probably not his account of Arianism with all its twists and turns, and not even his great work *Contra Gentes: De Incarnatione*, but his life of an ascetic monk, Antony. In modern terms, this work was a bestseller in both East and West and deeply influential in the development of Christian discipleship. It popularized monasticism in all its forms and set a gold standard of spiritual warfare with the devil which thereafter deeply impacted all Christian communities.

What has been called the flight to the desert, turning the desert into a city of hermits and monks, began in part because of the historical accident of persecution in the late third century.[24] Previously the kind of abstinence prevalent in the Church was one of earthly life itself. In other words, it was the embrace of martyrdom, as in the case of Ignatius, an early bishop of Antioch, who positively looked forward to his confrontation with lions in Rome, or St Perpetua, who willingly accepted martyrdom in 203 in Carthage as a young breastfeeding mother. Persecution had hastened flight, however, and in areas like Syria, Palestine, North Africa and Egypt, this meant the desert. Vast tracts of land were available near to great cities like Antioch, Jerusalem, Alexandria and Carthage. In the West and somewhat later, the habitats colonized by monks were remote islands, rocks, and out-of-the-way wildernesses on the Atlantic coastline or on the coasts of Gaul or Ireland. The environment may have been different, but the aim was the same: prayer, a disciplined life, the copying of the Scriptures, and a springboard for evangelism, as would be the case much later in Iona and Lindisfarne.

The move to the desert first occurred in Egypt, Syria and Palestine. In Egypt, as elsewhere, this withdrawal occurred in two ways: through *cenobitism* (living in community) or *eremitism* (living in isolation). Both were the preserve of what came to be called monasticism from the Greek word *monos*, meaning single. These two forms of monasticism were much in evidence in Egypt in the early fourth century. Pachomius (292–348), a one-time soldier turned ascetic, began a cenobitic community in the Thebaid in the Nile delta at Tabbenesi. Here a great number of monks were organized into a community life with military-style discipline.

Rules for the community were written by Pachomius and his successors, becoming the *Doctrina de institutione monachorum*, which was later translated from Greek by Jerome.[25] Elsewhere in Egypt, at Scetis in Wadi-el-Natrun, a young monk named Macarius settled and there pursued an eremitic life for over 30 years. "Nitria is the gateway of the Egyptian desert, Scetis is its citadel",[26] and it is here that Coptic monasticism of all kinds took root, and still exists today.

While Pachomius pioneered monasticism in community in the Nile Delta in the early fourth century, Antony the Great did the same for the eremitic lifestyle of a monk, with his biographer Athanasius advertising this way of life more than any other throughout the known world. The biography tells of Antony's call (§3,4), his all too vivid struggles with the Devil (§5,6), his defence of Nicene orthodoxy against the Arians (§69), his exorcism of those oppressed by the Devil (§§8–10, 63), his healing of a virgin girl from worms (§58) and his unassuming and unpretentious treatment of letters from emperors seeking advice (§81). Antony settled in ever more remote locations, residing first in the Nile Delta (§§8–10), then moving towards the Sinai in eastern Egypt, before he finally went from "the outer mountain to the inner mountain" at the bidding of an internal voice (§§49,50). In many ways, this biography by Athanasius set the template for many other monks or hermits in Christendom: Cassian, Benedict, Columba, Aidan and Cuthbert, for example. The same combination of self-disregarding humility, spiritual struggle, commitment to the Scriptures and healing power also characterized their lives and ministries.

If the seeds of monasticism were first sown in Egypt, they quickly spread elsewhere in the Near East and thence to western and northern Europe. Not surprisingly, the biblical lands of Palestine and Syria were receptive to monasticism in all its forms, especially when close to a holy site, whether in the Old or New Testament tradition. In Syria, a tradition of solitaries took root with the notion of *ihidaya* or singleness becoming prominent.[27] By the mid-fourth century, many church leaders and bishops in Syria and further east were also solitaries. And in Palestine, there were soon many solitaries or coenobitic communities, like that of the influential Evagrius Ponticus (345–99) near Jerusalem, with Melania the Elder and Rufinus nearby. These vocations were not met with universal acclaim from an educated society, however. One young man with a good education going off to join a community of monks on a local hillside was greeted with the following reaction: "Incomprehensible! He is the son of respectable upper middle-class parents, with a good education, and excellent prospects for a steady comfortable life, yet he has left home and gone off to join a lot of dirty vagrants!"[28] Nevertheless, monasticism in all its varied forms had caught the imagination of those wanting to make a mark in their discipleship. It appeared to offer a decisive challenge in Christian living which transfigured the normal. More than this, in some places, monasticism was harnessed to the task of mission. This occurred in Cappadocia and was largely the inspiration of the Cappadocian Fathers.

It is hard to overemphasize the influence of the Cappadocian Fathers in the development of monasticism, for they gave it both a missional and a theological edge. To put it simply, Basil of Caesarea (330–79) gave monasticism the clear missionary tasks of sharing the faith and of helping the needy, just as he himself did in his *Basileiados* in Caesarea, his hospice for the poor, sick and infirm.[29] Gregory of Nazianzus demonstrated the more theological side of monasticism by showing how it was the handmaid of writing and reflection. More than the others, Gregory of Nyssa linked monasticism to the contemplative tradition at the heart of the quest to know and experience the love of God. The discipline of *epinoia* or contemplative reflection lay at the heart of much of the Cappadocians' theologizing. Although they reckoned that the *ousia* or substance of the Godhead was beyond human knowing and shrouded in mystery, disciplined reflection on the characteristics of the Trinity or their *idiomata* would lead to a deeper appreciation of each person of the Godhead. Monasticism was no longer an end in itself or just a higher form of Christianity for the very serious. It was an essential tool for mission, contemplation and theologizing, and at its best would never depart from those ambitions.

In brief, this was the ascetic and spiritual movement that spread across the Near East and was soon to enter Europe, where the organizing genius of Benedict (480–547) would give it a rule and form by which it was readily established.

This then is the background to the early spiritual life of John Chrysostom. When he was born in *c.*349, the Arian controversy still had years to run, and, as we shall see, had a deep impact on the Christian communities in Antioch, where John lived, much of it for ill. The controversy would remain at its height for a further 30 years. Chrysostom entered a Church that was acutely aware of the suffering and endurance that was still part of the living memory of the oldest church members who had known the Great Persecution. The ascetic movement would deeply influence his own Christian formation and ambitions throughout his life. It would bring him into conflict, and it would also equip him for that conflict. Like all of us, he was shaped by the characteristics of his age. One further influence determined the course of his life and the shape of his ministry, however, and that was the ecclesiastical rivalries that existed between the great sees of the empire: Antioch, Alexandria, Constantinople and Rome. It is to them we must now turn.

Notes

1. See Apostolic Fathers, Ignatius, Letters.
2. Henry Chadwick, *The Early Church* (Harmondsworth: Penguin, 1993), p. 35.
3. Chadwick, *The Early Church*, p. 86.
4. Chadwick, *The Early Church*, p. 89.
5. Origen, *On First Principles* II.2.
6. Rowan Williams, *Arius: Heresy and Tradition* (London: SCM, 2001), p. 143.
7. Williams, *Arius*, p. 143.
8. Athanasius, *De sententia Dionysii*, in *Nicene and Post-Nicene Fathers: Second Series, Vol. IV: Athanasius: Select Works and Letters*, ed. Philip Schaff (Edinburgh: T&T Clark, 1987), pp. 176ff.
9. Williams, *Arius*, p. 3.
10. Williams, *Arius*, p. 144.
11. Chadwick, *The Early Church*, p. 124.
12. Chadwick, *The Early Church*, p. 124.
13. Athanasius, *Contra Arianos*, in *Nicene and Post-Nicene Fathers: Second Series, Vol. IV*, p. 309.
14. Athanasius, *Contra Arianos* I.2, op. cit., p. 310.
15. Sozomen, I.VI, *Nicene and Post-Nicene Fathers: Second Series, Vol. II: Socrates, Sozomenus: Church Histories*, ed. Philip Schaff (Grand Rapids, MI: Eerdmans, 1987), p. 3.
16. Williams, *Arius*, p. 54.
17. Williams, *Arius*, p. 67.
18. Williams, *Arius*, p. 70.
19. Lewis Ayres, *Nicaea and its Legacy* (Oxford: Oxford University Press, 2009), pp. 118–19.
20. R. P. C. Hanson, *The Search for the Christian Doctrine of God: The Arian Controversy 318–381* (London: T&T Clark, 1988), p. 362.
21. Hanson, *The Search for the Christian Doctrine of God*, p. 380.
22. Ayres, *The Legacy of Nicaea*, pp. 171ff.
23. Ayres, *The Legacy of Nicaea*, p. 171; Athanasius, *De Synodis* §41, in *Nicene and Post-Nicene Fathers: Second Series, Vol. IV*, p. 472.

[24] Derwas J. Chitty, *The Desert a City: An Introduction the Study of Egyptian and Palestinian Monasticism under the Christian Empire* (Crestwood, NY: St Vladimir's Press, 1999), p. 1.

[25] P. J. Whitworth, *Constantinople to Chalcedon: Shaping the World to Come* (Durham: Sacristy Press, 2017), p. 299.

[26] Chitty, *The Desert a City*, p. 13.

[27] Andrea Stark, *Renouncing the World yet Leading the Church: The Monk-Bishop in Late Antiquity* (Cambridge, MA: Harvard University Press, 2004), pp. 20–1.

[28] Stark, *Renouncing the World*, p. 24, citing *PG* 321B.

[29] Philip Rousseau, *Basil of Caesarea* (Berkeley, CA: University of California Press, 1998), pp. 133ff.

3

A tale of four cities: Antioch, Constantinople, Alexandria and Rome

The world in which John Chrysostom (*c*.349–407) grew up, and in which he ministered from 386 to 407, was dominated by an ecclesiastical quadrilateral revolving around Antioch, Constantinople, Alexandria and Rome. Questions of theology, church discipline and hierarchy reverberated around and between these historic centres like ping pong balls in a wind tunnel. Each of these centres, with its concurrent theological trajectory, had a particular set of circumstances that made it what it was. The Antiochene Church was like a revered scholastic, an ageing uncle: respected in the family but prone to bouts of inflexible independence. Constantinople was the new kid on the block: recently founded and eager to flex its muscles and show its new position in the empire, but dependent on Alexandria for grain. Alexandria was proud of its intellectual traditions, displayed in its neo-Platonic schools and Jewish scholarship, and of its church, which was accustomed to displaying power and influence in a pharaonic fashion. Ecclesiastical Rome kept itself apart, above the fight, assured of its own importance as the ancient and populous capital of the West and the resting place of Saints Peter and Paul. The protracted controversy over the definition of the Trinity that took up most of the fourth century meant that there was plenty of opportunity for rivalry between these centres, and for political power plays to mingle with theological questions, which they certainly did. Indeed, there were ecclesiastical rivalries which fuelled the fire of controversy over the years.

To understand these city-based ecclesiastical power plays, we will look at these four great centres in turn. There were other great and important cities, such as Jerusalem, Carthage, Milan, Thessalonica and Trier, but these four retained supremacy in the development of the Church.

Antioch

Antioch (present-day Antakya in the southwestern corner of Turkey in the *vilayet* of Hatay) had for generations been one of the most splendid and powerful cities in the Roman Empire. Founded in 300 BC by Seleukos I Nikator, one of Alexander the Great's generals, it remained the Roman imperial centre in the East until it was eventually overtaken by Constantinople in the fifth century. Here the Roman legions were garrisoned, and from here rebellious provinces, such as Judea and Palmyra, would be invaded and repressed. Antioch occupied a spectacular site on the left bank of the river Orontes, which then flowed south to Hama and Homs—cities, like nearby Aleppo, made prominent in the tragic Syrian civil war of the early twenty-first century. In a bend in the river, which formed an island, long since silted up, was situated the imperial palace, the hippodrome, and the recently completed Great Church, begun by Constantine and formally opened by his son Constantius II in 341, a time that coincided with the Dedication Council and its drafting of further creeds (see above).

The city was impressive with its well-lit marble streets, colonnades, chequer board design and 18 public baths. Its environs were also very pleasant. To the south was the garden suburb of Daphne, with the shrine of Christian martyr Saint Babylas in a disused temple of Apollo (which the apostate emperor Julian had sought to revive) and surrounded by impressive hills to the southeast. At the foot of Mount Silpios was the theatre of Caesar, while its precipitous upper slopes became the favoured location for many hermits, solitaries and anchorites. From the city, the Governor of the Province of Syria and the Comes of Oriens governed a vast region or diocese that comprised 15 Roman provinces. With good communications from east to west, the city quickly became a cultural and intellectual centre for the region and home to a number of well-known teachers.

The city had a particularly notable Christian heritage, probably becoming the most dynamic and important church in the first century. It was here that followers of The Way, the Jewish sect which followed Jesus of Nazareth as the Messiah, were first called Christians (Acts 11:26b and Acts 11:19–30). It was to Antioch that Barnabas brought Saul (Paul) from Tarsus in 46 to teach this rapidly growing and diverse church.[1] And it was from here that the first missions were sent out as led by the Holy Spirit (Acts 13:1–3) to Cyprus and the interior, and later to Europe. Other leaders were to follow Saul and Barnabas, notably Peter and, at the end of the first century, Ignatius. It was this Ignatius who travelled under Roman guard from Antioch to be martyred and who wrote these heroic words to the Smyrneans: "But why then have I handed myself over to death, to fire, to the sword, to wild beasts? But to be near the sword is to be near God, to be in the presence of the wild beasts is to be in the presence of God—so long as it is in the name of Jesus Christ."[2]

Despite this heritage, the Antiochene church had fallen from its dizzy spiritual heights during the fourth century because of the effects of the Arian controversy in the city. For some time, the intellectual climate of Antioch, open as it was to the philosophic traffic from East and West, meant that it was fertile soil for speculation and sometimes dissension. Indeed, it was here that Arius would learn his defective theology about the Trinity from Lucian the Martyr, and the neo-Platonist Iamblichus.[3] When it came to theologizing, Antioch had an open mind, influenced by philosophical classical thinking and a literal form of biblicism, and was quite ready to pick over the terms used in the Trinitarian controversy, not least the concept of *ousia* and its derivative *homoousios*, so prominent in the Nicene Creed. By 360, Antioch was wedded to the idea of there being three *hypostases* in the Godhead, in line with the thinking of the Cappadocian Fathers. This meant that each person of the Trinity had their own individuated existence, but shared a common substance.[4] By 361, however, and in his *Tome* to Antioch, Athanasius was willing to recognize the validity of this expression. However, much damage had already been caused by the schism of the previous 40 years.

Following the Council of Nicaea in 325 and its adoption of a creed designed to isolate and anathematize Arius and his theology (which at root maintained that the Son was a created being and hence subordinate to the Father), there was a reaction in the East to Nicene theology and the terminology used at Nicaea. In particular, by 331 a large body of Christians in Antioch saw the Nicene definition as a form of Sabellianism, driven by an overreaction to Arius's propositions. Sabellianism, which came from third-century Rome, tended to diminish the unity of the Godhead at the expense of upholding the diversity of Father, Son and Spirit. The dissenting Antioch Christians preferred to describe Father, Son and Spirit as being "like in all respects",[5] and in this way maintained the monarchy of the Father whom the Son and the Spirit, we are told, resembled, although this was quite inadequate for the Nicene party. By 331, Eustathius, the bishop of Antioch, who was overwhelmingly committed to Nicaea, was deposed, causing a schism in the city. Although he was succeeded by a line of bishops committed to a more moderate form of Arianism, there was still a remnant of Christians and leaders who were committed to Nicaea. Among these were Paulinus, who became a rival bishop in the city, together with two influential ascetic lay leaders, Diodore and Flavian.

In 359, the See of Antioch fell vacant and the Arianizing Bishop Eudoxius was appointed but translated to Constantinople the following year. Meletius of Sebaste in Armenia was promoted to Antioch, but he was not supported by the more hardline Nicene Paulinus and his followers, who in turn convinced Rome and Alexandria that they alone were truly waving the banner for Nicene orthodoxy. The waters were further muddied by the exiling of Bishop Meletius soon after his appointment and the installation of yet another bishop, Euzoius, who was more Arian. It was during this period of ecclesiastical confusion and theological stand-off that John Chrysostom began to pursue his vocation as a monk, first in community, and then in isolation on Mount Silpios.

New opportunities beckoned and after the defeat of the Emperor Valens at Adrianople in 378, and with the arrival of Theodosius as the new Eastern emperor, a new council was called at Constantinople in 381. Initially chaired by the greatly respected and eirenic Meletius, his tragic and sudden death at the start of the proceedings left the Council to be chaired by Gregory of Nazianzus, who found himself unable to control the unruly and wrangling bishops.[6] It had been Meletius's wish that the equally aged Paulinus should succeed him, but others would not accept Paulinus. Flavian was appointed bishop of Antioch instead, and the schism continued.[7] The combination of this long-running dispute and the founding of the city of Constantinople in 324 meant that regional pre-eminence was gradually passing from Antioch in the East, the ancient seat of the emperors and of the Church-outside-Jerusalem, to Constantinople. Nevertheless, the rise of Constantinople was matched by the rivalry, and at times resentment, of Alexandria.

Constantinople

The distance from Constantinople to Antioch through Ankara, already an important regional city in the Roman Province of Phrygia, was almost exactly a thousand kilometres. Although a considerable distance away, Antioch must have felt the growing influence of Constantinople by the mid-fourth century. There had been a city on the north side of the Bosphorus for hundreds of years. Constantinople was established on the foundations of firstly a Persian, and then a Greek city called Byzantion in Greek, or, in Latin, Byzantium. At some point in the late fifth century BC, this town, with its wonderful position on the Bosphorus, was taken by the Spartan general Pausanias, who had defeated the Persians but was later suspected of conniving with them to his personal advantage and assassinated by his own people. By 470 BC, Byzantion began its long history as a Greek city in league variously with Sparta, Athens and Macedon. In 334, Alexander the Great cemented Byzantion under Greek hegemony in the Aegean and the Black Sea, but by 146 the city was falling under Roman sway. It was now linked to Rome by the Egnatian Way. By 73 and under the rule of Emperor Vespasian, Byzantium was fully integrated into the Roman Empire. Emperor Septimus Severus would then consolidate its position in 196, building new walls around it, but it was Constantine the Great, after his defeat of his co-emperor Licinius in the East, who saw its potential as the new Rome. And indeed, when Rome fell to Gothic invaders in 410, Constantinople would continue as the centre of Eastern Roman power and the Orthodox Church for 1,000 years, until the final victory of the Seljuk Turks under Mehmed II in 1453.

Soon after the defeat of Licinius at Chrysopolis, Constantine began a building programme which would turn Byzantium into the New Rome, although the city would not be officially named or formally "opened" until 330. Tens of thousands of Goths, now prisoners, began the vast public works required. New walls were built 53 metres high and four metres wide, and the city limits were moved a further 2,500 metres inland up the peninsula from the original Severian or Roman Walls of *c.*200.[8] New churches were built: Hagia Eirene (Peace), still standing today, simple and compelling in its style; Hagia Sophia, which would become the backdrop to John Chrysostom and the Empress Eudoxia's greatest confrontation (later rebuilt in the reign of Justinian to become the great church it is today); and, further inland, the Church of the Holy Apostles, where Constantine was to be buried alongside other Apostles, but which is no longer in existence. Around the First Hill, close to the Bosphorus, were the hippodrome, the basilica, a public assembly space, a theatre, the imperial palace and the senate. And, leading from this centre of the city, the Mese, a great marble street which connected the centre with the Egnatian Way at one of its many gates. From there the route continued across land and over sea to Rome itself. It was the artery that connected the beating hearts of East and West.

Since Constantinople was to be the New Rome, with buildings and churches to match—especially the great Hagia Sophia, first completed under Constantius II but magnificently rebuilt under the patronage of Emperor Justinian (527–65)—it needed leaders or bishops to project this aspiration. It was the misfortune of Constantinople to be built and finished during the theological storm and divisions created by the Arian controversy, however. With Constantinople, the New Rome, becoming the seat of imperial power in the East, bishops were very much the emperor's choice. And since the two emperors who ruled for most of the time between 337 and 380 were Constantius II and Valens, the brother of Gratian, emperor of the West, and since both were Arian, it meant that at least until the reign of Theodosius, Constantinople remained very much an Arian stronghold. A succession of Arian bishops were appointed until Gregory of Nazianzus became bishop of the city briefly in 380, following the defeat of the Goths by Theodosius and his appointment as emperor in the East.

The effect of this was to heighten the suspicions of Alexandria, which now saw Constantinople not only as a new political rival in the eastern Mediterranean, but also as theologically suspect. At the forefront of this theological struggle was Athanasius, advocate of Nicaea and bishop of Alexandria from 328–73 (although exiled five times during this period). At one point after Nicaea, in the interests of standing up to Arianism, and when there seemed to be a dangerous rapprochement between Constantine and Arius on the basis of a flimsy statement of faith in which the latter pretended to accept the Nicene Creed,[9] Athanasius threatened the Emperor Constantine with disruption to the corn supply from Alexandria to Constantinople. For this temerity, together with complaints orchestrated by the Arian party in Alexandria, Athanasius was sent to Trier for his first exile following the Council of Tyre in 335. From this period until well into the fifth century (indeed until after the Council of Chalcedon in 451), there was deep suspicion between Alexandria and Constantinople, sometimes with good reason, sometimes with none. This atmosphere became more settled after the Coptic Church split from the West and the Orthodox Church following the Council of Chalcedon.

When Gregory of Nazianzus was invited in 378 to preach Nicene Orthodoxy in a series of Orations (*Orations* 28, 29, 30 and 31) at the Anastasia Chapel, which belonged to an orthodox patron in Constantinople, he met with mixed messages from Alexandria.[10] Athanasius had died some five years earlier to be succeeded by Peter II, who spent much of his time in exile in Rome (373–8). There was then the reawakening of the Arian controversy in Alexandria itself, with rival factions re-emerging. But a little after that, at the Council of Constantinople in 381, Alexandria's fears proved real when it was announced that Constantinople should henceforth be granted "the privileges and rights of honour after the bishop of Rome".[11] In other words, Alexandria was to play second fiddle to Constantinople. To prevent this, and fearing or anticipating this move, Alexandria began under Peter II to manoeuvre an appointment of one of its own to the See of Constantinople.

At any rate, in May 380, after a torrid episode in which local Arians in Constantinople violently attacked Gregory's Easter celebrations in the Anastasia Chapel, an Egyptian contingent turned up to hear Gregory's justly famous theological *Orations* 28–30, which were preached that summer. Among these Egyptians was one Maximus, a lay philosopher from Alexandria who was thoroughly Nicene in his theology. Gregory was very taken with Maximus and gave him much support and encouragement. For his part, Maximus saw Gregory as vacillating and uncertain, which was probably true given his past and future record: not so much in doctrine, but in desiring the archbishopric of Constantinople and leadership in the Church.[12] At this point, the Egyptians in Alexandria began to canvas Maximus as a possible new Archbishop of Constantinople instead of Gregory, and a plot was hatched.

The extraordinary conspiracy involved a combination of Egyptians in the congregation at the Anastasia Chapel and a large number of Alexandrian sailors present in the port of Constantinople forcibly consecrating Maximus to the bishopric of Constantinople with the backing of the Nicene party and Peter II. A motley crowd marched to the church one evening, requisitioned it, and the liturgy of consecration began for this episcopal usurper. Gregory was not present, as he was recovering from an illness.[13] Others in the city got wind of the scheme and a combination of supporters of Gregory and Arian Christians (on opposite sides theologically) broke into the church to break up the consecration. The ceremonies of Anastasia were smashed by the Arian mob and the consecration ended. No one comes out of events well: the Alexandrian Nicene party for wanting Maximus, Gregory for being deceived by a charlatan, and the Arians for their second use of force in the chapel in almost as many months. In his autobiographical poem *De Vita Sua*, Gregory pours out his heart as one deceived and in searing and lengthy words of invective against Maximus says, "What was it that threw me headlong? The Egyptian's fickleness."[14] He had been taken in by the man he goes on to excoriate in his poem for his effeminate looks, his long hair, his curls, his mincing gait and his superficial faith.

Nor was that the end of the rivalry between Alexandria and Constantinople. It was to burst out again in the final years of John Chrysostom's ministry, leading to the Council of the Oak (403) to which we shall come. And finally, the great theological debate and controversy about the nature of Christ led to the Council of Chalcedon and the theological chasm between Archbishop Nestorius of Constantinople and Pope Cyril of Alexandria becoming permanent. The Nestorians left Constantinople. They were banished, but regrouped further east in Erbil, in present-day Iraq, while the Coptic Egyptian Monophysite Church broke from the Orthodox Church to create the first permanent schism in Christendom.

Alexandria

There is no doubt that Alexandria was one of the greatest cities in the ancient world, so it is not surprising that Constantinople should have been jealous of its standing and reputation. Founded in 331 BC by Alexander the Great on his way to consult the oracle at Siwa in the western Egyptian desert before his invasion of Persia, it flourished during the dynasty of the Ptolemies. The Ptolemies, Greek successors of Alexander's general and Macedonian companion, Ptolemy Lagides, who became the pharaoh or ruler styled Ptolemy I Soter (Saviour), moved their capital to Alexandria. It was here that Pompey's life ended in 48 BC, where he was assassinated on the orders of the Ptolemies, and it was here that Julius Caesar came, taking the city in 47 BC, and, with Cleopatra, fathering Caesarion. And finally, it was here that Octavian (Augustus) came after the defeat of Antony at the Battle of Actium 31 BC, where both Antony and Cleopatra died by suicide. Few cities had so many historical events—apart from Rome herself; few can boast being a hinge in history in the way that Alexandria was.

It was not only a city where dynasties rose and fell but was also one of great intellectual and commercial powers. Situated as a port on the Mediterranean and defended by lake Mareotis on the southern side, the city was located on a peninsula or spit of land with natural harbours to the north from where it was able to export the plentiful produce and grain from the Nile Delta. The city was laid out in a classical grid structure and at its height housed up to half a million citizens. On the coast were twin harbours, lying back to back: the original old harbour—natural and undefended—which gave way to the newer port, capable of handling the grain trade and with greater sea defences, and the great Pharos lighthouse to guide shipping. The districts were divided into three areas:

the old town of Rhakotis settled by Egyptians; the Bruchium, where the professional classes of Greek and Roman origin tended to live in spacious villas; and the Jewish quarter to the east of the Great Harbour. The city was made up of these competing and diverse communities: Egyptian, Roman, Greek and Jewish. This mix of peoples, together with the evident wealth of the city from trade and its position on the Nile Delta, made it a patron of the arts and of intellectual enquiry.

Under the Ptolemies, this intellectual quest took shape in a religious library: that is, a library whose roots lay not only in philosophic enquiry but in a deeper religious quest. The archive, called the Serapeum, was originally part temple and part library, but it was probably the largest deposit of books, be they codices or scrolls, in the ancient world, numbering at its height as many as 400,000 texts. Before its eventual tragic destruction, the Serapeum suffered damage over the years, such as when Julius Caesar besieged the city after his victory at Pharsalus in 48 BC; and it was finally destroyed in AD 495.[15] Yet such a library was nevertheless a magnet for study, teaching and research of all kinds.

In the third century BC, and quite possibly under the patronage of Ptolemy II (285–247 BC), 72 scholars in Alexandria, six, it is said, from each of the 12 tribes of Israel, were given the task of translating the Hebrew scriptures into Greek. By then, the Hebrew scriptures had been extensively used from the period of the Second Temple (i.e., from the end of the exile, or *c*.450 BC). By the third century BC, the Septuagint was produced and constituted a "publishing phenomenon". The fact that it was completed in Alexandria not only gave the Jewish community there great kudos, but also fired up Jewish studies in general. In particular, it inspired studies of the relationship between the Jewish Scriptures and Stoic Greek philosophy, a line pursued by Philo (*c*.20 BC–AD 50). This led to a further investigation of common ground between philosophy, especially Plato, and the Jewish Scriptures, and birthed the idea of the *Logos* as mediator of wisdom in both Greek philosophy and in the Second Temple wisdom literature or pseudepigrapha (e.g., the Wisdom of Solomon). What arose from this was the quest to build bridges between classical thought and the Jewish canon, which was mirrored in Philo's desire to bring amity between the Jewish and Greek communities there, for which he tirelessly worked. Indeed, it is said that he was so set on achieving this goal that he went on a mission to Emperor Caligula in Rome, that most capricious and unprepossessing of all emperors, in order to improve Jewish–Greek relations, which nevertheless remained rocky.

Alexandria was to remain a centre of Jewish and classical studies, inspiring both philosophical and Christian thinkers, with its great library a beacon for the intellectuals and teachers who gravitated there. According to Porphyry, Ammonius Saccas (c.175-242), the founder of neo-Platonist philosophy, taught both Origen and Plotinus philosophy. This would have given Origen knowledge of Greek philosophy, particularly of Plato, Aristotle and the Stoics, and he would have treated this as a means of understanding Scripture and of gaining wisdom. Scripture and philosophy were not considered at odds, as long as the latter was used only for endorsing the former (see Paul at Athens, Acts 17:16–33). Theological or catechetical schools were also established in Alexandria, no doubt drawing on the resources of the library to train future clergy. One such school was founded by Pantaenus, who subsequently went on a mission to India. He was succeeded then by Clement of Alexandria (c.150–215), and later, Origen.

Christian studies were also marked in Alexandria. In the late first century, the Evangelist Mark brought Christianity to the city, which proved fertile soil for the gospel and especially for stimulating theological enquiry. There is little evidence of a strong Christian presence in Alexandria before the second century, and in the second century there would be a serious struggle with Gnosticism.[16] The Coptic (Egyptian) Church would not be firmly established until the episcopacy of Demetrius I (189–231). It was around this time that the early and influential Alexandrian Christian teachers began to emerge. As we have seen, the catechetical school, led successively by Pantaenus, Clement and Origen, began to take root. Origen started writing works of theology, such as his seminal *On First Principles*, as well as exegetical works and his magnum opus, the *Hexapla*, which combined six existing translations of the Old Testament into Greek in a massive work numbering 6,500 pages of text on parchment. The growing influence of the catechetical school was to be challenged by the bishops of Alexandria, notably Demetrius I, however, and it was incorporated into the diocese under Bishop Heraclas

(214–247),[17] at which point, in 231, Origen left Alexandria for a second career as principal of a new college he started in Caesarea, Palestine.

By 300, the power of the Alexandrian see was greatly enhanced and looking to consolidate its authority further over a large and often unruly archdiocese. Persecution under Diocletian, and later under Galerius, effectively split the Church, with bishops and clergy under Melitius's sway seceding because of what they saw as Bishop Peter I's failure to withstand persecution by himself going into hiding.[18] The Melitians considered this flight by Peter a dereliction of pastoral oversight, although later Peter, like Cyprian, would be martyred by Galerius, once he decided that valour was the better part of discretion. This schism, which like the Donatist schism in Latin North Africa persisted, did not prevent the bishops of Alexandria accruing further authority, although a new challenge in the form of Arianism was only years away.

We have already taken into account the course of Arianism, which was birthed by Arius around 312–21, and which quite probably originated in present-day Libya, after taking some of its shape from Platonism and also from the more literal and Jewish-leaning school of biblical studies at Antioch. Although the authority of a bishop like Alexander (312–28) in Alexandria was increasing, there were still fissures in the Church there, caused by the Melitian schism and a group of more-or-less independent churches in the city. These fissures allowed heresy to take root,[19] especially from someone like Arius, who was plausible, capable of subtle argument, and compelling. After Nicaea, and his election as bishop in 328, Athanasius remained in the position until 373, although his tenure was punctuated by five exiles. Athanasius's powerful advocacy of the Nicene cause gave him prominence throughout the empire. His thorough narrative of the Arian controversy, his popular book on the *Life of Antony* and his theological writings, such as *Contra Gentes: De Incarnatione*, gave him and the Alexandrian see a high international profile. With the support of the newly founded monastic communities, and in particular of the monk Antony the Great, who gave him unswerving allegiance, Athanasius's stature was greatly enhanced. By 380, Alexandria saw itself as one of the foremost sees in Christendom. It had spiked the guns of Arianism; it had ensured the support of literally hundreds of monks; it was heir to a great theological and catechetical school; and it was well known throughout the empire. It would not sit idly by and see its place usurped by another, particularly the newly created capital of Constantinople. It was this trajectory which in time was to prove so destructive to Chrysostom and so useful to the empress. Ecclesiastical ambition began to suborn doctrinal orthodoxy.

This antipathy came to a head under Athanasius's successors. We have already noted the intervention of Peter II (373–80) in the appointment of a new bishop of Constantinople, ahead of Gregory of Nazianzus, in the person of Maximus.[20] But worse was to come under the episcopacy of the iconoclastic Theophilus (385–412), who was responsible for the destruction of the library or Serapeum, and the bizarre dispute with the Tall Brothers, which, as we shall see, effectively ended Chrysostom's ministry in Constantinople. If ever there was a case of ecclesiastical aggrandizement allied to political conspiracy and theological expediency, it was this; but we must leave the explanation of this episode until the dispute between empress and bishop. It is enough to note here that this rivalry between the great sees of the empire led eventually to the existence of the three different denominations of Orthodox (Constantinople), Catholic (Rome) and Coptic (Alexandria). There may have been evident theological differences, but there was also more than an ounce of human ambition mixed in, and here Rome was no exception.

Rome

By the beginning of the fourth century, the glory days of Rome had passed, although it was probably still the largest city in the world. Great emperors, such as Octavian (or Augustus), Hadrian or Marcus Aurelius were not to return. Although Alexandria had settled at about half a million inhabitants, and likewise Constantinople had quicky grown to that figure by the end of the fourth century (being only founded in 324), Rome was still a city of about a million people at the time of Constantine's conquest of Rome and his defeat of the usurper Maxentius at the Battle of Milvian Bridge in 312. Arguably, the division of the empire into a *quadrivium* with two *augusti* and two *caesars* served to diminish the political and symbolic importance of Rome. Instead, new regional capitals developed at places of greater strategic importance to the divisions of the empire, such as Trier in the north; Milan guarding access to the Alps from the south; and Constantinople, Thessalonica and Antioch in the east. By the time of the accession of Arcadius in the East in 383 (the heir of Theodosius I and husband of the Empress Eudoxia, whose story we shall soon follow), there were less than 30 years before Rome would be taken and sacked by the Goths in 410. In other words, Rome was in a time of transition, not only in its political and military importance but also in terms of moving from a pagan metropolis of unsurpassed importance to becoming the centre of the Western Catholic Church. And this by virtue of its history and association with Saints Peter and Paul, the most influential followers of Christ.

The changes began when Constantine entered Rome after the decisive battle of Milvian Bridge. He was 39 years old, at the peak of his powers, and had, just before the battle, proclaimed allegiance to Christ. This conversion followed a vision of some kind, as recorded by Eusebius and Lactantius.[21] Constantine commanded in consequence that the new Christian Chi-Rho emblem be placed on his soldiers' shields and banners. When he entered the city, the emperor did not sacrifice at the Temple of Capitoline Jupiter as former emperors did after victory, but instead restored to the Church property confiscated during the Great Persecution.[22] Furthermore, he endowed new churches, taking properties either from pagan temples or from his defeated opponents and handing them over to church authorities. Constantine also built the Basilica Constantiniana, now St John's in Lateran, having seized the property from the Laterani family.[23] Although a different structure, the church survives there today. It was a huge five-aisle basilica, 55 metres wide and 95 metres long.[24] Further churches were built in a flurry of construction: the Basilica of St Peter and St Marcellinus with a mausoleum attached for the burial of Constantine's mother, Helena; the Basilica of the Apostles (now San Sebastiano); St Peter's Basilica in the Vatican, outside the old Aurelian walls; the Basilica of San Paolo (St Paul's Outside the Walls) on Via Ostiense near the Tiber; the Basilica of St Laurence; and the Chapel of the Holy Cross close by the Lateran (now Santa Croce in Gerusalemme). Many of these structures were completed during Constantine's life, and they underlined the transition of the city from pagan to Christian.

The church in Rome had survived for 250 years before this imperial endowment, which included not only property, but also privileges for the clergy, especially bishops. From the very beginning, it seemed that the church in Rome, rather than being a large unitary entity, was split into many home churches with loose connections. The final chapter of Romans, written in about 57, bears witness to this with the greetings Paul makes to the leaders of these home or villa churches (Romans 16:1-16).[25] It is because of this dispersed and possibly divided church that Paul appeals for unity "within the scattered and quite possibly mutually suspicious churches in Rome".[26] It is quite probable, given the tenor, scope and direction of Paul's letter to the Romans, that these home churches were divided essentially between Jews and Gentiles.

The Church was under pressure both from within and from without in the first three centuries. There was the pressure of being out of step with pagan aspirations and the pervasive culture of Rome, which was based on military power, intrigue, cruelty and conquest. The Church was also, as Tertullian suggests in his *Apologia*, the convenient scapegoat for anything that went wrong, from the great fire of Rome under Nero in July 64 to a temporary flooding of the city by the Tiber.[27] For these things, Christians were killed in the amphitheatres. In the first 250 years of the Church's life in Rome, as many as 28 bishops were martyred, and the almost ceaseless pressure meant that divisive disputes emerged over how to treat the lapsed after the Decian persecution in *c.*250.

Alongside the effects of persecution were a number of doctrinal disputes as well as heresiarchs threatening the church in Rome. Among these were Marcion of Sinope, a shipbuilder and Christian (*c.*85-150), who challenged the authenticity of the Bible aside from the Gospels and Pauline epistles, and who initially found favour in Rome because of his wealth and patronage. Later, there was the Gnostic Valentinus, who came from Alexandria and was very nearly elected bishop of Rome. This was followed by the monarchical controversy (198 onwards) involving Bishop Callistus of Rome (*c.*218-22) and his theological opponents Hippolytus and Tertullian in the early third century, which anticipated the much greater Arian controversy of the fourth century in terms of its debates about the Trinity. In effect, the controversy revolved around those like Callistus, and later Paul of Samosata, who stressed the monarchy of the

Father, and those like Origen (c.185–253) and Hippolytus (c.175–235), who stressed the individuated divinity of Son and Spirit, which they described with the term *hypostasis*. The lawyer and theologian Tertullian encapsulated the Latin view of the Godhead with the tag that God is "one substance consisting in three persons".[28] It was this definition that would become a bulwark of orthodoxy in the Latin Church of the West.

It is no surprise then, given its past, that the Church in Rome has been characterized in recent scholarship as having "multiple Christian identities and communities [which] were continually created and transformed".[29] Nevertheless, there was a sense of there being a great Church from which orthodox catholic leadership would come.[30] It was not until the early fourth century and the Edict of Milan, together with the incorporation of Christianity into the empire as a legitimate religion, thereby giving Christians freedom of worship, that the Roman Church began to take on a more authoritative role outside the city. In many ways, the Arian controversy served only to strengthen its position as such. It was from the mid-fourth century, around 337, soon after Nicaea and the death of Constantine, that Rome had strong bishops or popes in succession. These were Julius (337–51), Liberius (352–66) and Damasus (366–84). Each of them saw Athanasius as the torch bearer for Nicene and Western orthodoxy, and all of them, especially Damasus, were willing to use strong-arm tactics to achieve their objectives.

With these three relatively long-ruling popes, the authority and confidence of Rome grew, both in intervening in the Church's affairs further afield, even in the East, and in shaping the Western response. In 341, following Athanasius's first exile, Julius held a small council in Rome at which, after examination, Athanasius was exonerated of all charges. Julius then wrote to the Eusebians at Antioch on the issue.[31] Although Julius may not have understood the intricacies of the Greek use of the word *homoousios* and its derivatives, he was confident enough to intervene and give support to the Alexandrian position, as Rome had traditionally done, as well as to caution the Eusebians. Despite the fruitful creed-making at the Council of Antioch in 341, the West paid little attention to the creeds enacted there. The next council, actually at Serdica in 343 as we have seen, was a debacle with neither Eastern or Western bishops meeting, being profoundly split over Athanasius. The meeting of Western bishops at Serdica two years after Antioch showed some serious grappling with the terminology of the East, however. There appears to have been genuine disagreement over the use of language: with the West using the term *hypostasis* and applying it to the Godhead as whole; and the East increasingly using *hypostases* to describe each member of the Godhead.[32] To put it simply, the East recognized the threeness of the Godhead, while the West acknowledged the singleness, in which a common substance was shared.

Liberius, who succeeded Julius, continued the stand-off with Emperor Constantius and his Arianizing policies. A council requested by Liberius at Milan in 355 failed to get off the ground, and in 356 Liberius refused to accept gifts from Constantius for the memorial chapel of Peter's tomb.[33] A further council was called at the request of the emperor at Sirmium on the Sava in present-day Serbia in 357, and under imperial pressure several Nicene bishops, notably the very elderly Ossius, signed up to an Arianizing creed. Constantius began to see a way of establishing a consensus in the Church around the *homoiousion* position, by excluding the extremes at both ends: the extreme Arians like Eunomius and committed Nicenes like Athanasius. In 359, a council was called for the Eastern bishops at Seleucia and for the Western bishops at Rimini or Ariminum. The Eastern council steered clear of all *ousia* language, holding that Father and Son were just like (*homoios*), while the Western bishops were firm in their support of Athanasius. Liberius did not go to either council, and by 361 the reign of Constantius and his policies ended with his death, although the latter would be resurrected by the later Eastern emperor, Valens. Five years later, in 366, Damasus succeeded Liberius.

By all accounts, Damasus was a belligerent pope, intent on extending Rome's sway. J. N. D. Kelly maintains that he was not above using a gang of thugs to attack his opponents and their churches. He was willing also to face down Ursinus, a rival for the papacy and someone who was expected to succeed Liberius at his death.[34] It does seem that he was something of an aggrandizing pope seeking to further establish Rome's authority. He did this by forceful interventions in church affairs, sending commissaries to councils, as at Constantinople, to combat heretics like the Spirit-fighters from Macedonia (who did not accept the divinity of the

Spirit) and the Apollinarians (who argued that Jesus had a human body but a divine mind). Most importantly he commissioned Jerome to begin writing the Latin Vulgate Bible, having established the books of the Bible in a council in Rome in 382. This was to be the text of Christendom in the West until the Renaissance and the Reformation, with new translations forthcoming with the advent of Erasmus, Luther and Tyndale. In this way, Damasus laid the foundation of Roman Catholic influence or power.

As Rome's confidence about intervening outside its own region increased to the point of consciously holding a right or mandate to intervene in the Church in matters of doctrine and practice, so its relationships with other ecclesiastical centres became more strained. As far as Antioch was concerned, Damasus, like popes before him, supported the more extreme Nicene position of Paulinus and so cut the ground from the Nicene-supporting but more tolerant leader, Bishop Meletius of Antioch, and his successor, Flavian. Although very much in sympathy with Athanasius after his death, Rome became increasingly suspicious of Alexandrian influence in Constantinople, for seeking to elect a bishop amenable to Alexandria and hence opposing Gregory of Nazianzus in 380 and John Chrysostom later on. In effect, this ecclesiastical quadrilateral, subsequently reduced to three with the decline of Antioch's influence, would dictate Church affairs from the fifth century onwards and would lead to two schisms, firstly with the Coptic Church over the Chalcedonian definition of Christ's nature, and then much later with the Orthodox Church in 1054. These churches were not prepared to accept Rome's hegemony in matters of doctrine or practice; nor were these great cities prepared to play second fiddle to Rome.

It was into this all-too-human power play of ecclesiastical politics that John Chrysostom was born and, to his cost, these tensions only became more evident during his lifetime. This was the complex church background into which John arrived.

Notes

1. Tom Wright, *Paul: A Biography* (London: SPCK, 2020), pp. 86ff.
2. Ignatius, *Letter to the Smyrneans 4*, in *The Apostolic Fathers I*, Loeb Classical Library, Vol. 24 (Cambridge, MA: Harvard University Press, 2003), p. 299, p. 301.
3. Rowan Williams, *Arius: Heresy and Tradition* (London: SCM Press, 2001), p. 31.
4. Lewis Ayres, *Nicaea and its Legacy* (Oxford: Oxford University Press, 2009), p. 174.
5. J. N. D. Kelly, *Golden Mouth: The Story of John Chrysostom, Ascetic, Preacher, Bishop* (Ithaca, NY: Cornell University Press, 1998), p. 12.
6. Gregory Nazianzen, *Oratio 42*, in *Nicene and Post-Nicene Fathers: Second Series, Vol. VII: Cyril of Jerusalem, Gregory of Nazianzen*, ed. Philip Schaff (New York: Cosimo, 2007), pp. 385ff.
7. John A. McGuckin, *Saint Gregory of Nazianzus: An Intellectual Biography* (Crestwood, NY: St Vladimir's Seminary Press, 2001), pp. 350–1.
8. Bettany Hughes, *Istanbul: A Tale of Three Cities* (London: Weidenfeld & Nicolson, 2017), p. 113.
9. See *Socrates Scholasticus*, Chapter XXIX (Philadelphia, PA: Aeterna Press, 2016), pp. 53ff.
10. McGuckin, *Saint Gregory of Nazianzus*, pp. 229ff.
11. Stephen J. Davis, *The Early Coptic Papacy: The Egyptian Church and its Leadership in Late Antiquity* (Cairo: American University in Cairo Press, 2004).
12. McGuckin, *Saint Gregory of Nazianzus*, pp. 312ff.
13. McGuckin, *Saint Gregory of Nazianzus*, p. 317.
14. Gregory Nazianzen, *De Vita Sua*, tr. Caroline White (Cambridge: Cambridge University Press, 1996), pp. 67–93, lines 113–1272.
15. See Luciano Canfora, *The Vanished Library: A Wonder of the Ancient World*, tr. Martin Ryle (Berkeley, CA: University of California Press, 1989).
16. See Walter Bauer, *Orthodoxy and Heresy in Earliest Christianity* (Philadelphia, PA: Fortress Press, 1971).
17. Davis, *The Early Coptic Papacy*, p. 27.
18. Davis, *The Early Coptic Papacy*, pp. 34ff.
19. Williams, *Arius*, p. 44.

20 Gregory Nazianzen, *De Vita Sua*, op. cit., pp. 67–93, lines 728–1112.
21 Jonathan Bardill, *Constantine: Divine Emperor of the Christian Golden Age* (Cambridge: Cambridge University Press, 2015), pp. 220ff.
22 David Potter, *Constantine the Emperor* (Oxford: Oxford University Press, 2013), p. 145.
23 Bardill, *Constantine*, p. 237.
24 Bardill, *Constantine*, p. 237.
25 Wright, *Paul*, p. 434.
26 Wright, *Paul*, p. 336.
27 Tertullian, *Apologia*, in *The Ante-Nicene Fathers: The Writings of the Fathers down to A.D. 325 Volume III Latin Christianity: Its Founder, Tertullian,* Vol. III:1 (New York: Cosimo, 2007), p. 47.
28 Henry Chadwick, *The Early Church* (Harmondsworth: Penguin, 1993), p. 89.
29 David Brakke, *The Gnostics: Myth, Ritual and Diversity in Early Christianity* (Cambridge, MA: Harvard University Press, 2010), p. 12.
30 John Behr, *Irenaeus of Lyons: Identifying Christianity* (Oxford: Oxford University Press, 2015), p. 9.
31 R. P. C. Hanson, *The Search for the Christian Doctrine of God: The Arian Controversy 318–381* (London: T&T Clark, 1988), p. 271.
32 Hanson, *The Search for the Christian Doctrine of God*, p. 301.
33 Hanson, *The Search for the Christian Doctrine of God*, p. 340.
34 J. N. D. Kelly, *Oxford Dictionary of Popes* (Oxford: Oxford University Press, 1979).

4
John Chrysostom: Early years and vocation

John was born in Antioch, probably between 349 and 351. From a passing reference to a young widow in correspondence in later years, it seems that the likeliest date is 349.[1] He was born in the reign of Constantius II, Constantine's second son by his wife Fausta, and, as we have seen, an inveterate advocate of Arianism.

John's father, Secundus (quite possibly Roman, rather than Greek), worked for the imperial administration in Antioch. He was comfortably off and part of the ruling class, if not in the first rank. His mother, Anthousa, was a devout Christian, and after the early death of her husband when she was only 20 years old, and with two small children (John and his elder sister), she became responsible for the household. Like many devout Christian widows, she set herself against a second marriage, pursuing instead the much-lauded vocation of celibacy or chastity, albeit after a first marriage. It was a committed Christian household, located in a villa, probably in the garden suburbs of a city which by then numbered at least 200,000 inhabitants.

Anthousa struggled to bring up her family, not financially, but emotionally. In his work *De Sacerdotio* (*On the Priesthood*), John recalls his mother's pleas that he would not leave her for an ascetic life on the nearby Mount Silpios. *De Sacerdotio* is generally assigned to a much later period of 387–93,[2] but it was initially prompted by John's concern for his university friend Basil, who wanted to give up the idea of priesthood for a monk's existence. John sought to encourage Basil to consider becoming a presbyter, however demanding that role, and this he outlines in this work. He sensed Basil's call to the priesthood, something he did not want his friend to evade, although both men were anxious lest they should be dragged into it by the wider Christian community. The work recalls John's own memories of leaving home for a life of monasticism. He describes the moment his mother heard of his intention of taking up a monastic or eremitic existence:

> When she perceived that I was meditating [on] this step, she took me into her own private chamber, and, sitting near me on the bed where she had given birth to me, she shed torrents of tears, to which she added words yet more pitiable than her weeping.[3]

She recalled sorrowfully her all-too-brief marriage before the death of her husband and pointed out John's resemblance to his father and the trials of widowhood: being fleeced by servants, being sponged on by relations, and facing the costs of an expensive education for her promising son, now considering throwing away all its benefits. At the end of this heartfelt plea, Anthousa made one last attempt at dissuading John from his proposed course of action:

> My foremost help indeed was the grace from above; but it was no small consolation to me under those terrible trials, to look continually on thy face and preserve in thee a living image of him [John's father] who had gone, an image indeed which was a fairly exact likeness . . . Yet do not think that I say these things by way of reproaching you, only in return for all these benefits I beg one favour: do not plunge me into a second widowhood: nor revive the grief which is now laid to rest; wait for my death—it maybe in a little while I shall depart.[4]

It was a heartfelt cry and few could have resisted it, yet despite his mother's pleas and tears, John demonstrated that single-mindedness that would characterize his life and for which he would become well known. He left home and pursued his ascetic calling.

Prior to this, John had been given a first-rate education in one of the great intellectual centres of the empire, and also familiarity with one of its great churches from infancy. From the age of seven, he would have attended an elementary school where the basics of reading, writing and arithmetic were instilled. From this primary education, he would have progressed to the grammar school, where, as the name implies, he would have concentrated on classical literature and Greek authors such as Homer, Herodotus and Thucydides, as well as the tragedians: Euripides, Aeschylus and Sophocles. Presumably the tragedians would have taught him the elements of drama and speech, which would prove useful for his later ministry.

The last stage of his education might well have proved the most useful and consisted in rhetoric. In this, John would also have been exposed to the thinking of Plato and Socrates, as well as the ethics of Aristotle. He was taught by the great pagan teacher Libanius (314–93) and also attended the lectures of Andragathios, who was probably a philosopher.[5] Various other pupils were John's constant companions: Basil, for whom he wrote *De Sacerdotio* (1:1) and another Theodore, who would become bishop of Mopsuestia and one of the great theologians and biblical commentators of his generation. John would later persuade him to pursue an ascetic calling when he was thinking of giving it up.[6] Almost without exception, many of the Greek and Latin Fathers, such as Basil of Caesarea,[7] Jerome and Rufinus, publicly repudiated, or least questioned, the spiritual worth of a classical education because of its pagan influence. Nonetheless each benefited from their work and from the insights and disciplines gained. John himself gained a purity of diction and an elegance of expression that would stay with him throughout his life and ministry. "Modern connoisseurs of Greek literature have united in acclaiming him an almost pure Atticist." Only Demosthenes stood comparison with him.[8] When his old teacher Libanius lay dying and was asked who should succeed him, he answered, "It ought to have been John had not the Christians stolen him from us."[9]

Thus, equipped with the best education that Antioch could supply, coming from the elite of its society, and most probably known to the imperial administration, John might well have completed his training in law and prepared for a glittering career in Roman administration in the East. Not so. For a time, he toured the law courts with his close friend Basil, gaining familiarity with the legal system and the skills of advocacy, but the pull of his faith and insistent vocation began to lead him in a different direction. There was an inner stirring and his biographer Palladius said that having left the schools of Libanius, his superstitious but talented teacher, he was now considering "the service of the divine oracles".[10]

We have only sketchy knowledge of the church in Antioch then, but we do know that Arianism had created bitter divisions in the Church as a whole, and especially in Antioch, where it would be divided for at least two generations. By 331, just six years after Nicaea, those, like the Eusebians, who opposed the Nicene Creed and the employment of the *homoousios* definition of the Son being of the same substance (*ousia*) as the Father managed to eject the Nicene-supporting Bishop of Antioch, Eustathius, much loved though he was by the church there. The exact charge against Eustathius is unknown,[11] but it was probably one of Sabellianism (that is, believing that the persons of the Trinity were different modes of divine being—in other words he stressed the unity of the Godhead over the Trinity (to individual beings sharing a common substance)). He went into exile, but the church split and a Nicene-supporting church called the Eustathians came into being, holding out a more fundamental Nicene position. Eventually led by Paulinus, it was supported by Rome and Gregory of Nazianzus.

In 341, almost a decade before John's birth, a council at Antioch was attended by some 90 bishops for the dedication of the new Great Church begun by Constantine and completed under Constantius II, and to hammer out new creeds.[12] The so-called Dedication Creed came very close to the Nicene position, but did not state the eternal nature of the Son's Kingdom, holding instead that the Son was "the exact image of the Father", which most Arians would not accept.[13] A succession of Arian bishops would follow, culminating with Eudoxius, an imperial placeman, who was only briefly bishop of Antioch before being appointed to Constantinople. By 361, the godly, but less theologically intransigent Meletius, had been appointed to Antioch. Although by no means Arian or ultra-Nicene, he nonetheless displeased Emperor Constantius II, and on three occasions was sent into exile. John took Meletius's position in these controversies. He was Nicene in outlook, if not as ultra-Nicene as Paulinus, as he makes clear in his book on the priesthood, in which he writes, "The Godhead of the Father and of the Son and of the Holy Ghost, is all one, while we add thereunto a Trinity of Persons ... and maintain they are of the same substance."[14]

John completed his studies aged 18, in or around 367,[15] and for a time thereafter considered the possibility of a legal career. He was still at home and had not yet had that painful bedside conversation with his mother about his intended future. His friendship with Basil and Theodore deepened. He may well have worshipped as a child at the newly opened Great Church along with his family, rather than at the Church of the Apostles, where the congregation supporting Paulinus gathered. By 365, aged 15, he had most probably worshipped with the followers of Meletius outside the Great Church on the banks of the Orontes.[16] He had not at that point been baptized, but he soon fell under the sway of Meletius and his followers and offered himself for baptism at Easter 368, aged about 18.[17] For the next three years, he attached himself to Meletius and moved into a more committed form of Christianity. He became an official reader of the church (an *anagnostes* in Greek, or lector in Latin) but was soon looking for more. Having attended a kind of ascetic school led by two notable laymen, Diodore and Flavian, and having been an aide, mentee or apprentice of Meletius, he was ready for a more committed and demanding step.

Meletius remained in exile until 378 when the Arian emperor Valens was killed at the Battle of Adrianople by the Goths. He then returned to Antioch, and with the appointment of Theodosius as *augustus* in the East, a whole new future opened up. Those intervening years from 372 to 378 were the ones when John left home to live the life of a solitary, aged about 23, and perhaps triggered by the absence of his mentor Meletius. Likewise, he encouraged Basil, and then Theodore, to do the same. These six years of isolation, so different from what his mother had envisaged, devout though she was, and so out of keeping with what his élite education had prepared him for, gave John a spiritual foundation from which he never departed.

John the Ascetic

As we have already seen, the ascetic movement took off in the early fourth century, especially in Egypt, Syria and Palestine. Building on the idea of the philosophical life prevalent in classical times, it centred on withdrawal, contemplation and abstinence, especially abstinence from luxurious food, sex and marriage. By 372, a year before the death of Athanasius (*c.*295–373), and well after the death of Pachomius (292–348), manuscripts on the ascetic life were probably circulating in the Ancient Near East, not least Athanasius's *Life of Antony* and the monastic rules of Pachomius and Basil of Caesarea. So many of the leading Christians espoused and advocated the ascetic life, while works on virginity—which meant not just abstinence from sex, but the embrace of a disciplined life of abstinence, contemplation and prayer—abounded. Indeed, it would not be long before John himself wrote a work *On Virginity*. Nor is it surprising that a serious-minded and talented young man like Chrysostom should embrace this now popular, almost fashionable, and defining movement. However popular, even fashionable, the movement became, it was still a radical break with the *cursus honorum* (the Roman career path) which a man like John would have been expected to take given his education, skills and family background. Nor was it surprising, therefore, that his mother should weep on the bed beside him, having survived 20 years of widowhood and having brought up her son in the way her beloved husband would have wanted, only to see him throw it all away for the life of an income-less hermit on a nearby mountain. Indeed, the sacrifice was as much hers as his; maybe it was even greater for her since it was not of her choosing. Her future was rendered more insecure with no breadwinner in the household and her friends surely mostly pitied her, rather than instinctively applauding.

Sometime in 372, while in his early twenties, John, along with Basil and Theodore, finally left home. Palladius of Galatia, his biographer, tells us that "he betook himself to the nearby mountains".[18] In so doing he avoided ordination during a time of uncertainty, when Meletius and a number of other clergy were removed once more into exile. Furthermore, Palladius suggests that this drastic step was also due to John wanting to put to death the passions which might overwhelm his soul, not least his burgeoning sexuality as a young man. In *On the Priesthood*, which is directed in part both at himself and his friend Basil, he writes, "For even now I am taken captive by vainglory, but I often recover myself, and I see at a glance that I have been taken, and there are times when I rebuke my soul, which has been enslaved; outrageous deists even now come over me, but they kindle only a languid flame, *since my bodily eyes cannot fasten upon any fuel to feed the fire.*"[19] This was a roundabout way of saying he had removed himself from the presence of women. In other words, by removing himself to a hut on the side of a mountain, bereft of society, and where he could not see women, he believed he was more likely to keep himself pure. The witness of the Desert Fathers is that this was not so simply achieved, for they were pursued by lustful thoughts even in their solitary loneliness, sometimes even more so, with such thoughts developing into obsessions.[20]

Naturally, John made for Mount Silpios on the southeast side of the city, which rose to about 400 metres and had become a kind of holy mountain favoured by the hermits and contemplatives of Antioch. The historian and bishop Theodoret (*c.*393–466) of Kyrrhos, north of Antioch on the Orontes, called it as beautiful as a flower-decked meadow, although it was in fact very rocky, craggy and uninviting. Here John began his ascetic career, initially among the other solitaries who lived in a collection of huts. It seems that from the outset John was in some form of community, where he feared he would be given endless back-breaking tasks and go short of food or be given "a diet of wretched lentils with little meat or bread".[21]

There was a daily regimen: an early wake-up call from a community leader who may or may not have been John's mentor, and four services of prayer each day equivalent to the Latin monastic offices of terce, sext, nones and vespers. At these services, the community sang psalms in unison, quite probably from memory, and Scripture was read. There was meditation on Scripture and further prayer in each person's cell, and the rule of silence was strictly observed. Between these prayer services, there was work to do: they grew their own food, sold produce to others, wove baskets and made clothes. Diet was most simple: lentils, vegetables, bread and salt, and often no olive oil. There would be fasting in the weeks leading up to Easter, now known as Lent. Theodoret was the single greatest chronicler of the Syrian monks and wrote about 28 male ascetics and three women whom he revered, particularly in his *Philotheus* (or *Historia religiosa*).[22] Theodoret presents these monks, like those in Egypt, as champions of Nicene orthodoxy, although in Antioch, as we have already seen, there were different shades of such orthodoxy, ranging from that of Paulinus to Meletius. For nearly four years, John followed this way of life, but being John, was also ready for the most demanding form of asceticism. Having mastered himself, perhaps learning that "chastity is born of tranquillity, and silence, and inner prayer",[23] and having met the demands of this lifestyle, he was ready to face the toughest test: living totally alone on the mountainside.

At this point, and for two more years, John embarked on a form of monasticism that might strike us as either totally bizarre or heroic, and which was, in his case, health-breaking. He withdrew to a lonely cave on another part of the mountain. His abstinence was complete. There was no society, and he was alone for the best part of two years. He abstained from all but the most frugal food, barely enough to keep him alive. Furthermore, in another twist of the monk's ascetic tale, he hardly slept, but followed the discipline of *stasis*, which was then being practised by monks, especially by the end of the fourth century and the early fifth. *Stasis* meant not lying down, and enduring sleep deprivation by standing in one's cell day and night. If these were the negatives of this extreme form of monasticism, the positive purpose was to maintain an uninterrupted communion with God. "Their supreme objective was, as far as possible, to commune with God continually, and any practice or indulgence that stood in the way of this was to be rigorously excluded."[24] At the same time, John pursued a feat of memory not unknown in the monastic community and quite possibly true of Antony himself: he learnt the entire Old and New Testament.[25] In later life, as a consummate preacher, this absolute recall of the biblical text must have been of inordinate value, but at what cost!

By the end of these two years, John's health was broken by sleep deprivation, lack of basic food and self-mortification. Nevertheless, he always considered the life of a monk the life of a full and committed Christian, and he arguably believed that even though living in the world, both laity and clergy should follow such precepts as much as they were able. In fact, he never departed from this way of life himself, even when great influence and power became his. If the harsh environment of solitary monasticism had established in him a way of life he would keep for the rest of his life, in whatever way he practically could, two further great facets of his ministry, those of writer and preacher, would be added to this ascetic base.

Ascetic writings

It was about this time (372–8) that John began writing. It may not have been in his solitary sojourn in the cave, but it was soon after or even just before. John did not have a library in his cave such as the one Jerome was later to secrete into his. Jerome, an ambitious 33-year-old, had arrived in Antioch from Rome and Aquileia in 373, just as John was beginning his own ascetic seclusion, and he would remain in Antioch and its environs until 376.[26] For most of this time, Jerome resided locally with the monk Evagrius, an ascetic scholar and role model who had translated Athanasius's *Life of Antony* into Latin. Like John, Jerome also sought utter seclusion, and so, for 18 months likewise lived in a cave in the hinterland of Antioch, quite possibly near to John on Mount Silpios. While Jerome was writing his *Life of Paul*, who he considered the first Christian hermit, John too wrote three works, in keeping with this mix of asceticism and literary output. They were not only written to make a literary name for himself in the burgeoning world of Christian ascetism, but also stemmed from pastoral concern for two of his friends who needed encouragement to remain on the path of renunciation. The three main works to consider in this matter are *On the Priesthood*, *To Theodore When He Fell Away* and *A King and a Monk Compared*. Later works that similarly defend monasticism and renunciation are *On Virginity* and *Against the Enemies of Monasticism*, along with pastoral letters that reflect their thinking.

On the Priesthood was written either before or soon after John's monastic withdrawal. Of the two possibilities, it is more likely to have been before his monastic experience, as the work serves as both an encouragement to his friend Basil to consider the possibility of priesthood, and also a warning about not entering such an office hastily. And perhaps more germane: no one should place themselves in a position where they might be forced into the priesthood by others. It is clear that at the time of writing, which was around 372, John thought his friend Basil was more suited to the priesthood than himself. He may have either encouraged or acquiesced in his friend being seized for ordination, to the point where Basil felt himself manipulated when John was not himself willing to take the same step.[27] It was not unusual for men to be almost press-ganged into the office of priest or bishop in those days. The selection process involved a person's peers or pastors and their own evident skills, rather than any personal sense of calling. In other words, community calling was more important than personal conviction. This was the experience of many, and notably of Ambrose of Milan and Augustine of Hippo, who were both made bishops forcibly, and also of Gregory of Nazianzus, who felt press-ganged into ordination by his powerful father.[28]

Whatever the exact circumstances or reason for its writing, *On the Priesthood* is a great summary of the scope and responsibility of priestly ministry, and a forerunner to such works as Gregory the Great's *Pastoral Rule*, Richard Baxter's *Reformed Pastor* and, much later, Michael Ramsey's *The Christian Priest Today*. At the outset, John says that priestly ministry, as laid on the Apostle Peter to care for the sheep (see John 21:15–17), is the greatest proof of love for Christ (1:§1). He quickly goes on to say that it is the most demanding of tasks, as Gregory of Nazianzus himself said.[29] John elaborates, using a medical metaphor:

> Much skill is required so that our patients may be induced to submit willingly to their treatment prescribed by the physicians, and not only this, but that they may be grateful also for the cure. The Pastor has need of much discretion, and a myriad of eyes to observe on every side the habit of the soul. For as many are uplifted to pride, and then sink into despair of their salvation, from inability to endure severe remedies; so, there are some, who from paying no penalty equivalent to their sins fall into negligence, and become far worse, and are impelled to greater sins. It behoves the priest therefore to leave none of these things unexamined, but, after a thorough inquiry into all of them, to

apply such remedies as he has appositely to each case, lest his zeal prove to be in vain.[30]

Later John would say "more billows vex the soul of the priest than the gales which disturb the sea".[31]

While Book II proceeds along the lines of a dialogue between Basil and John about the demands of the priesthood, indicating how Basil might be ready but John, in his own estimation, is not, Book III only heightens the sense of the awesome responsibility of being a priest. There is more than a hint of John making a defence of his own reluctance to enter the priesthood in the face of the charge that he seeks worldly glory elsewhere. Nothing could be further from the truth, John argues. It is in fact the very greatness of the office, "ranking among the heavenly ordinances" that deters him.[32] Indeed, "what priests do here below, God ratifies above, and the Master confirms the sentence of his servants".[33] Such is the authority and responsibility of priests that the sins forgiven by priests on earth are forgiven by God in heaven.[34] John also shows his prejudices and suspicions: his was impatience with women in ministry, of whom he says, "The divine law has excluded women from the ministry, but they endeavour to thrust themselves into it; and since they can effect nothing of themselves, they do all through the agency of others,"[35] and he was suspicious of those who "lust for the office of bishop".[36] He abhorred the use of violence by some seeking office, such as Damasus of Rome, of whom it was said of the 367 people that were slain in the churches in sectarian rivalry over succession to the papacy, 137 perished in a single day.[37] Lastly, in this section, John itemizes the administrative load on the priest in administering benevolence towards widows, the poor and virgins who seek a celibate life. It was said that in Antioch the Church was responsible for 3,000 souls in this category. For John, eternal vigilance was the price of good order in the Church.[38]

The final three sections of this work focus especially on the necessity of preaching and governing well. John begins by saying that "there is but one method and way of healing [the soul] appointed, after we have gone wrong, and that is, the powerful application of the word".[39] For John, preaching is the most effective "physic". Even with the power of miracles, the minister should apply himself to the application of the word. It is the means of waging spiritual warfare against evil.[40] It means wrestling with the Greeks (i.e., pagan philosophy), with the Jews, the Manichees, the Gnostics, the Sabellians and with Arians. Indeed, rightly handling the word of God means showing the deficiencies of each; and in exposing one set of falsehoods the preacher might well prevent others.[41]

He briefly sets forth his own orthodox beliefs on the Trinity here and then answers Basil's interjection that Paul calls himself an unskilled speaker (1 Corinthians 2:2,3). *On the Priesthood* takes on the style of a Platonic dialogue in this respect, much like Gregory of Nyssa's piece on the Resurrection (*On the Resurrection*), which is a dialogue with his dying sister Macrina. John responds by saying even without opening his mouth, the very presence of Paul "was terrible to the demons". Indeed, spiritual authority was more than polished preaching. It was the mediated power of God through the Spirit. What follows in the remainder of Book IV of *On the Priesthood* is an *encomium* (praise) of the Apostle Paul: his miracles, his ministry and his teaching, found especially in his epistles:

> For as a wall of adamant, so his writings fortify all the churches of the known world, and he, as a most noble champion, stands in the midst, bringing into captivity every thought to the obedience of Christ, casting down imaginations, and every high thing which exalts itself against the knowledge of God, and all this he does by those Epistles which he has left to us full of wonders and of Divine wisdom.[42]

Finally, in a cascade of Pauline teaching, mostly taken from the pastoral epistles, John exhorts his readers, and indeed future ministers, to be apt teachers of the Word in combating error, for no amount of austerity can make up for mishandling the teaching of Scripture.[43]

The penultimate book, Book V, continues with the theme of the importance of public preaching, which was to become so central to John's own life. Preachers must contend with the audience's desire to be entertained rather than illuminated or challenged. They must not give in to being merely people-pleasers without challenging their lifestyle. The preacher must rouse the audience's best spiritual instincts by raising their own spiritual expectations. Furthermore, the church leader or bishop must be irreproachable, impervious to slander or envy, and must not give in to despondency or depression, or be suborned by flattery, or a desire only to please. Then their words will carry weight and their teaching will be an extension of their lives. Indeed, John says "it is especially necessary to be trained to be indifferent to all kinds of praise", to subdue the wild bear of seeking men's good opinion.[44] In view of all these warnings, it would be surprising if anyone put themselves forward as a priest or presbyter.

The final book, Book VI, continues the theme of the responsibility of the priest or preacher and there follows a comparison between the value of the recluse and that of a priest. John is realistic about the trials of a priest. He warns, "The soul of the Priest ought to be purer than the very sunbeams, in order that the Holy Spirit may not leave him desolate, in order that he may be able to say, 'Now I live; and yet no longer I but Christ lives in me'" (Galatians 2:20).[45] Such purity for John means resisting the blandishments of women, which he enumerates vividly:

> The beauty of face, elegance of movement, an affected gait, and lisping voice, pencilled eyebrows and enamelled cheeks, elaborate braiding and dyeing of hair, costliness of dress, variety of golden ornaments, and the glory of precious stones, the scent of perfumes, and all other matters to which womankind devote themselves, are enough to disorder the mind unless it happens to be hardened against them, through much austerity of self-restraint.[46]

While the recluse faces milder temptation on this score, the priest, ministering in a community like Antioch, well known for its love of luxury and sophistication, has a greater task to remain pure.[47] After all, he will see such women continually. Indeed, the contrast between the recluse and the priest when it comes to temptation and struggle is "like a commoner (recluse) to a king (priest)".[48] The privileges are nevertheless many for the priest: not least in celebrating the Eucharist, when John says he believes that "a multitude of angels, clothed in shining robes, encircle the altar, and bending down, as one might see soldiers in the presence of their King".[49] The role of the priest is thus far more highly valued than that of a recluse or hermit, for the former profits the entire community, while the latter profits mostly himself. Last of all, John shares with Basil some grievous thoughts about not possessing that which has been promised him in Christ because of unworthiness and the need to contend in a spiritual battle which is both fierce and prolonged.[50] Nevertheless, John believes that Basil is called to this ministry of priesthood, whatever the cost, and that he shall never want for power to fulfil it.[51] Basil should remain a recluse, but should also become a priest despite all the warnings!

Basil did indeed go into the ministry and quite probably became the bishop of Raphnea in Syria. Some years later John followed suit, first as a priest in Antioch, but then in the greater Diocese of Constantinople. For a time, however, he followed the life of a recluse, evading any formal church leadership. Although John had successfully encouraged Basil to take up the ministry of priesthood and then episcopal service, he wrote very differently to his friend Theodore, who was contemplating giving up his ascetic life to marry a woman called Hermione who had captured his heart. Here John pressed on his friend not priesthood, but renunciation and abstinence. John's two *Letters to Theodore* reveal his own youthful enthusiasm for asceticism and renunciation, as much as they reveal the conflicted soul of Theodore, who is pulled between asceticism and the love of a woman. They are almost certainly the earliest letters of John that we possess. They show passion and eloquence, and echoes of the Apostle Paul, not least at the start.

John's opening words to Theodore do not spare his friend. He quotes Jeremiah, saying, "Oh, that my head were a spring of water, and my eyes a fountain of tears" (Jeremiah 9:1). As John begins, so he continues throughout this correspondence, proclaiming how much he has mourned and wept for Theodore over his change of heart, his renouncing of renunciation. Ironically, John's appeal is the opposite of his advice to Basil in *On the Priesthood*. Whereas Basil is encouraged to give up the indulgence of a solitary life and take on the burden of the priesthood with all its demands, Theodore is encouraged, nay implored, to keep to his life of renunciation. The truth was that Theodore had fallen in love with Hermione and wanted to cast off his monastic life for her. With copious examples from Scripture, John shows Theodore that God is well able to use the slightest inclination towards repentance in re-establishing a person in their intended vocation. Thus, "for such is the loving kindness of God that he never turns his face away from a sincere repentance, but if anyone has pushed on to the very extremity of wickedness, and chooses to return thence towards the path of virtue, God accepts and welcomes [him], and does everything so as to restore his position".[52]

Here repentance would mean restoration to a life of renunciation, which John considers Theodore's true calling. John goes on to give an almost classical description of the benefits of repentance, warnings of persisting in disobedience, and the need to get back on the right track. He writes, "For to have fallen is not a grievous thing, but to remain prostrate after falling, and not to get up again, and play the coward and the sluggard, to conceal feebleness of moral purpose under the reasoning of despair is culpable."[53] With these words and many like them, John encourages Theodore to journey towards Christ on the Mount of Transfiguration and see his shining glory.[54] Coming to that point John says, "I know that thou art admiring the grace of Hermione, and thou judgest that there is nothing in the world to be compared to her comeliness; but if you choose, O friend, you shall yourself exceed her in comeliness and gracefulness, as much as golden statutes surpass those which are made of clay."[55] It is persuasive language.

Having cajoled Theodore with the "carrot" of the surpassing beauty that comes through renunciation, John then uses a far cruder physiological argument or "stick", maintaining that Hermione's beauty rests on phlegm!

> For the groundwork of [her] corporeal beauty is nothing else but phlegm, and blood, and humour, and bile, and the fluid of masticated food. For by these things both eyes and cheeks, and all other features, are supplied with moisture and if they do not receive that moisture, daily ascending from the stomach and the liver, the skin becoming unduly withered, and the eyes sunken, the whole grace of the countenance forthwith vanishes; so that if you consider what is stored up inside those beautiful eyes, and that straight nose, and the mouth and the cheeks, you will affirm a well-shaped body to be nothing else then a whited sepulchre.[56]

That was severe.

John's onslaught against Theodore's proposed change of vocation continues. He writes: "All that we ask for is that you would release yourself from your accursed bondage, and return to your former freedom".[57] John promises the blessings of future achievements if Theodore returns to his original vocation and shakes off "any cloud of despondency" that comes with his struggle.[58] John further cites from his own day the story of a once-flamboyant young man who gives up his life of abstinence and contemplation and returns to one of revelry and show, but is won back by a group of holy men in Antioch.[59] Likewise, the runaway slave Onesimus in the Bible (Philemon 8–11) is brought back by Paul to a life of meaning and purpose in Christ.

There is no doubt that in his writing, John does not pull any punches, confronting Theodore with the challenge of not leaving his original vocation, of calling for repentance, and of describing human beauty, in particular that of Hermione, in terms that would be extreme to our ears and minds. Yet in the setting of his times, the ascetic life, the pursuit of abstinence and the rejection of marriage were frequently seen as the highest calling, and all else as second best. And so John uses all the firepower of his bold speech, which is to be so much a mark of his ministry, both then and in the future, to achieve his considered objective. In later times, we shall see this *parrhesia* (bold speech) overstep the mark, as in his diatribes against the Jews. At other times, he will not sit on any fence, but will confront the worldliness of the court or corruption in the Church, as he will do in Constantinople. As for Theodore, having received this blistering letter, and another much shorter one, which must have been very hot to handle, he did return to his original intention of a life of renunciation. He gave up his affection and love for Hermione, becoming a much loved and revered bishop of Mopsuestia near Tarsus in modern-day Turkey. He also became a biblical commentator and the writer of a long work upholding the Incarnation, in which he rebuked both the logician Eunomius and the Apollinarians, who misunderstood the true nature of Christ. After his death, Theodore's words and teachings were caught in the Nestorian Controversy, his reputation was tarnished, and his works supressed. What is in no doubt, however, is his devout life, his commitment to biblical teaching, and his orthodoxy on the Trinity.

In fact, John's own time of monastic withdrawal was coming to an end. He would ever remain a monk in his spirit, but he was now being called to a more public ministry than is generally possible in a cave on a mountain. (Simon Stylites [*c*.390–459] would show that even that was possible in exceptional times.) John made clear his deep personal attachment to the monastic spirit in *Against the Enemies of Monasticism*,[60] and how much he valued the nobility of the ascetic calling in *A King and a Monk Compared*, but great events in the empire were happening which would profoundly impact his life. At these, and no doubt at the invitation of his beloved bishop and mentor Meletius, John would forsake the fastnesses of Mount Silpios for Antioch and the Great Church to which Meletius had been restored as bishop. The cause was a catastrophic defeat of Roman arms at Adrianople on 9 August 378, the death of the Eastern, Arianizing emperor, Valens, and the recall of all bishops previously exiled to their sees by the 19-year-old emperor, and nephew of Valens, Gratian.

Notes

1. J. N. D. Kelly, *Golden Mouth: The Story of John Chrysostom, Ascetic, Preacher, Bishop* (Ithaca, NY: Cornell University Press, 1998), p. 249.
2. Kelly, *Golden Mouth*, p. 37.
3. John Chrysostom, *De Sacerdotio (On the Priesthood)* I:5, in *The Nicene and Post-Nicene fathers of the Christian Church, Volume 9: Saint Chrysostom: On the priesthood; Ascetic treatises; Select homilies and letters; Homilies on the statues*, ed. Philip Schaff (Grand Rapids, MI: Eerdmans, 1975), p. 34.
4. Chrysostom, *De Sacerdotio* I.5, op. cit., p. 34.
5. Sozomen §8, *Nicene and Post-Nicene Fathers: Second Series, Vol. II: Socrates, Sozomenus: Church Histories*, ed. Philip Schaff (Grand Rapids, MI: Eerdmans, 1987), p. 399.
6. Chrysostom, *Letters to the Fallen Theodore*, in *The Nicene and post-Nicene fathers of the Christian Church, Volume 9: Saint Chrysostom: On the priesthood; Ascetic treatises; Select homilies and letters; Homilies on the statues*, ed. Philip Schaff (Grand Rapids, MI: Eerdmans, 1975), pp. 87ff.
7. See Basil of Caesarea, *Letters* 337, 339, 342 etc. to Libanius, Loeb Vol. 270 (Cambridge, MA: Harvard University Press, 2003), pp. 285ff.
8. Kelly, *Golden Mouth*, p. 7.
9. T. E. Ameringer, *The Stylistic Influence of The Second Sophist on the Panegyrical Sermons of St John Chrysostom* (Washington D.C.: Catholic University of America, 1921), cited in Kelly, *Golden Mouth*, p. 8.
10. Palladius, *Dialogues*, in *Dialogue sur la vie de Jean Chrysostome/Palladios*, ed. and tr. Anne-Marie Malingrey with Philippe Leclercq, *SC* 341, Vol. 4 (Paris: Les Éditions du Cerf, 1988), p. 107.
11. R. P. C. Hanson, *The Search for the Christian Doctrine of God: The Arian Controversy 318–381* (London: T&T Clark, 1988), p. 209.
12. Hanson, *The Search for the Christian Doctrine of God*, p. 284.
13. Hanson, *The Search for the Christian Doctrine of God*, p. 286.
14. Chrysostom, *De sacerdotio* IV.4, op. cit., p. 66.
15. Kelly, *Golden Mouth*, pp. 296–7.
16. Kelly, *Golden Mouth*, p. 17, citing Theodoret, *Ecclesiastical History* II, in *Histoire ecclésiastique Tome 1 (livres I–II)*, ed. and tr. L. Parmentier, G. C. Hansen, J. Bouffartigue, A. Martin and P. Canivet, *SC* 234 (Paris: Les Éditions du Cerf, 2006), p. 228.

17 Kelly, *Golden Mouth*, p. 17.
18 Palladius, *Dialogue* 5, op. cit., p. 108.
19 Chrysostom, *De sacerdotio* VI.16, op. cit., p. 80.
20 Benedicta Ward (ed.), *The Desert Fathers* (Harmondsworth: Penguin, 2003), pp. 34ff.
21 Chrysostom, *De compunctione cordis* I.6, PG 47.403.
22 Andrea Stark, *Renouncing the World yet Leading the Church: The Monk–Bishop in Late Antiquity* (Cambridge, MA: Harvard University Press, 2004).
23 Ward, *The Desert Fathers*, p. 41.
24 Kelly, *Golden Mouth*, p. 33.
25 Palladius, *Dialogue* 5.
26 Megan Hale Williams, *The Monk and the Book* (Chicago, IL: University of Chicago Press, 2006), p. 29.
27 Chrysostom, *De sacerdotio* II.4, op. cit., p. 42.
28 Gregory Nazianzen, *Oratio I: On Defence of his Flight to Pontus*, in *Nicene and Post-Nicene Fathers: Second Series, Vol. VII: Cyril of Jerusalem, Gregory of Nazianzen*, ed. Philip Schaff (New York: Cosimo, 2007), pp. 203ff.
29 Gregory Nazianzen, *Oratio* I.10 and 16, op. cit., p. 207 and 208.
30 Chrysostom, *De sacerdotio* II.4, op. cit., p. 41.
31 Chrysostom, *De sacerdotio* III.7, op. cit., p. 49.
32 Chrysostom, *De sacerdotio* III.4, op. cit., p. 46.
33 Chrysostom, *De sacerdotio* III.5, op. cit., p. 47.
34 John 20:23; Chrysostom, *De sacerdotio* III.5, op. cit., p. 47.
35 Chrysostom, *De sacerdotio* III.9 op. cit., p. 49.
36 Chrysostom, *De sacerdotio* III.10, op. cit., p. 50.
37 Chrysostom, *De sacerdotio* III.10, op. cit., p. 50.
38 Chrysostom, *De sacerdotio* III.16, op. cit., pp. 55–9.
39 Chrysostom, *De sacerdotio* IV.3, op. cit., p. 64.
40 Chrysostom, *De sacerdotio* IV.4, op. cit., p. 65.
41 Chrysostom, *De sacerdotio* IV.4, op. cit., p. 65.
42 Chrysostom, *De sacerdotio* IV.7, op. cit., p. 68.
43 Chrysostom, *De sacerdotio* IV.9, op. cit., p. 69.
44 Chrysostom, *De sacerdotio* V.8, op. cit., pp. 71–3.
45 Chrysostom, *De sacerdotio* VI.2, op. cit., p. 75.
46 Chrysostom, *De sacerdotio* VI.2, op. cit., p. 75.
47 Chrysostom, *De sacerdotio* VI.3, op. cit., p. 75.

[48] Chrysostom, *De sacerdotio* VI.5, op. cit., p. 77.
[49] Chrysostom, *De sacerdotio* VI.4, op. cit., p. 76.
[50] Chrysostom, *De sacerdotio* VI.12, op. cit., p. 81.
[51] Chrysostom, *De sacerdotio* VI.13, op. cit., p. 83.
[52] Chrysostom, *First Letter to the Fallen Theodore* 6, op. cit., p. 95.
[53] Chrysostom, *First Letter to the Fallen Theodore* 7, op. cit., p. 95.
[54] Chrysostom, *First Letter to the Fallen Theodore* 11, op. cit., p. 100.
[55] Chrysostom, *First Letter to the Fallen Theodore* 14, op. cit., p. 103.
[56] Chrysostom, *First Letter to the Fallen Theodore* 14, op. cit., pp. 103–4.
[57] Chrysostom, *First Letter to the Fallen Theodore* 14, op. cit., p. 104.
[58] Chrysostom, *First Letter to the Fallen Theodore* 16, op. cit., p. 107.
[59] Chrysostom, *First Letter to the Fallen Theodore* 17, op. cit., p. 108.
[60] *PG* 47.349–86.

5

Pastor, polemicist and preacher

The defeat of the Roman army by the Goths at the battle of Adrianople in August 378 was to have almost immediate effects on John, and on Antioch itself. In the spring of 378, Valens, the emperor, had moved his court from Antioch to Constantinople. He quickly made peace with the Persians over the disputed territory of Armenia,[1] and, spurred on by his much younger nephew Gratian's victory over the Goths in Illyricum (which is south of present-day Vienna), prepared himself to face a combined force of Goths and others nearby in Thrace. If anything, Valens was overconfident: too eager for personal glory and too proud to be seen to rely on reinforcements from his young nephew, the Emperor Gratian. The Goths, who were led by Fritigern, had combined with a large force of Greuthungi cavalry and were ready for battle. Fighting in full armour after a prolonged march and in the heat of the hot August sun, the Romans found themselves overwhelmed, and their lines broken by the impact of Gothic forces. While trying to escape, Valens was struck by an arrow, much like Harold at the Battle of Hastings. The historian Ammianus tells us that "he was mortally wounded by an arrow and died immediately".[2] The death of the emperor precipitated a change that would deeply affect the Church. A single arrow, as at Hastings in 1066, changed the course of history.

As emperor, Valens combined boorish manners with cruel actions and, according to Ammianus, was "insatiable in the pursuit of wealth," and "bow-legged with a somewhat protruding stomach".[3] More significantly, he had advanced the Arian cause. With the help of the much-loved Ulfilas, their bishop, "who invented Gothic letters" and was himself appointed by Valens, the Goths embraced the Arian view of Christianity, a move which would influence them for generations to come.[4]

Furthermore, Valens's Arianizing was felt throughout the East. He actively opposed Nicene orthodoxy, sent bishops like Meletius of Antioch into exile, and opposed both Basil of Caesarea and Gregory of Nazianzus. After Valens's death, however, Gratian swiftly appointed Theodosius, whose dynasty would come to lead the empire in its closing years. Theodosius was the last emperor to reign over both the Eastern and Western halves of the empire before it was split again between his two sons.

Theodosius was both a proven general of Spanish origin, and, as a Western Christian, firmly committed to Nicene Orthodoxy, and hence an Orthodox view of the Trinity. Coming from Italica (near present-day Seville) in Spain, he became a military commander, served with his father in Britain in 368 where they quelled a revolt, and was then appointed a military commander of Moesia in 374, aged only 27. However, with his father's trial and execution for unknown causes, Theodosius fell from grace and returned prematurely to his property in Spain during Valentinian I's reign. Aware that he was a skilled and dependable commander, Gratian recalled him to take on, and eventually defeat, the Goths. After being made *magister militum* (master of the army) at Sirmium, and having rapidly defeated the Sarmatians, on 19 January 379 Theodosius was acclaimed *augustus* and given direct rule over the Eastern provinces of the empire. He entered Constantinople as emperor on 24 November 380, after his successful campaign against the Goths, and took charge.

Theodosius famously declared his faith in an edict of 28 February 380, affirming the "religion handed down by the Apostle Peter to the Romans and now followed by Bishop Damasus (of Rome) and Peter, Bishop of Alexandria, a man of apostolic sanctity: that is, according to the apostolic discipline of the evangelical doctrine, we shall believe in the single Deity of the Father, the Son and the Holy Spirit under the concept of equal majesty, and of the Holy Trinity".[5] It was an extraordinarily clear statement from a clear thinking and plain-speaking general. With the appointment of this no-nonsense soldier, who also had many social graces, considerable experience of command, and the respect of his troops, the religious and political landscape of the Eastern empire changed at a stroke.[6] It was a sudden switch from all that had gone before, and was quickly seen by the Nicene party as a great providence of God. Theodosius was the new Constantine, willing to uphold orthodoxy and see off its opponents, as well as work for the unity of the Church. It was the opinion of Gregory of Nazianzus that Theodosius did not adequately settle the Antiochene schism in favour of Paulinus and the extreme Nicene party, however; nor did he press for the explicit statement that the Spirit was *homoousion* (of the same substance) with the Father and Son at the forthcoming Council.[7]

This constellation of events in both Church and State, which happened at the same time, created a new opportunity for John. Theodosius now ruled in the East. He had finished the war with the Goths (for the time being), judiciously settling them in the Balkans for the most part, although by no means finally. After all, Rome would fall to the troops of Alaric the Visigoth (*c*.370–410) in 410, just 30 years later, and Theodosius's own daughter, the remarkable Galla Placidia, whose beautiful mausoleum can still be seen in Ravenna, would be captured by Alaric and married to his successor, Aetius. Goths were now settled within the borders of the empire but pressure from the east, especially from the Huns, and the demands for more space drove the Goths ever further south and west. They were given land but were expected to fight as *foederati* for the Romans.

Meanwhile, in Antioch, Meletius had swiftly invited John to join the staff of the Great Church as a reader but had not yet ordained him as deacon or presbyter, something that would not occur until 386. At the same time, Paulinus continued to pastor the ultra-Nicene congregation in the town and was still recognized as the legitimate bishop by the West.[8] These then were the changed circumstances of Church and State in 378, when, after his monastic seclusion, John's public ministry began. They were times full of opportunity and hope after the years of confusion under Valens, and there seemed to be settled leadership ahead. Indeed, John would minister in Antioch for all of Theodosius's reign (379–92), and his elevation to the Bishopric of Constantinople would be made by Theodosius's son, Arcadius, in 397.

John the pastor and polemicist

Having ended his monastic seclusion permanently scarred by an ascetic experience that had left him half-starved and with physical effects that would last a lifetime, and at the same time, with a knowledge of the Bible that would also serve him all his days, John began a different life in the city of Antioch. He came from the isolation of his monastic life and the virtual solitary confinement of his cave into a sophisticated and bustling city. To go from such isolation to a public position must have been disorientating at best and bewildering at worst. His duties would have involved personal counselling, instruction, especially of those to be baptized, liturgical services, and functioning as a kind of aide-de-camp or chaplain to his bishop. Chaplains also had the responsibility of looking after the poor, the sick and the mentally deranged, often called "demoniacs".[9] Throughout the history of the Church, such a post has often been a stepping stone to much greater responsibility, and so it proved for John. He also gave himself to writing.

John served as a reader for two years and was then ordained deacon by Meletius,[10] shortly before the latter left to go to Constantinople to open the Council of Constantinople in January 381, of which he was chairman. Theodosius had himself arrived in Constantinople, victorious from his campaigns against the Goths in November 380. But much to John's shock and sorrow, soon after the opening of the Council, Meletius fell ill and died suddenly. At this point, Gregory of Nazianzus became the putative Bishop of Constantinople, although he was never fully consecrated, and for a short while was also chairman of the Council. However, given his thoughtful and irenic character, he found the infighting of the bishops extremely testing,[11] and in the end he took flight from the Council to write up his great Orations in Nazianzus.

Back in Antioch, Flavian was appointed to succeed Meletius. He was someone to whom John became equally devoted, although the Western Church still recognized Paulinus, rather than Flavian as the legitimate bishop of Antioch. John began his ministry as a deacon, continuing in this role until his priesting five years later in 386. Not yet licensed to preach, he was determined nevertheless to teach through pamphlets and short works, and then later, once ordained presbyter, through much more extensive preaching. Being John, his output was immense, and we can divide these early writings into two main groups: the pastoral and the polemical. The former focussed on issues connected to marriage, widowhood, virginity, repentance and suffering, that is, issues that have to do with our humanity in every generation, while the latter were more to do with paganism, Judaism and Greek philosophy.

One of the effects of returning from his monastic vigil to the city—a city well known for its luxury, sophistication and wealth—was the need to deal with the age-old questions of marriage, celibacy and sexuality. For John, who had gone into isolation to overcome his own passions and sexual desires, and who had strongly counselled Theodore against marriage to Hermione, was now confronted by issues of sex, celibacy and marriage, presumably on a daily basis. Indeed, this very subject was one of the main features distinguishing Christianity from the pagan or semi-pagan world around it (e.g., of the Manichees and Gnostics). And on the subject of marriage, the teaching of Jesus and Paul separated Christian teaching from the lax position on divorce found in large parts of Judaism (for instance, in the teaching of Rabbi Hillel, who allowed divorce for quite trivial reasons). In other words, in the ancient world, Christian teaching on sex, marriage and celibacy was unique when compared to paganism, Judaism and the neo-pagan sects. Furthermore, the fourth century emphasis on virginity or permanent celibacy, which was to take root in the Catholic Church in the Middle Ages, but which in the fourth century was strong throughout the Church and based in part on the idea of the perpetual virginity of Mary, was a step beyond the tenets of paganism and of much of Judaism.

John was well aware of the sexual mores of the age that were affecting the Church. In *On The Priesthood*, which must have been in gestation during this period, although not formally published until after 386, John makes clear the temptations women offer to the presbyter. As we have already noted from his writings, he took the view that "all those matters to which womankind devote themselves are enough to disorder the mind, unless it happens to be hardened against them through much austerity and self-restraint".[12] Earlier in the third century, in *The Instructor*, Clement of Alexandria had written extensively about the lengths to which both men and women will go to attract each other, and had recommended simplicity and sobriety of dress.[13] Furthermore, throughout the fourth century and before, the church fathers counselled, indeed powerfully taught, the need for sexual purity and the virtue of celibacy, and sometimes expressed a preference for abstinence over marriage. (In this respect, they were not far removed from the Stoic philosophers like Epictetus [80–135].)

In the early third century, Tertullian advocated the veil for all virgins or unmarried women outside the home: "Put on the panoply of modesty; surround yourself with the stockade of bashfulness; rear a rampart for your sex, which must neither allow your own eyes egress nor ingress to other people. Wear the full garb of woman, to preserve the standing of the virgin."[14] He also wrote *On Modesty*, *On an Exhortation to Chastity* and *On Monogamy*. He was quite clear: "Whoever enjoys any other than nuptial intercourse, in whatever place, and in the person of whatever woman, makes himself guilty of adultery and fornication."[15] When the fourth century ended, church leaders were writing almost prolifically on the subject. In Milan in 377, and greatly influenced by Athanasius's *On Antony*, Ambrose wrote *On Virginity*, praising the calling of singleness with typically forthright language.[16]

Gregory of Nyssa, the most mystical of the Cappadocians, who also gave the funeral oration for Bishop Meletius of Antioch, wrote his version of *On Virginity* in 368. Although married, which he appeared to regret,[17] he extolled the life of virginity for sparing a woman from the pain of childbirth, from the grief of losing her children through untimely death, and from neglect by her husband or his untimely loss.[18] More positively, he argued virginity frees a woman (or a man) to pray, contemplate and be sanctified, thereby creating "a union of the soul with the incorruptible deity which can be accommodated in no other way but by herself attaining by her virgin state to the utmost purity possible".[19] Virginity was not simply the absence of sex; it was the devotion of the whole person to a single cause. Basil of Caesarea likewise extolled the celibate state in his works and in his correspondence, strictly enforcing church canons or discipline with those who had fallen from their celibate intentions. This seemed to apply especially to virgins who had taken a vow of abstinence, or to widows who had done likewise.[20] Finally, Jerome, another contemporary who was actually living in Antioch from

376–80, extolled celibacy to his protégée Eustochium, who later joined him in Bethlehem, in his famous *Letter* 22.[21] Jerome was critical of John and Meletius, having joined the ultra-Nicene group in Antioch under Paulinus, and saw the celibate life as full-blooded Christianity.

Perhaps it is not surprising that, fresh from the caves of Mount Silpios, John should write first about the calling and blessings of virginity. To our contemporary minds it is an unusual subject to write on, but for almost all well-known church leaders in the late fourth century it was nearly, if not actually, top of their list of spiritual disciplines and topics for teaching. John's work was about 250 pages. Whether as monks or laypeople, many aspired to virginity as the better way. At the outset of his *De Virginitate*, John makes an important disclaimer.[22] He is not of the opinion that marriage should be rejected as some extreme ascetics believe.[23] Such people show a Manichaean or Gnostic contempt for life in the flesh, an attitude carried over from a Platonic dualism which discredits the flesh and its appetites. Nevertheless, John swiftly moves to "a sustained eulogy of virginity",[24] and like his contemporary Gregory of Nyssa, argues that virginity is a way of life that encompasses much more than abstinence from sex. It embraces also fasting from luxurious food, simplicity of clothing, restraint in socializing, and a way of life committed to prayer and contemplation. These disciplines together enable a purity of soul and a close bond with Christ himself, as the yearned-for bridegroom of the Song of Songs (Song of Solomon 2:16–3:5). Furthermore, in a comparison with marriage, which was quite common among the church fathers of that period, John maintains that the trials of marriage—the anxieties of pleasing a husband or a wife, the pain of childbirth, the grief of infant mortality, the physical decline or loss of a partner and the bereavement of a husband or wife—are worse trials than those of abstinence or virginity. Many of course would now disagree. Despite his reprimand of the extreme ascetics and his contention he is not like them, he nevertheless misinterprets the Apostle Paul as saying that the voluntary decision of a couple to desist from sex for their prayers found in 1 Corinthians 7:3–7 is in fact a covert signal that at root virginity is superior to marriage.

We will return later to look at the wider view of Chrysostom's teaching on marriage, sex and family life, or as Peter Brown has construed it in his important book *The Body and Society*. John's tendencies are widely on view in *De Virginitate*. Behind it all is his negative, disparaging view of women as the source of men's undoing: from Eve to Delilah and beyond.[25] *De Virginitate* is a long work of 70 chapters. The first 24 comprise general teaching on virginity; the next 26 are an exposition of Paul's teaching in 1 Corinthians 7:1–27, and something of a proof text on the subject. The remaining 20 are a comparison between virginity and marriage, stressing the inconvenience of the latter and the trouble it can bring. There is little on the positive side of the marriage balance sheet, such as the celebration of the love between a man and a woman, family life, and the enriching relationships that come through the birth of children and their progeny. John ends his work with a paean of praise to the blessings of virginity.

A further Church issue upon which John wrote more briefly was the care and vocation of widows. This took the form of an open letter titled *To a Young Widow*, addressed to someone he had met in the course of his pastoral work.[26] He also addresses the issue in a further piece called *De non iterando coniugio*.[27] The Church was caught in a dilemma of its own making: on the one hand it encouraged widows to remain single and aspire to a life of sexual abstinence or celibacy. On the other, the Church did not wish to bear the burden of young widows who might then become reliant on financial support. The fact was that there were many young widows in their early twenties. After all, most marriages were contracted in a woman's mid-teenage years and many husbands died young. John's open letter *To a Young Widow* was written to the wife of a very promising officer, Therasios, who served and died in Emperor Theodosius's campaign against the Goths of 379–81. John wrote to his widow in mostly impersonal terms, encouraging her to consider a single life and make some form of a pledge to that effect. These widows were treated almost as rigorously as those who had vowed to live a life of celibacy. Thus Basil of Caesarea counselled his fellow Bishop Amphilocus "that if a widow lies under a very heavy charge, on the ground that she has made void her faith in Christ [by breaking a public vow of celibacy] what must we think of the virgin who is the spouse of Christ and the sacred vessel dedicated to the Lord!"[28] In other words, the virgin who broke her vow of celibacy was to be placed under a charge of adultery for forsaking her bridegroom, Christ, for which there were exacting penances. At the same time, the "widow as a corrupted handmaid" who had vowed celibacy and remarried was also condemned.[29] Behind this sentiment there is undoubtedly the underlying thought that the single state is superior to the married (however much denied), and that young widows are to be encouraged to remain single and condemned if they remarry. However, as single women, the issue of their support becomes central.

In 1 Timothy 5:14, the Apostle Paul suggests that young widows *should* remarry, because their sensual desires are strong, and they are vulnerable and economically unstable. Only widows over 60 should be enrolled on the list of those needing church support (1 Timothy 5:9). In his letter to the young widow, John starts with his personal knowledge of this particular woman, who, unlike those whose husbands died suddenly in battle, had the chance to tend her dying husband, kiss his eyes when dead and lay flowers on his grave. He then moves on to rhetorical devices, including a fictitious dialogue mixed with panegyric. As a piece of writing, it is a hybrid of personal empathy mixed with literary devices better suited to more impersonal classical moral teaching. Nevertheless, John has one overriding theme, which is "the praise of the widow who rejects the temptation to marry again" and the view that widowhood is as "superior to a second marriage as virginity is to marriage".[30]

John's teaching on virginity, sexuality and abstinence was almost complete at this point, but there was one more area in which he felt compelled to instruct, and this was the growing practice of monks taking single women into their houses to care for them or keep them company. Since many of these male monks came from the better-off classes and were used to domestic service in their households, it became common practice to engage the services of a woman to cook, wash and clean. However, while common, the practice was specifically legislated against in the third Canon of Nicaea, which said, "It is stringently forbidden for any bishop, presbyter or deacon to have dwelling with him any woman except a mother, sister or aunt or such persons who are above suspicion." In his *Quod regularis viris cohabitare non debeant*, John suggests that it is impossible for an unrelated man and woman to live together in purity, even if there are plausible reasons for doing so: e.g., the man giving financial security, the woman practical help.[31] It is *a morally dangerous way of life* for both, which might at worst bring about fornication, and at best a state of frequent sexual arousal. Never short of vivid language to embellish and drive home his point, John describes women practising the arts of seduction, using alluring walks and enticing glances to net their unsuspecting male companions![32] Equally, John's imagination is fertile enough to envisage a monk visiting a sick woman in her bedroom, or performing services for her which were suitable only for a female companion. "These may be small things, but they bring to birth big coals of lust."[33] In short, he condemns the practice of house-sharing and sought in later life to end it. By way of compensation, he encourages all ascetics to look forward to heaven, where amidst the sexless life of the angels, men and women might enjoy unlimited social intercourse.

Nor is it surprising, given John's pastoral responsibilities within the community of the Great Church, which was responsible for 3,000 older widows, virgins, the poor, the disabled, hospital patients and prisoners, that John should write on matters to do with suffering and need.[34] One such letter is to Stageirius, a young friend who must have found John's advice as abrasive as bleach. Stageirius, also a monk from a high-class background and who had earlier indulged himself in good times, found himself unaccountably suffering from epilepsy and seizures, in those days often thought to be the result of possession by evil spirits. In a diffuse address spread over three books, John seeks to stiffen Stageirius's resolve that he might avoid a worse fate. Despite many attempted cures, nothing had so far prevailed, whereupon John writes that such attacks might well be the result of a "slack, uninstructed and indolent" mind.[35] He goes on to say that there is nothing to be ashamed of in such seizures, for the only thing that matters is not falling into sin. Another book written at this time was *On Contrition*,[36] a long work first listing all the moral demands of the Gospels and then advocating true inner contrition as the only safeguard against forbidden pursuits.

As well as writing powerful open letters of instruction, which leave little to the imagination as to their meaning and intent, John was also always prepared to deal with current issues in a more polemical fashion. As we have already gleaned, like so many church leaders of his time, John was always an ascetic at heart, willing to renounce a more normal human life for a greater calling (as he saw it). Although widely practised by late fourth-century church leaders, as well as by others, monasticism or a life of renunciation was not accepted by all, least of all by parents who had spent large sums on their children's education. They expected their sons to take prestigious positions in society (not least in the *cursus honorum*, the Roman career structure), and their daughters to "marry well". They were not to seek a life of celibacy and dependency with no hope of producing children. It was not uncommon for monks in Antioch to be set upon, beaten up and ridiculed, sometimes by well-educated people, incensed at the way these men were leading their children astray. It was as part of this debate, fuelled by some bitterness about the role of the Church, that John wrote *Against the Enemies of Monasticism*. Over three books, he reveals "not only the extreme irritation which the proselytizing activity of monks was causing in the leading circles of Antioch, but also the disenchantment he himself was feeling with the classical tradition".[37] Like Basil of Caesarea, Gregory of Nazianzus, Jerome and others, John was questioning the value of the classical education he himself had enjoyed.

Not surprisingly John comes at the problem head-on, maintaining in Book II that monks make the best of teachers and the most virtuous of guides. The monk can guide his pupils into greater riches than those of worldly success.[38] Not only that, but this instruction can improve a pupil's character so that they might become more considerate, gentle and biddable. By contrast, many schools or teachers enforced discipline through the cane, and in the schools there was often rampant sexual abuse and homosexuality.[39] Presumably John did not think such problems would arise if the schools were run by monks. He thus proposes that monks should be responsible for a child's whole education from start to finish, and that the curriculum should be based on the Bible, rather than on classical studies. Only after a thorough schooling by monks could men be admitted into society, ready, aged 20, to share their wisdom, because for John, "True wisdom and true education consists only in the fear of God."[40] Whether John succeeded in changing Antiochene society is uncertain, but what we can be sure of is that from 787 onwards, in the later medieval Europe of Charlemagne, teaching was almost entirely in the hands of monks and monasteries and later cathedrals, before the start of the universities led by Franciscan and Dominican friars in

Bologna, Paris, Oxford, Cambridge, Naples, Salamanca and elsewhere. At the very least, John must have started the ball rolling, along with some of his other contemporaries. By around 379, John had fully embraced an almost fanatical monastic life, and "was driven to propose extreme measures which he must have known to be impractical by his disgust at the meretricious attractions of life in the great city".[41] Ten years later, in his more considered work *On Vainglory and How Parents should Educate Children*, his proposals were more considered. But this early polemical foray into education shows John's utter distaste for the vainglorious and false values of his day, and his willingness to be countercultural whatever the cost. It was a characteristic that would shape his ministry profoundly in the years ahead, and of course cause him considerable difficulty.

The preacher

In 386, Bishop Flavian ordained John presbyter in Antioch, ministering for the most part in the Great Church. He was already a well-known figure on account of his writing, his willingness to go out on a limb in making known his ideas, and his assiduous pastoral work. He was now to become even more influential and his voice more forceful and persuasive in the affairs of the city. Although John's biographer Palladius writes little about his preaching at this time, he does note that his ascetic life, particularly his sleep deprivation, prepared John for his exacting ministry.[42] The difference now was that whereas John was previously known for his pastoral work and his extensive writings, as well as for his closeness to the bishop, he now quickly became known for his preaching, which in turn led to the appellation of Chrysostom or Golden Mouth.

Amazingly, we have a record of his very first sermon after ordination.[43] He was now 37 years old and had had a long and demanding apprenticeship. It was 15 years since the start of his time as a monk and then as a complete recluse. When he stepped up to the raised dais (or ambo) at the east end of the Golden Church, where hundreds if not thousands of Antiochenes were waiting for his words, on either 13 or 14 March 387, he was following a long line of preachers in Antioch, including the Apostles Paul and Peter, Barnabas (Acts 11:19–30), Ignatius, Babylas, and more recently the beloved Meletius. It was thus a moment of great historical resonance. For John, addressing the congregation for the very first time, it was something beyond his wildest dreams. He said he felt panic-stricken and too inexperienced to be effective in public speaking. Nevertheless, from this self-deprecation and proffered inadequacy, he moved deftly on to praise his patron, Bishop Flavian, for his rule of life, his austerity, his disdain for luxury and high living, and for his care of the Church, all of which made him appear like Meletius reborn. And alongside this typical piece of fourth-century praise (*encomium*), in an aside which reflects the true John, he declared unequivocally that "nothing so impedes our advance to heaven as wealth and all the evils which flow from it".[44] He started as he meant to go on: exalting simplicity and decrying all semblance of luxury in a city well known for it. Indeed, this decrying of the evils that come from the love of wealth would remain a constant theme of his preaching both in Antioch and later in Constantinople (1 Timothy 6:6–10).

Although John still had other duties as a presbyter, such as accompanying the bishop and helping in the irksome duty of administering the church's property, he now gave himself to preaching. His style of preaching appears to have been extempore, without a note in his hand, and reflecting his deep knowledge of the Bible, his years of preparation, and his ability to think and respond on his feet. John was to become the most famous preacher in the city in the remaining years of the fourth century, the leading pulpit orator of Antioch from 386–97.[45] For the most part, he preached in the Great Church, so recently completed, and to a large congregation who came to relish the regular mixture of encouragement and profound challenge that he wove together in his preaching. His style appears to have been almost always expository of Scripture, direct and informal so that he could respond to the reaction of the congregation: quelling their applause or galvanizing their attention. His use of Scripture was in the Antiochene style, following the teacher Diodore. This means that he sought the literal unvarnished meaning of the text and did not look for allegorical or mystical meaning as was the case with Origen and much preaching elsewhere.

Like his contemporaries, the Cappadocians, John fully grasped the notion of the incomprehensibility of God,[46] his apophatic unknowable qualities (e.g. his invisibility, incomprehensibility, infinity and ineffability). He makes this clear in five initial sermons delivered in the Great Church at the Eucharist. In the first of these homilies, John warns: "Flee from those men who are obstinately striving to know God *in his essence*".[47] John maintains the essence of God is not given to humans to know fully, for, as Paul says, some things are beyond our comprehension now (see Romans 11:33, 1 Corinthians 13:12). Here John draws a very clear line between himself and logicians like Eunomius, who maintained the extreme Arian position that *the Son was unlike the Father*. Rather, for John, Jesus shares fully in the apophatic qualities of the Godhead, but, as the Word made flesh, he comes to make the Godhead known to human beings (see John 1:18; 14:9,10). Indeed, the then recently designated celebration of the Incarnation at Christmas or on December 25—a festival begun by Pope Julius (337–52) in the mid-fourth century—gave Christians the chance to celebrate close to the winter solstice and so overlay a previously pagan festival with a newly defined Christian one. The celebration also gave John the opportunity to preach on the mystery of the Incarnation, the Epiphany and the baptism of Christ in these opening sermons on the incomprehensibility of God in the Great Church from September 386 to early 387, which included Christmas and the Epiphany (also used in the Eastern Orthodox Church to celebrate the Baptism of Christ). In this way, John tackled this subject, which was probably the central theological issue of the day. Nevertheless, he did not make these more topical sermons the basis of his preaching, for that was derived from Scripture itself.

John's preaching thus falls into two general categories: peaching on specific issues and topics (one of which we will look at in greater detail in the next chapter) and expository preaching from the Bible. In addition, there were particular themes germane to the period which we will look at separately later, especially in relation to sex and the body, wealth, and the Jewish community.

Preaching on particular subjects

John was never one to shirk a difficult subject, nor did he ever mince his words. He preached both from Scripture and on the great themes of the faith at its main festivals. Thus, in c.386/7, John preached on the Resurrection, the Ascension and Pentecost, strongly maintaining the divinity of the Spirit against the so-called spirit-fighters (*pneumatomachoi*),[48] while also addressing other lurking dangers. He warned his listeners against the heresies of false sects. In this way, he set a tradition for all preaching thereafter: the need for both affirmations and warnings. One such false sect, whose adherents were circulating in Antioch, was Manicheism, a religious movement akin to Gnosticism and Marcionism. Marcion (85–160) was a leading Gnostic who moved to Rome from the Black Sea city of Sinope, where he had been a successful shipbuilder. He maintained that the God of the Old Testament was distinct, indeed quite unrelated to the Father of the Lord Jesus Christ. He thus discounted the Old Testament as a preparation for the New. He even characterized the God of the Old Testament as vacillating, and responsible for evil.

Like the Gnostics and indeed like some Greek teaching that followed Plato, Marcion despised the flesh and in particular the humiliating and, to him, banal act of sexual intercourse with its dis-orders of pregnancy and birth. Tertullian addressed these views extensively in *Against Marcion*, but some of his ideas were to reappear in Manichaeism. Mani (216–74), the Persian-based founder of Manichaeism, believed, as did the Gnostics, in an ascending order of enlightenment through which an individual could progress from being a "hearer" and become part of the "elect". Hearers could be married or have mistresses and could have intercourse but must avoid procreation. Procreation would only multiply bringers of darkness, or unenlightened humanity. Augustine of Hippo records in his *Confessions* that he followed the way of Mani for a time as part of his search for salvation and peace.[49] In the end, he came to see Manichaeism as a hollow and pretentious religion, whose leaders did not practise the tenets of celibacy. However, many on the fringes of the Church were influenced by this seemingly rigorist teaching. Aware of the Manichees' presence in and around Antioch, Chrysostom answered their siren calls to become enlightened with a powerful riposte, not so much denouncing their tenets outright, but by showing that it was in fact through the flesh that God in Christ works our salvation in the incarnation and crucifixion.

John chose the text of Jesus in the Garden of Gethsemane where he prays, "My Father, if it is not possible for this cup to be taken away unless I drink it, may your will be done" (Matthew 26:42). He sought to show that it was only through suffering in the flesh, and through no other way (for no other way other was possible) that Jesus procured salvation. By taking on flesh, and dying an excruciating death *in the body*, Jesus opened up the way to salvation.

John has this to say about the cross:

> For the cross destroyed the enmity of God towards man, brought about the reconciliation, made the earth heaven, associated men with angels, pulled down the citadel of death, unstrung the force of the devil, extinguished the power of sin, delivered the world from error, brought back the truth, expelled demons, destroyed temples, overturned altars, suppressed the sacrificial offering, implanted virtue, founded churches.... The cross is the will of the Father, the glory of the Son and the rejoicing of the Spirit.[50]

He makes the point from Jesus's own words (Matthew 26:42) that this suffering in the flesh was the only way by which the world might be redeemed:

> Indeed, he clothed himself with our humanity like any other person. He did not enter once for all into a man matured and completely developed, but into a virgin's womb, so as to undergo the process of gestation and birth and suckling and growth, and by the length of time and the variety and stages of growth to give assurance of what had come to pass. And when bearing the body of flesh, he suffered it to experience the infirmities of human nature and to be hungry, and thirsty, and to sleep and feel fatigue; finally also when he came to the cross, he suffered it to undergo the pains of flesh.[51]

Of the teachings of Marcion, Valentinus (a leading Gnostic) and the Manichaeans, John says the following:

> [They have sought to] overthrow the doctrine of the Incarnation and have vented a diabolical utterance declaring that he did not become flesh, nor was clothed with it, but this were a mere fancy and illusion, a piece of acting and pretence although the sufferings, the death, the burial, the thirst, cry aloud against this teaching. For this reason, just as he hungered, as he slept, as he felt fatigue, as he ate and drank, so also did he deprecate death, thereby manifesting his humanity, and that infirmity of human nature which does not submit without pain to be torn from this present life. For had he not uttered any of these things, it might have been said that if he were a man, he ought to have experienced human feelings. And what are these? In the case of one about to be crucified: fear and agony, and pain in being torn from the present life; for a sense of the charm which surrounds present things is implanted in human nature: on this account wishing to prove the reality of the fleshly clothing, and to give assurance of the incarnation he manifests the actual feelings of man with full demonstration.[52]

It is a majestic piece of insightful apologetic and a defence of the true meaning of the Incarnation against the speculative and tawdry propositions of the Gnostics in their various guises. While the above is an example of a sermon in response to a circulating heresy, John could also give an *encomium* as good as any, in remembering the great martyrs of Antioch from the past. Two sermons remembering Ignatius and St Babylas, who were martyred respectively in the second century and in the Great Persecution, have come down to us. Firstly, John praises Ignatius for his martyrdom in Rome in *c*.108, where he was devoured by the lions in the Colosseum. He praises Ignatius for his diligent care of the Church, his willingness to embrace "his time", which was one of great persecution, his care for the whole city of Antioch, and his joy in being martyred.[53] He also praises the locally martyred bishop Babylas. In praising Saint Babylas, John draws attention to the work of the Spirit being accomplished even through the dust of his decayed body. He recalls that in his brief rule of 362–4, Emperor Julian sought to bury Christianity and its martyrs and resurrect paganism and Greek philosophy in its place. Not only did he not survive long enough to have much effect, but for John the power of God was evidently against him throughout. One clear sign of this relates to the remains of Babylas, much venerated by Bishop Meletius and for whom Meletius built a new tomb and shrine at Daphne with the help of John. The tomb of Babylas and the Temple of Apollo were both in the outskirts of Antioch at Daphne and close by each other. Julian sought to suppress remembrance of Babylas and exalt the worship of Apollo. He thus desecrated the tomb and rebuilt the temple. Nevertheless, such was the power of God working through Babylas, that when Julian, "that wretched and miserable man",[54] moved the coffin from the shrine to the city "a thunderbolt came from upon the head of [the emperor's] image and burnt it all up".[55] Furthermore, the roof of the shrine of Apollo was damaged.

But the preaching which occupied far and away the greatest number of his sermons, and for which John is especially remembered, is his expository preaching, which for 11 years (386–97) he pursued thoroughly in the Great Church and elsewhere. Given all else he was doing, the quantity of his sermons is prodigious. There are some 600 pieces of exegesis from his years at Antioch. He started as he meant to go on, and in 386 began a Lenten series on Genesis, the traditional time in the Church to teach on that book and, in particular, on the six days of creation (the Hexameron). There were 32 sermons in Lent before Easter and a further 35 leading up to Pentecost. These were held in the early morning, probably in the Great Church. John approached these sermons with zest, frequently encouraging his listeners to remain awake and share what they learnt with those at home.[56] He said at the start, "Let no one be gloomy, let no one look sullen but exult and be glad and glorify the guardian of our souls, who shows us the best way [compared to Pagans and Jews] and let us welcome with great joy his approach."[57]

Much else was to follow. In 386/7, John preached a shorter series on Isaiah, while in his later years as a preacher in Antioch he gave himself to expositions of the Gospels, notably Matthew and John, and most of the Pauline corpus. The exposition of Matthew, which ran to 90 homilies,[58] was much more uneven in quality, relying on frequent recourse to moral exhortation and "shot through with Stoic presuppositions".[59] His series on John, which was preached in 391,[60] ran to 88 homilies, was more polemical, and acknowledged the role of the Spirit in the teaching of the Gospel and in the inner reflections of the Apostle.[61] The Pauline corpus was mostly tackled in John's later years in Antioch, and in particular the pastoral epistles and the later chapters of Ephesians gave John ample opportunity for his advocacy of the life of abstinence, his censure of luxury, his cautions against idleness, and his warnings against the advance of the Huns through the Caucasus into the empire.[62] His teaching on Romans—32 homilies—was given in 392, and is considered one of John's most polished productions. In fact, scholars explain the uneven quality of John's exegetical work in terms of whether or not they were subject to some post-delivery editing by John himself and/or his colleagues; or whether, as was the case in Constantinople, they were circulated in an unvarnished form during periods of great stress.[63]

Nevertheless, it was an extraordinary corpus of preaching in which his plain speaking was matched by his comprehensiveness, and his willingness to address the issues of the day. But there came a time, early on in his preaching career, which afforded him an opportunity to gain the attention of the whole city at a time of great jeopardy for its future prosperity. At this time of civic crisis, John's gifts would especially shine, and his voice would become the guide to the people's welfare, and *the* voice to be heard in Antioch.

Notes

1. John Curran, "From Jovian to Theodosius", in A. Cameron and P. Garnsey (eds), *The Cambridge Ancient History Vol. XIII, The Late Empire, AD 337–425* (Cambridge: Cambridge University Press, 1998), pp. 98–9.
2. Ammianus Marcellinus 31, in *The Later Roman Empire (A.D. 354–378)/ Ammianus Marcellinus*; selected and translated by Walter Hamilton with an introduction and notes by Andrew Wallace-Hadrill (Harmondsworth: Penguin, 1986), p. 436.
3. Ammianus Marcellinus 31, op. cit., p. 438.
4. See *Socrates Scholasticus* IV:33 (Philadelphia, PA: Aeterna Press, 2006), p. 205.
5. Stephen Williams and Gerard Friell, *Theodosius: The Empire at Bay* (London: Routledge, 1998), p. 53.
6. Williams and Friell, *Theodosius*, p. 26.
7. John A. McGuckin, *Saint Gregory of Nazianzus: An Intellectual Biography* (Crestwood, NY: St Vladimir's Press, 2001), p. 326.
8. J. N. D. Kelly, *Golden Mouth: The Story of John Chrysostom, Ascetic, Preacher, Bishop* (Ithaca, NY: Cornell University Press, 1998), p. 37.
9. Kelly, *Golden Mouth*, p. 39.
10. Palladius, *Dialogue* 5, Palladius, *Dialogues*, in *Dialogue sur la vie de Jean Chrysostome/Palladios*, ed. and tr. Anne-Marie Malingrey with Philippe Leclercq, SC 341, Vol. 4 (Paris: Les Éditions du Cerf, 1988), p. 111.
11. See Gregory Nazianzen, *Oratio 36: De Vita Sua*, in *Nicene and Post-Nicene Fathers: Second Series, Vol. VII: Cyril of Jerusalem, Gregory of Nazianzen*, ed. Philip Schaff (New York: Cosimo, 2007) p. 122.
12. Chrysostom, *De sacerdotio* VI.2, in *The Nicene and Post-Nicene fathers of the Christian Church, Volume 9: Saint Chrysostom: On the priesthood; Ascetic treatises; Select homilies and letters; Homilies on the statues*, ed. Philip Schaff (Grand Rapids, MI: Eerdmans, 1975), p. 74.
13. Clement of Alexandria, *The Instructor* III.2 (Savage, MI: Lighthouse Christian Publishing, 2014).
14. Tertullian, *On the Veiling of Virgins* XVI, in *The Ante-Nicene Fathers: The Writings of the Fathers Down to A.D. 325 Volume IV Fathers of the Third Century: Tertullian Part 4*, ed. Alexander Roberts, James Donaldson and Arthur Cleveland Coxe (New York: Cosimo, 2007), p. 37.
15. Tertullian, *On Modesty* IV.7.

16 Ambrose, *De Virginitate*, in Neil B. McLynn, *Ambrose of Milan* (Berkeley, CA: University of California, 2014), pp. 57ff.
17 Ambrose, *De Virginitate* V.3, in *Ambrose: Selected Works and Letters*, ed. Philip Schaff, NAPNF (Grand Rapids, MI: Christian Classics Ethereal Library, 2004), p. 545.
18 Ambrose, *De Virginitate* III, op. cit., p. 547.
19 Ambrose, *De Virginitate* XI, op. cit., p. 557.
20 Basil of Caesarea, Letter 199 To Amphilocus, Bishop of Iconium, in *Basil of Caesarea: Letters,* vol. III, tr. Deferrari, Loeb Classical Library, Vol. 24 (Cambridge, MA: Harvard University Press, 2003), p. 103.
21 Jerome, *Letter* XXII to Eustochium: *The Virgin's Profession*, tr. F. A Wright, Loeb Classical Library Vol. 262 (Cambridge, MA: Harvard University Press, 1975), pp. 53ff.
22 Chrysostom, *De Virginitate*, *PG* 48, pp. 533–96.
23 Chrysostom, *De Virginitate*, *PG* 48, pp. 114–18.
24 Kelly, *Golden Mouth*, p. 45.
25 Chrysostom, *De Virginitate* XCVIII.2, op. cit., p. 258.
26 Chrysostom, *Ad viduam iuniorem*, *PG* 48, pp. 599–610.
27 Chrysostom, *De non iterando coniugio*, *SC* 138.166.
28 Basil, Letter 199, op. cit.
29 Basil, Letter 199, op. cit.
30 Kelly, *Golden Mouth*, p, 47.
31 Chrysostom, *Quod regularis viris cohabitare non debeant*, *PG* 47, pp. 495–514.
32 *C. eos qui subintroductas habent virgi's*, *PG* 47, pp. 507–10.
33 *Quod regularis* 8, *PG* 47, pp. 528–9.
34 Kelly, *Golden Mouth*, p. 39.
35 Chrysostom, *Ad Stag 1.1*, *PG* 47, p. 426; Kelly, *Golden Mouth*, p. 44.
36 Chrysostom, *De compunctione cordis*, *PG* 47, pp. 393–415.
37 Kelly, *Golden Mouth*, p. 51.
38 Chrysostom, *Adversus oppougnatores vitae monasticae* 2:9, *PG* 47, p. 344.
39 Chrysostom, *Adversus oppougnatores vitae monasticae* 3:8, *PG* 47, pp. 360–3.
40 John Chrysostom, *How Parents Should Bring up their Children*, tr. A. M. Malingrey, *SC* 188 (Paris: Les Éditions du Cerf, 1972).
41 Kelly, *Golden Mouth*, p. 53.
42 Palladius, *Dialogue* 5.19–38, in *Dialogue sur la vie de Jean Chrysostome*, eds A.-M. Malingrey and P. Leclercq, *SC* 341 (Paris: Les Éditions du Cerf, 1988), p. 111.

43 *PG* 48, pp. 693–700.
44 *Jean Chrysostome: Sur le sacerdoce (dialogue et homélie)*, ed. A.-M. Malingrey, SC 272 (Paris: Les Éditions du Cerf, 1980), pp. 406–14.
45 Kelly, *Golden Mouth*, p. 57.
46 *Jean Chrysostome: Sur l'incompréhensibilité de Dieu*, ed. J. Daniélou, A.-M. Malingrey and R. Flacelière, SC 28 (Paris: Les Éditions du Cerf, 1970).
47 *Fathers of the Church*, Vol. 72, ed. Paul W. Hawkins (Washington D.C.: Catholic University of America, 1984), p. 59.
48 *Jean Chrysostome: Homélies sur la Résurrection, l'Ascension et la Pentecôte*, ed. N. Rambault (Paris: Les Éditions du Cerf, 2014), cited in Kelly, *Golden Mouth*, p. 61.
49 St Augustine, *Confessions,* tr. Henry Chadwick (Oxford: OUP World's Classics, 2008), pp. 48ff.
50 Chrysostom, *Against Marcionites and Manichaeans* 2, in *St. Chrysostom: On the Priesthood, Ascetic Treatises, Select Homilies and Letters*, ed. Philip Schaff, NAPNF, First series, Vol. IX (New York: Cosimo, 2007), p. 203.
51 Chrysostom, *Against Marcionites and Manichaeans* 4, op. cit., p. 205.
52 Chrysostom, *Against Marcionites and Manichaeans* 4, op. cit., p. 205.
53 Chrysostom, *On St Ignatius*, in *St. Chrysostom: On the Priesthood, Ascetic Treatises, Select Homilies and Letters*, ed. Philip Schaff, NAPNF, First series, Vol. IX (New York: Cosimo, 2007), pp. 135ff.
54 Chrysostom, *Homily on St Babylas* §1, in *St. Chrysostom: On the Priesthood, Ascetic Treatises, Select Homilies and Letters*, ed. Philip Schaff, NAPNF, First series, Vol. IX (New York: Cosimo, 2007), p. 141.
55 Chrysostom, *Homily on St Babylas* §3, op. cit., p. 143.
56 Chrysostom, *Fathers of the Church*, Vol. 74, ed. Robert Hill (Washington D.C.: Catholic University of America, 1985), p. 14.
57 Chrysostom, *Fathers of the Church*, op. cit., p. 15.
58 *St. Chrysostom: Homilies on the Gospel of St. Matthew*, ed. Philip Schaff, NAPNF, First series, Vol. X (New York: Cosimo, 2007).
59 Kelly, *Golden Mouth*, p. 92.
60 *St. Chrysostom: Homilies on the Gospel of St. John and the Epistle to the Hebrews*, ed. Philip Schaff, NAPNF, First series, Vol. X (New York: Cosimo, 2007).
61 Chrysostom, *Homily 1*, op. cit., p. 7.
62 Chrysostom, *Homily 7*, op. cit., p. 79.
63 Kelly, *Golden Mouth*, pp. 92–3.

6

Church and State

Soon after John's ordination as a presbyter in 387, a crisis of imperial proportions arose in Antioch. Only the historian Sozomen—who was born near Gaza around 400, and who wrote his *Church History,* which he dedicated to Theodosius II, between 439 and 450—and the rhetorician Libanius mention it. Sozomen tells us that

> the continuance of the war [against the Goths, and later the usurper Maximus] compelled the rulers to impose fresh taxes on the people, a sedition was [thus] excited at Antioch in Syria; the statues of the emperor and of the empress were thrown down and dragged through the city, and as is usual on such occasions, the enraged multitude uttered every insulting epithet that passion could suggest. With the emperor, determining to avenge this insult by the death of the principal conspirators, the whole city was [now] filled with terror.[1]

However sketchily these events are recorded by Roman historians, what does seem clear is that in and around the beginning of March 387, soon after John had preached on the Lenten theme of "use a little wine because of your stomach" (1 Timothy 5:23) on 21 February, arguing for moderation but not complete abstinence in the use of alcohol, a riot occurred in Antioch. Before John preached again the following weekend, and towards the end of that week, a new exorbitant tax was announced from the courthouse in the city. It was a demand that sent the population into rage and desperation, precipitating looting, rioting and criminal damage.

According to Libanius, even the city councillors (*decurions*) and other prominent citizens addressed tearful pleadings to the governor that the tax be lessened or withheld entirely.[2] What was such an affront and offence to the emperor, at a time of impending civil war in the empire, was the tearing down of his statue and that of the empress and the way they were dragged like refuse through the city. "Everyone knew that to insult or show disrespect to the images of the reigning emperor was equivalent to insulting him personally, and therefore counted as high treason."[3] No city could do such a thing with impunity, and Antioch, host to innumerable emperors down the years, knew this very well. During the riot, the governor's house was attacked and the public baths were ransacked. The disturbance was short but vehement. It was all over by noon as Libanius, the philosopher and former teacher of John, and the main recorder of these events, documented in his five speeches.[4] But in the cool light of the morning after the riot the city feared vengeance from the emperor's troops.

There were initial reprisals. Troops led by the Count of Oriens (the East) moved in, the ringleaders were rounded up and quickly executed, while the city waited on tenterhooks to see what an enraged emperor, now in Constantinople, would do. After all, only three years later, in 390, an equally angry emperor would order reprisals against a crowd in Thessalonica for rioting over the treatment of a favourite homosexual charioteer by his troops. In that case, some 7,000 citizens would be slaughtered, prompting Ambrose's famous demand for contrition on the part of the self-same Emperor Theodosius with the threat of exclusion from the sacrament.

John was the master of the moment, and with Bishop Flavian of Antioch determined to plead for mercy for the city by personally going to Constantinople where Theodosius was holding court, John found himself preaching the Lent Sermons for the next eight weeks at a time when the city was in a state of the highest tension over the possibility of reprisals. For those eight weeks, John had a virtually captive audience, as the normal entertainments of the city, such as horse or chariot racing and the theatre were in suspension, pending the emperor's decision. Given that Antioch followed the Alexandrian calendar, with Easter falling on 25 April that year, John would preach his homilies throughout that Lenten period. The turn of events during that time was the immediate departure of the elderly Flavian for Constantinople, the initial reprisals by the Count of Oriens, the setting up of a Commission on 15 March to investigate the riot and report back to the emperor, and the emperor's final decision about the fate of the city. With these events in train and the mood being one of anxious waiting, as a newly ordained presbyter with his bishop away, John addressed the city. He showed he was fully up to the challenge.

John preached 21 sermons or homilies in either the Old Church (the first two homilies) or the Great Church. The first homily he preached, on Sunday 21 February 387, dealt with human weakness in the service of God, and the virtues that may come from this.[5] Taking Timothy's frequent ailments of the stomach, for which Paul prescribes wine as an example of human weakness (1 Timothy 5:23), John identifies the benefit of weakness as being the demonstration of Apostle Paul's pastoral care for Timothy, as well as Timothy's dependence on the grace and strength of God. Having begun his series in this way, John was to be overtaken by events. The following week all had changed, except of course the city's reliance on God and Scripture. Once more preaching in the Old Church, John opens his second homily in dramatic fashion:

> What shall I say, or what shall I speak of? The present season is one for tears, and not for words; for lamentation, not for discourse; for prayer and not for preaching. Such is the magnitude of the deeds daringly done; so incurable is the wound, so deep the blow, even beyond the power of treatment, and craving assistances from above. Thus, it was that Job, when he had lost all, sat himself down on a dunghill; and his friends heard of it, and came seeing him, while yet afar off, they rent their garments, and sprinkled themselves with ashes and made great lamentation. The same thing now ought all cities around do, to come to our city and to lament with all sympathy what has befallen us.[6]

However, far from being a moment to give up on preaching, the riot proved a gift that emboldened John in his efforts, enabling him to preach more, if anything, rather than less. For during this time of heightened tension, he had the citizenry's ear like never before. And he would not lightly give up that opportunity. With accomplished, natural eloquence he paints the scene: "A foretime there was nothing happier than our city; nothing [more] melancholy has it now become."[7] The Forum was now "a cheerless spectacle". It was like a garden with a failed irrigation system, with the dried-up leaves stripped from both the plants and trees. It was like a beehive with just one solitary bee where there was once a working, thriving hive. Metaphor is built upon metaphor to heighten the sense of the plight of the city following the riot and the desecration of the statues. And then, into this dire situation, John planted his text from Paul: "Command those who are rich in this present world not to be arrogant nor to put their hope in wealth, which is so uncertain, but to put their hope in God, who richly provides us with everything for our enjoyment" (1 Timothy 6:17). This gave his homily its theme: the answer to the city's crisis lies not only in the clemency of the emperor but in the rich turning away from arrogance and unhealthy trust in mammon. It was one of John's most prevalent and most powerful themes, both in Antioch and Constantinople. "Therefore," he argued, "let us not adorn our houses but our souls."[8] It was a priceless one-liner.

John's second homily begins with a lament for fallen Antioch, once so prosperous and confident but now cowering anxiously, and leads on to a plea for simplicity in lifestyle and a rejection of the pursuit of riches. The third homily, probably preached on 28 February, brings the crisis centre stage once more, and focusses on Flavian's mission to the emperor in Constantinople. This homily was quite possibly preached in the Great Church with its larger seating capacity, as no specific mention is made of the Old Church as the venue. Once again John knows how to use the theatre of the moment. At the outset, drawing attention to the vacant episcopal chair or throne he said:

> When I look on the throne, deserted and bereft of our teacher, I rejoice and weep at the same time. I weep, because I see not our father with us! But I rejoice that he hath set out on a journey for our preservation; that he is gone to snatch so great a multitude from the wrath of the emperor. Here [the empty throne] is both an ornament to you, and a crown to him!"[9] John then pictures this elderly, physically frail bishop "hastening along borne up on the wings of zeal".

He points out that Flavian, "knowing our city is the head and mother of all the East", was willing "to encounter every danger and nothing would avail to detain him here".[10] John goes on to describe how Flavian will speak with wisdom before the emperor, how he will invoke these holy weeks of Lent as a reason for clemency, where mercy should follow contrition; how he will plead only a small proportion of the city were guilty of rioting and vandalism, and how some of those were in fact "strangers and adventurers".[11] In other words, the citizens of Antioch were hardly to blame. Using biblical models such as Esther, who delivered the Jews in the Persian Empire from slaughter, and Jonah, who secured the repentance and saving of Nineveh, John urges his listeners to commit to prayer and fasting and intercession for their city.[12] They are to ask forgiveness for their sins, however long ago committed, and seek with hope deliverance from further punishment.[13] There must have been a chastened, sombre, yet hopeful mood in the Great Church after this third homily.

And so the homilies continued, at the rate of at least two a week over the eight-week period of Lent. Some focus on the biblical examples of patience and fortitude as displayed by Job and Daniel.[14] Others focus on a particular fixation of John's, which is the misuse of oaths in swearing about the truthfulness of something (see Matthew 5:33–6).[15] But these calls for abstinence and spiritual discipline, typical of Lent, were intermingled with news and spiritual lessons about the ongoing plight of Antioch, awaiting the emperor's decision about a suitable punishment.

Homilies XII, XIV, XV, XVI, XVII and XXI especially focus on the plight of Antioch. Once again John uses the fear and anxiety about the emperor's impending decision as a springboard for encouraging repentance, amendment of life and the avoidance of sins such as the use of oaths. These later homilies, which climax in Flavian's return from Constantinople with news from the Imperial Court, revolve around the developing narrative of this crisis.

Homilies XII to XV reflect the continuing sense of fear about the future of the city. Remembering the city's anxiety, John once again praises God for Antioch's deliverance thus far. He speaks vividly, but not without a measure of hyperbole, to underline his point: "For who hath seen, who hath ever heard of sufferings such as were ours? We were every day in expectation that our city would be overturned from its foundations together with its inhabitants. But when the Devil was hoping to sink the vessel, then God produced a perfect calm. Let us then not be unmindful of the greatness of these terrors, in order that we may remember the magnitude of the benefits received from God."[16]

A week later, in late February, there were new false rumours of impending doom. Nevertheless, John calls for calm, saying in Homily XIV:

> Let us not be desponding, nor let us despair of a change for the better; but let us hope that speedily there will be a calm; and, in short, casting the issue of all the tumults which beset us upon God, let us again handle the customary points; and again, bring forward our usual topic of instruction.[17]

For John, this "customary" instruction was about not misusing oaths, which you might say was an obsession with him. But by the next homily customary teaching on fasting is put on hold as the crisis is once again addressed.

Word had come from Emperor Theodosius that far from there being bloodletting or looting by his soldiers, a Commission would be appointed to investigate the causes of the destruction of the statues and apportion blame. The Prefect of the East, the highest official in the great Diocese of Antioch, entered the Great Church to reassure the congregation and to explain the emperor's method of proceeding. John was embarrassed that it had been necessary for a pagan official to enter a Christian church and reassure the congregation.[18] The Commission of Enquiry that was announced included Caesarius, the Master of Offices, and Hellebichus, the Commander of the Army. The accused were brought to court in front of the Commissioners, but the punishments were less severe than expected, and a sense of relief began to seep into the city. Nor was John slow to portray the punishments they were saved from, and the need for rejoicing and praise.[19] He was also quick to compare favourably the ministry of the monks, who had come down from their caves to encourage the populace, with the actions of the pagan philosophers, who had slipped away and deserted the city altogether. The true shepherds had stayed with the flock and were not hirelings. Of the latter, he said:

> Where now are those who are clad in threadbare cloaks, and display a long beard and carry staves in the right hand: the philosophers of the world who are more abject in disposition than the dogs under the table, and do everything for the sake of the belly.[20]

In other words, in times of crisis the monks showed real concern, while the philosophers looked after themselves. As ever, John does not mince his words. Furthermore, in closing the theatre, the Hippodrome and the baths, the emperor had reduced the possibility of wickedness.[21]

But the climax was still to come with the return of Flavian after a slow journey, perhaps by sea, having interceded with the emperor on behalf of the city. Although the two sources of these events, the account of the pagan rhetorician and philosopher, Libanius, and the homilies of John entitled *Concerning the Statues*, differ on who secured the result, the outcome was beyond question. John typically praises Flavian for securing the clemency of the emperor, while Libanius says nothing of Flavian and attributes the result to the wisdom of Caesarius, the emperor's Master of Offices, who had acted as a commissioner and magistrate and had found the principal offenders. He had recommended the death penalty but referred the final decision to the emperor himself.[22] It seems that Flavian had travelled ahead of Caesarius, who was detained by the Commission, reaching Constantinople a little earlier to make his plea before Caesarius arrived with his own account. Theodosius decided to lift the death sentences on the culprits and restore all the privileges of the city. Caesarius then travelled more swiftly back to Antioch with the emperor's letters of pardon and announced the decision at festivities held in the main square of the city, which was festooned with garlands and lit by torches. Flavian arrived a little after these festivities, before Easter, which fell on 25 April, and was most probably present in the church when John preached his final homily "On the Statues" as his Easter Sermon.

Kelly refers to this sermon as one of John's most accomplished and most tendentious orations.[23] Naturally it was a sermon which lent itself to great drama. The city had been on tenterhooks for weeks, the good news that no retaliatory measures were to be taken had been proclaimed, the frail bishop was back with his flock and the Church was celebrating Easter. The sense of deliverance was all around, and John was not one to let such an opportunity pass by. He was lavish in his praise of Flavian, who was willing to travel, who was prepared to be away from home even during Easter, and who "took not his age into account and dispatched this long journey with just as much ease as if he had been young and sprightly!"[24] It seems that he may have travelled overland to Constantinople and returned mostly by sea.[25] Not only was the bishop to be praised, but the emperor, with splendour "beyond that of a diadem" also.[26] The loving kindness of God, the magnanimity of the emperor and the wisdom of the bishop combined for the city's deliverance. But John was not content to leave it there without conjuring up an affecting scene of the bishop's intercession:

> He stood before the emperor at a distance, speechless, weeping, with downcast eyes covering his face as if he himself had been the doer of the mischief and then began an apology on our behalf.[27]

The emperor was melted by the tears of contrition and abject penance of Flavian. He was then called to act with that virtue which is most becoming, so that new statues of the emperor and his consort might be robed, not in precious stones or gold but in the most valuable of all clothes, "humanity and tender mercy".[28] Recalling past acts of clemency to prisoners by Theodosius, the example of Constantine, who refused even to notice damage to a statue attacked by his opponents,[29] and the certainty that this act of clemency would be a legacy of his imperial rule for generations to come, Flavian moved Theodosius to mercy and, like Joseph, who wept secretly having recognized his brothers (Genesis 43:30ff.), Theodosius also wept. Only he did so "mentally", and "did not let it be seen for the sake of those who were present".[30] Faced with such an intercession, what else could the emperor do but remit the offences of Antioch and envelop it in his pardon? Meanwhile Flavian humbly entrusted to another the good news that would delight the city of Antioch. There is little doubt that to have been present in the Great Church that

Easter Sunday in 387 and hear John's account, however confected, would have been a memory to take to the grave.

Given that John had been a priest for a little over a year[31]—he was still under 40 years old—he was nevertheless among the most arresting and well-known voices in Antioch. In ten years, he would be the Bishop of Constantinople. In that period, as we have seen, both in his publications and preaching, he would continue to build his reputation as a fearless speaker and as a gifted expository preacher—if at times prolix and digressive in style and sometimes disjointed in form. Although wholly committed to the ascetic lifestyle, he was now free to lead a secular congregation in the challenges of urban life. The opportunity afforded John by the city's crisis and by an absent bishop was boldly and eloquently taken. His pulpit oratory was probably unmatched. His mix of Attic Greek and the more unclassical Greek of the New Testament and Septuagint made him different from the teachers of the schools, such as Libanius, and he was certainly more direct and confiding in his approach. At the same time, he was deeply conservative in outlook. He upheld the right of the emperor to tax as he wished. He supported the actions of the magistracy in quelling the riots. He deplored citizens rising up against legitimate authority, but he welcomed the emperor's right to be merciful, which he regarded as a further garland around his head. Theodosius was to be supported and praised in all weathers. He had returned the Eastern empire to Nicene orthodoxy and would see off the rivals who sought his throne. For Chrysostom, Theodosius's reign was a golden age much like Constantine's. It was not altogether surprising that after a further ten years as a presbyter, John should be chosen by Theodosius's son, Arcadius, and his advisers, to follow Bishop Nectarius, who himself had followed the all-too-brief episcopacy of Gregory of Nazianzus. In inviting John, the court was certainly inviting someone of proven loyalty to the dynasty, but it would not be at any price. John's severe simplicity, his criticism of wealth, ill-gotten or wrongly obtained, and his unwillingness to compromise his principles would make him an uneasy chaplain to a court bent on luxury and self-importance. Just as Henry II thought by appointing Chancellor Thomas à Becket as archbishop he could tame and subject the Church, so Arcadius thought that John would follow his wishes, and those of his wife the empress. He had the wrong man. As with

Becket it would end with the death of the archbishop, but also, as with Becket, John made a reputation which would far outlive and outshine those of his enemies.

After the settling of the riot and the emperor's response, the relative calm of Antioch would have seemed like a backwater compared with the ecclesiastical complexities and the imperial complications of Constantinople. John must have felt his days in Antioch had provided him with a platform for addressing a city which he would never have again. The ebbs and flows of politics, the power struggles, and the ecclesiastical jealousies would make Antioch seem like a haven where the business of teaching and applying Scripture to a city population had been a real possibility. Those ten years or more of teaching in Antioch following his baptism of ascetic fire in the nearby hills would not come again, but he had provided an example of applied expository preaching which would recur down the ages: in Geneva with John Calvin, for example; in Glasgow with Dr Chalmers in the eighteenth century; and with the great Baptist preacher Charles Haddon Spurgeon in London. John had a lit a fire which would be reignited down the centuries.

Notes

1. Sozomen, *Church History* XXIII, in *Ecclesiastical history: a history of the church in nine books, from A.D. 324 to A.D. 440 by Sozomen*, a new translation from the Greek, with a memoir of the author (London: Bagster, 1846), pp. 360–1.
2. Libanius, *Orations*, 19:15–26.
3. J. N. D. Kelly, *Golden Mouth: The Story of John Chrysostom, Ascetic, Preacher, Bishop* (Ithaca, NY: Cornell University Press, 1998), p. 74.
4. Libanius, *Orations* 19–23.
5. Chrysostom, *Concerning the Statues Homily 1*, *PG* 49.22, NAPNF Series I, Vol. 19 (Grand Rapids, MI: Eerdmans, 1975), pp. 331–44, especially p. 336.
6. Chrysostom, *Homily on St Babylas II* §1, in *St. Chrysostom: On the Priesthood, Ascetic Treatises, Select Homilies and Letters*, ed. Philip Schaff, NAPNF, First series, Vol. IX (New York: Cosimo, 2007), p. 344.
7. Chrysostom, *Homily on St Babylas II* §3, op. cit., p. 345.
8. Chrysostom, *Homily on St Babylas II* §16, op. cit., p. 349.
9. Chrysostom, *Homily on St Babylas III* §1, op. cit., p. 354.
10. Chrysostom, *Homily on St Babylas II* §3, op. cit., p. 355.
11. Chrysostom, *Homily II* §3, op. cit., p. 355.
12. Chrysostom, *Homily II* §11, 12, op. cit., p. 359.
13. Chrysostom, *Homily II* §21, op. cit., p. 363.
14. Chrysostom, *Homilies IV and V*, p. 364, op. cit., pp. 371ff.
15. Chrysostom, *Homilies X and XII*, op. cit., pp. 406ff. and 418ff.
16. Chrysostom, *Homily XII* §3, op. cit., p. 419.
17. Chrysostom, *Homily XIV* §2, op. cit., p. 431.
18. Chrysostom, *Homily XVI* §1, op. cit., p. 445.
19. Chrysostom, *Homily XVII* §3, op. cit., p. 453.
20. Chrysostom, *Homily XVII* §5, op. cit., p. 454.
21. Chrysostom, *Homily XVII* §9, op. cit., p. 455.
22. Kelly, *Golden Mouth*, op. cit., p. 79.
23. Kelly, *Golden Mouth*, p. 80.
24. Chrysostom, *Homily XXI* §4, op. cit., p. 483.
25. Chrysostom, *Homily XXI* §19, op. cit., p. 488.
26. Chrysostom, *Homily XXI* §5, op. cit., p. 483.
27. Chrysostom, *Homily XXI* §6, op. cit., p. 484.

28 Chrysostom, *Homily XXI §10*, op. cit., p. 485.
29 Chrysostom, *Homily XXI §11*, op. cit., p. 485.
30 Chrysostom, *Homily XXI §18*, op. cit., p 488.
31 Kelly, *Golden Mouth*, p. 55.

7

A new broom in Constantinople

When not on military campaigns, Theodosius made his base at Constantinople from 382, but would not fully reside there until 391.[1] There is no doubt that Theodosius, a Spanish Roman general in origin and a firm adherent of the Nicene Creed, was a very powerful force in the annals of Roman history, particularly in the final days of the empire which included East and West. Perhaps it is ironic that the disintegration of the empire began soon after the rule of this remarkable leader. But by then the inherent problems of an empire stretching from Hadrian's Wall in the north to Alexandria and Egypt in the south, and as far east as the Danube, the Black Sea and the Euphrates, ensured it would eventually collapse under the scale of its own size. It was simply too big to defend and administer, especially in the face of growing incursions from the east of the Goths in their many tribes, the Huns, the Alamani, the Quadi, the Alans and the Persians, among others.

A Roman emperor must be a successful general before anything else, and Theodosius was certainly that. Like his father before him, he was able to see off the enemies of the empire. By 382, after the catastrophic reverse of Adrianople in 378 and the death of Valens, he had been able to subjugate the Goths,[2] but he had settled them in lands inside the borders of the empire, thus storing up problems for the future. During Theodosius's reign two usurpers emerged to try and seize power, both in the western half of the empire where Gratian was emperor until 383. The first usurper, Magnus Maximus, the *Comes Brittaniarum*, was the leader of the notoriously fickle British legions. Gratian, who was more at home in a philosophy class than on the battlefield, fled from combat near Paris and was executed together with his senior ministers at Lugdunum (Lyon) by some supporters of Maximus.[3] Perhaps Gratian's greatest act had been to appoint Theodosius *augustus* in the East in 378. In 387, Maximus continued to advance and overwhelmed Valentinian II, the successor to Gratian in the West, who now fled to Thessalonica and into the orbit of Theodosius. Theodosius swiftly advanced against Maximus in the Balkans, defeating and executing him, and then went to Rome exhibiting his four-year-old son Honorius as a future *augustus*. The second usurper against Valentinian II, Eugenius, now emerged in the West and once again Theodosius came to the rescue. However, following tensions with his chief commander, Abrogast,[4] Valentinian was found dead in Vienne in Gaul in May 392. Although he briefly declared himself emperor, Eugenius was defeated at the River Frigidus in 394 by Theodosius (who had already declared his son Honorius Augustus in the West and his other son Arcadius in the East). Then, for nearly three years, Theodosius was the last emperor to rule both East and West.

Not only was Theodosius an extremely effective military commander, he was also determined to advance the Christian cause, especially that of Nicene orthodoxy. He also began a more systematic suppression of paganism, which would be further extended in future years, especially during the reign of his grandson, Theodosius II (408–50). Theodosius accelerated the process of dismantling pagan worship: visits to temples or any forms of sacrifice were forbidden. Even practising pagan rites or haruspicy at home was proscribed under the Theodosian Decrees (389–91). Later in his reign, he fostered the destruction of the Serapeum in Alexandria, and the Temple of Apollo in Delphi. He supported the earlier edicts of Gratian in extinguishing the eternal fire in the Temple of Vesta in Rome, abolishing the Altar in the Senate House, and exiling the chief pagan senator and orator Symmachus.[5] The toleration Constantine had encouraged and which Theodosius had adopted in the earlier part of his reign was now abandoned in the wake of this more uncompromising policy.[6]

After he had defeated the two usurpers, Maximus and Eugenius, it became clear that Theodosius was in a position to found a dynasty. The western part of the empire had become dependent upon him, both for suppressing the political rivals of Gratian and Valentinian II, and for providing a successor to the latter in the West after his murder. In January 393, Theodosius appointed his younger son Honorius as co-ruler with him in the West, ruling from Milan, while his older son Arcadius was already co-ruler in the East, and reigned from Constantinople. After the death of his first wife, the Spanish Aelia Flacilla, Theodosius married Galla, the daughter of Valentinian I, and had one surviving daughter, Aelia Galla Placidia, one of the most remarkable women and empresses in Roman history. Theodosius, however, had less than two years to enjoy his family dynasty before he died in January 395 from severe oedema in Milan. Ambrose preached at his funeral, highlighting his suppression of paganism and his defence of Nicene Orthodoxy. This was the same Ambrose who had curtailed Theodosius's power by criticizing the massacre of citizens in Thessalonica by his troops, following a disturbance after a chariot race.

On 26 September 397 came the death of the much-respected Bishop of Constantinople, Nectarius. He had been Theodosius's choice to succeed Gregory of Nazianzus, who had resigned his post because he found the politics of church government overwhelming. Nectarius, like Ambrose, had been in the imperial administration as a *praetor* (a senior elected magistrate) before being chosen for his skill and tact in leading the often prickly and disputatious bishops of the province in a Nicene direction. Now Arcadius summoned John to the imperial city. He did so on the advice of his influential court eunuch Eutropius, who was superintendent of the bedchamber and at that time, before his dramatic fall, the mastermind behind many imperial decisions. An order was issued that John should be escorted from Antioch to be appointed the next Bishop of Constantinople, one of the four senior posts in the Church. John was no doubt chosen for his eloquence and clear teaching, his support of the emperor during the earlier crisis over the statues, and his generally conservative approach to authority. Arcadius, however, was no Theodosius and John was much less likely to support him and his court, or, when he got to know her, the highly influential Empress Aelia Eudoxia. Although a synod was called to consult over the appointment, little attention was paid to their deliberations and the appointment was essentially a court one.[7] Worse still, Theophilus, Patriarch of Alexandria, responded to the summons to come to the synod, only to learn that the candidate had already been chosen. This was a snub as far as he was concerned, and one for which John would pay dearly. Sozomen tells us that "The clergy and the people were unanimous in electing [John] and their choice was approved by the emperor."[8] In truth, it was the other way round. The emperor (or Eutropius) chose John and the synod approved the choice, but this would store up trouble for the future.

Nectarius, the previous Bishop of Constantinople, died on 26 September 397. By late October, John had been summoned by imperial decree to leave Antioch for Constantinople without initially being told why. En route at Bagras, some 25 kilometres from Antioch, the Governor of Syria informed the startled John that he had been chosen as the next Bishop of Constantinople. John would be the twelfth bishop since the founding of Constantinople by Constantine in 324. On the whole, Constantinople would not prove a happy see for many of them: it was a hotbed of Arianism over the years, the target of Gothic invasion, and the object of conspiracy from an Alexandrian Patriarchy jealous of its growing prominence. A later archbishop, Nestorius (428–31), who stoked a new controversy over the person of Christ and how his divinity and humanity were combined (or not fully combined as he would hold), only added to this tradition of unhappiness. Undoubtedly, John was summoned to Constantinople as the most eloquent preacher in the Eastern Church, and one who had hitherto shown himself a staunch supporter of Theodosius and his rule. He was now expected to strengthen the bond between court and Church and root out opposition to the emperor. How differently it would all turn out.

When John arrived in Constantinople, he moved into the bishop's residence or *episkopeion* which stood to the southeast of the Great Church, which itself came to be known later as Hagia Sophia. Completed in c.360, the Great Church was mostly built during the reign of Constantius II, although badly burnt in the reign of Theodosius. It would burn down again during riots caused by the empress's treatment of John and be rebuilt by Theodosius II. It would then burn down yet again during serious riots in Justinian's reign (527–65), at which time it was entirely and majestically rebuilt into its present magnificent form by the architects Anthemius of Tralles and Isidore of Miletus. (In recent years it has shuttled from a being a church, then a mosque, to a museum, and at the time of writing, a mosque.) Other prominent churches in the city were Hagia Eirene, still visible and wonderfully restored, and the Church of the Apostles, where Constantine had been buried. Nearby was the

Augustaion, a vast porticoed piazza which Constantine had named after his mother, Augusta Helena. To the east rose the senate house and to the southwest of that the great Hippodrome, where chariot races and games were held. On the far side of the Hippodrome was the imperial palace. Leading northwest from this collection of very imposing buildings was the great marbled Mese or street which went through the forums of Constantine and Theodosius before exiting through the walls near the Church of the Apostles. A further great street led off the Mese beyond the Forum of Theodosius, went out of the city through the Golden Gate to the Via Egnatia, past the shrine built to hold the head of John the Baptist, through Thrace, and on to Rome. The Via Egnatia was one of the great arteries of the empire.

Close by his own residence and on the south side of Hagia Sophia and connected to its narthex was a "sprawling convent". It was founded and presided over by a remarkable woman named Olympias, who would play an important part in John's story. She was a woman of great intelligence and character. Palladius writes that she was renowned for her asceticism, her knowledge of the Scriptures and her fortitude in the vicissitudes of life.[9] She was also a woman of immense wealth. As the granddaughter of Constantine's Prefect of the Praetorian Guard, she held vast estates in Thrace, Galatia, Cappadocia and Bithynia.[10] She had been briefly married to Nebridius, the city praetor, but he had died soon after, and, like many, she refused to marry again, seeking instead a celibate life of devoted service through a convent, modelling herself on the great Melania the Elder, who had accompanied Rufinus of Aquileia to the Holy Land where she likewise built a convent. In Olympias's convent, the number of nuns rose to 250. Olympias was to find in John a kindred spirit: both were formerly members of the Roman élite, both were well educated, committed to the ascetic lifestyle, and in need of mutual support under taxing and often lonely circumstances. Hers was an extreme asceticism. She ate very little, rarely took baths, and even then did not remove her undergarments so that neither she nor her maids should see her naked body.[11] Nevertheless, these two single-minded ascetics found a connection in their human needs and gave each other mutual support. Food was cooked and despatched to John from her kitchens. Conversations about ecclesiastical business were had. His clothes were mended. Indeed, there was no one in Constantinople with whom he was to have a deeper or more sympathetic understanding, no one with whom he was to feel more at ease or to whom he was to pour out his heart more unreservedly, than this independent, strong-willed but also intensely emotional woman.[12]

And at the time of his own greatest need and when she was at her lowest ebb, John provided touching support and counsel and at the same time received consolation himself. This then was the context in which John found himself as he began his work in the city.

A new broom sweeps clean

When John arrived in Constantinople, he was a tried and tested servant of the Church aged about 48. There was much behind him: a fine classical education; years of asceticism in the caves near Antioch (in part entirely on his own); the experience of managing a great church in Antioch with its large numbers of dependants, as well as experience dealing with a major crisis of Church–State relations in the time of Theodosius. He had also delivered and written many sermon series of biblical expositions and numerous clearly targeted books. He arrived in Constantinople surprised, if not overwhelmed, at his sudden elevation to this great see. He came to a city which in recent times had been racked by the divisions of the Arian controversy.

It was in Constantinople that the doctrines of the more extreme Arians, as promulgated by Eunomius, had taken root. Working from rational logic rather than scriptural authority, Eunomius maintained that the Son was unlike the Father. Both Basil of Caesarea and Gregory of Nyssa had written lengthy works against him. Yet from 339 until 380 there had been a succession of Arian bishops in Constantinople. These included the famous Arian and court bishop Eusebius of Nicomedia (339–41), Macedonius (342–6 and 351–60), who openly preached against the divinity of the Holy Spirit as a *pneumatomachi* (Spirit-fighter), Eudoxius of Antioch (360–70), and Demophilius (370–80), both Arians, before the brief tenure of Gregory of Nazianzus following his Orations on Nicene orthodoxy in the Anastasia Chapel. It was during these times that Gregory of Nyssa famously characterized conversation in Constantinople as follows:

> If you ask anyone for change [when out shopping], he will discuss with you whether the Son is begotten or unbegotten. If you ask about the quality of the bread, you will receive the answer that, "The Father is greater, the Son is less". If you suggest that you require a bath, you will be told that there was nothing before the Son was created.[13]

John's predecessor had been the urbane and diplomatic Nectarius, plucked from Roman bureaucracy like Ambrose of Milan to oversee the step change from outright Arianism to Nicene orthodoxy, although he was not as forthright as Ambrose. It was a long process of weeding out Arian-minded clergy and monks and installing new Orthodox ones.

Although it was 17 years since the start of Nectarius's episcopal reign, John suspected there were still residual Arian sympathies in the city, but he also desired the support of ordinary people. The note he struck in his early preaching was populist, and in his second sermon in Constantinople he deliberately set out to woo the people, not only to galvanize their orthodoxy but also to begin to form an unshakeable bond with them. His words were fulsome:

> I have already addressed you once [his first sermon in Constantinople now lost], but from that day I have come to love you as if I had grown up among you from childhood. The chains of affection which bind me to you are as strong as if I had enjoyed your most pleasant company for time past counting. And this has come about, not because I am especially given friendship and love, but because you are of all people most desirable, the most lovable. For who would not marvel at your zeal tested in the flames, your unfeigned love, your warm regard for your teachers, the unity you maintain among yourselves.[14]

While John was setting out to win the affection of the people, he was also careful not to alienate the court, or, at this stage at least, Emperor

Arcadius and Empress Eudoxia. At the same time, while John was willing to go to some lengths to ingratiate himself with court and city, he was as severe on the Church as he was emollient with these powerful leaders.

We have seen from his time at Antioch that John was a demanding church leader. He expected a great deal of himself in his role as preacher and pastor, and he expected little less from others. As Sozomen tells us, from the outset, John "devoted his attention to the reformation of the lives of his clergy, and to the regulation of their pursuits and conduct".[15] Sozomen goes on to say that, unlike his more easy-going predecessor Nectarius, "he was naturally disposed to reprehend the misconduct of others and to feel excessive indignation against those who acted unjustly".[16] This authoritarian style, which can in part be seen as a weakness, only intensified in his new office. He carefully scrutinized the accounts, for example, and was shocked by the sums being spent on hospitality. Accustomed to eating extremely frugally himself, he expected the same of others. He refused official or private dinners in his own palace, but this had the effect of isolating him, with the news of him eating alone circulating in the city.[17] His biographer Palladius goes to great lengths to defend John's reputation in this regard, arguing that had he entertained the rich in his palace he would have become popular in the court and among the powerful, but might well have been thought worldly and to be currying favour. If, on the other hand, he used church resources for the poor, without going out of his way to entertain the rich, his reputation would be that of a killjoy and miser.[18] As so often with leadership, it was a case of damned if you do and damned if you don't! John did start a hospital for lepers outside the city, much as Basil had done in Caesarea. In this respect, John was following the examples of a previous Arian bishop of Constantinople, Macedonius, of the early 340s, as well as the philanthropy of Theodosius's first wife, Flacilla.

If John's style did not suit all and alienated some, his discipline of the clergy and monks led to complaints about, and objections to, his interventions. This in turn stored up trouble for the future. Although this discipline was often justified, in some cases it led to a festering resentment which was later exploited against him. One practice John had already written and spoken against in Antioch was that of single men, whether monks or clergy, sharing premises with members of the opposite sex, who had the title *suneisaktoi*—i.e., unmarried sisters dedicated to God, but not related to the males of the household. This was widely practised but had been challenged and indeed stringently prohibited by the Canons of Nicaea (e.g. Canon 3). John enforced this prohibition severely and created some resentment on account of doing so. He also investigated the behaviour of virgins in the Great Church, insisting on modest dress, a minimum number of baths (which were considered a breach of ascetic living), and an assessment of each celibate's dedication to the vow of celibacy. If they were found wanting in this investigation, they would be encouraged to marry again. Even Olympias was counselled to stop giving her money away to the undeserving and instead encouraged, almost commanded, to place her huge wealth at John's disposal for the good of the Great Church. Such legacies or endowments made the bishop extremely powerful and the Church very influential, but they were also a hostage to fortune.

John also sought to regulate the burgeoning numbers of monasteries and monks. It is quite clear from earliest times that the wandering monks, prophets or apostles, as they were called then, were prone to prey on the hospitality of others. This was an issue in the Early Church. Indeed, in the *Didache*, the early Christian handbook on church life at the end of the first century, there is a warning about them:

> Every apostle [literally "messenger"] who comes to you [should be] welcomed in the Lord. But he should not remain more than one day. If he must, he may stay one more. But if he stays three days, he is a false prophet. When an apostle leaves, he should take nothing except bread, until he arrives at his night's lodging. If he asks for money, he is a false prophet.[19]

In other words, the Christian duty of hospitality (see Hebrews 13:2; 1 Peter 4:9) was always going to be open to abuse. Written in *c*.100, the *Didache* came well before the explosion of monasticism in the early fourth century. And although the monastic movement was something in which John had himself participated while in Antioch (and in many respects he was to remain a monk in spirit for his whole life), he was nevertheless quick to distinguish between the genuine and the counterfeit, the sponger and the truly spiritual. Perhaps it was for this reason that he quickly came to criticize the large numbers of monks who were milling around Constantinople at this time. Sozomen, the historian, records that

> John had several disputes with many of the monks, particularly with Isaac. He commended those who, in conformity with the rules of their profession, remained in quietude in their monasteries; he protected them from all injustice, and supplied all their wants. But the monks who made their appearance in cities were severely censured by him, and declared to be the disgrace of monasticism.[20]

Isaac was to become an implacable enemy of John. As with many of the Desert Fathers and Mothers, John saw the cave, the cell or the communal monastery as *the* place within which the discipline of the ascetic life must be worked out.[21] Indeed, when in the sixth century Saint Benedict came to list the rules of the monastic life, he made this an essential feature of the truly ascetic life.[22] Although the Franciscan and Dominican Friars were to change all this in the thirteenth century in the West, it would nevertheless only be a temporary change since most Dominicans and Franciscans in the end built friaries.

The monk Isaac, whom Palladius described as "the little Syrian, the lay about, the troop leader of bogus monks who had worn himself out with incessant slander of bishops",[23] became the main opponent of John's reforms. Isaac was well connected: he had been ordained by Athanasius the Great, further trained in Rome, and was known to Evagrius, the ultra-Nicene Bishop in Antioch in succession to Paulinus. All of this made him confident about defying his new bishop, John. Furthermore, Isaac had played a large part in condemning Arianism and establishing communities of monks in the city. He therefore resented John's interference and his attempt at changing what he had himself established in the city, however lax it all might have become. He was therefore a dangerous enemy. By the end of this period of seeking to bring these monks in hand, Sozomen tells us that John had incurred "the hatred of the clergy, and of many of the monks, who represented him as a hard, passionate, morose and arrogant man".[24] The need to reform the Church and restore discipline was therefore far from popular, and in Isaac there was an opponent who would not go quietly.

While John's attempt at restoring discipline among clergy and monks led to a hostile response from many, more powerful voices would be needed to join that chorus for it to become truly dangerous for him. In the meantime, John's popular preaching and clear-eyed spiritual vision won him the support of the rank-and-file laity, and in one particular way he was able to garner further popularity. This was through the entombing of martyrs and through celebrations of their feast days or anniversaries at their tombs. The fourth century was the beginning of the cult of martyrs. For much of the century, it was still only decades since the end of the Great Persecution (303–13), and part of the Church's life was to recall the lives of the martyrs with thanksgiving, representative as they were of countless Christians who had suffered during that time, and indeed in the preceding two centuries also. Gathering at a tomb to celebrate a martyr became an important devotional act, and also, inevitably, a reason for a party or a demonstration of civic pride. By the fifth century, Augustine of Hippo was warning against the abuses of such occasions and seeking to quell them. But worship around tombs persisted and many became sites of miraculous healings as reported several centuries later, as was the case in Britain by Bede (672–735). We have seen how in Antioch the tomb of St Babylas supplanted the Temple of Apollo, while Ambrose was deeply engaged in the burial of two saint-martyrs in Milan. Because Constantinople was founded after the persecution, the people did not have martyrs of their own. So, a trade in martyrs' bones began, in which some places imported and others exported the sacred remains. If that seems a crude way of putting it, it was nonetheless the case. Thus, in 381 Theodosius I had a "martyr" originally from Constantinople brought back. He was a bishop who had been exiled to the Caucasus for his Nicene Orthodoxy and was now buried in Constantinople in a tomb prepared for his Arian successor, Macedonius. The irony here is that it was friendly fire: a tomb prepared by and for an Arian bishop was now occupied by his Orthodox predecessor who had been exiled. No doubt it was seen by many as Macedonius getting his just deserts.

In 398–9, John himself took part in the reception and burial of relics, along with the imperial court. The first such burial happened with the arrival of the relics of one Phokas, a gardener who was to become patron saint of sailors.[25] His remains arrived by ship from Sinope on the Black Sea (from whence the second-century Gnostic Marcion came) and were greeted by a welcome party led by the emperor and empress and by John, who preached at their arrival. The party then escorted the ship in other boats to Phokas's final resting place.[26] The second of these occasions was when the Empress Eudoxia herself, later to become a thorn in John's side, was proclaimed *augusta* in January 400. In this instance, there were apparently three martyrs to bury: possibly Sisinnius, Martyrius and Alexander, who had been brutally killed in north Italy near Trent.[27] With the empress walking alongside the relics, the procession, which practically emptied the city, went at night from the palace to a point some 13 kilometres west of the city, along the Via Egnatia. There at the Church of Saint Thomas Drypia, John preached an ecstatic sermon of great elation.[28] He praised the numbers of people attending, the lights of their torches which lit up the sea as if it were on fire, and the Empress Eudoxia for casting off her diadem and purple robe and walking the entire distance just like an ordinary pilgrim, touching the biers to gain spiritual energy as she did so. In a climactic ending, John declared that future generations would recall her piety and humility. It was the honeymoon period of his relationship with the empress. Who could have guessed how rapidly their mutual respect would wane. Meanwhile, not wanting to walk the entire distance, the Emperor Arcadius arrived with a full military bodyguard and "did respectful obeisance", but left before John preached for a second time! In little over a year, relations would become strained between bishop and empress, but for the moment she showed she could be as pious as any pilgrim, and John as laudatory and extravagant in his praise of her as any Byzantine prelate.

International relations

It is clear that John had a real sense of his own authority when appointed Bishop of Constantinople. Although not yet formally archbishop of a wider province or even an ecumenical patriarch, which the office would eventually become, John considered his position one of ecclesiastical parity with the other three great positions in the Church: Bishop of Antioch; Archbishop of Alexandria and Pope of the Coptic Church; and the Bishop of Rome, soon to become Pope of the Western Catholic Church.

Shortly after his arrival in Constantinople, John dispatched a delegation offering fraternal greetings to the Bishop of Rome, Pope Siricus (384–99), and to gain recognition for his own appointment and begin the process of breaking the deadlock between Rome and Antioch that had gone on for 20 years since the appointment of Meletius. As we have seen, Roman Bishops (later popes) tended to support the ultra-Nicene church in Antioch led by Paulinus and Evagrius, and had no formal relationship with the godly Meletius and his successor, Flavian. John therefore sent a hand-picked delegation in the hope that his association with Meletius and Flavian would not see him blackballed as the new Bishop of Constantinople, and that there would be fraternal bonds between Constantinople and Rome in the future. He was also seeking re-establishment of fellowship between the Bishop of Rome and Flavian, Bishop of Antioch. With this aim in mind, John chose Acacius of Haleb (present-day Aleppo), who was well known for his orthodox views on Arianism, and Isidore, who had nearly been appointed Bishop of Constantinople himself, and was the preferred choice of Theophilus of Alexandria and his envoys. John hoped that between the two of them they would secure recognition for himself as Bishop of Constantinople and for Flavian as Bishop of Antioch. With the support of Theophilus of Alexandria, the mission proved doubly successful. Both John and Flavian received letters of fellowship from Rome and, in the case of Flavian, fellowship was restored for the first time in 20 years.[29] It was a clear indication that when Alexandria and Constantinople worked together, they were effective in whatever they did. Sadly, this was far from always the case.

While John was successful in gaining ready recognition from Rome and also in demonstrating that he could work effectively with Alexandria, his relationship with the Novatian Church in Constantinople, led by Agelius and then by Sisinnius, was not so promising. The Novatians were formed in third-century Rome when their founder and theologian Novatian (c.200–58) split from Pope Cornelius over the treatment of lapsed Catholics (i.e., lapsed in the sense of being apostates who had burnt incense to the gods under the threat of imprisonment, torture or execution). For Novatians, such lapsed Christians could not be restored by penitence and forgiveness, while Pope Cornelius and Cyprian believed that, after due repentance, they could be. The Novatians initially lived in Rome, but eventually spread throughout the empire. Hence what the Melitians were to Athanasius, and the Donatists to Augustine of Hippo, the Novatians were to John. They were the extreme puritans of the age, calling themselves the *katharoi*, the pure ones, and even refusing to accommodate in the church any who committed major sins, such as adultery and theft. But whereas Nectarius, John's predecessor, made a friend of Agelius by consulting him about the treatment of Arian Christians in the city and allowing them to worship separately with the permission of Theodosius I, John preferred a more confrontational approach. In many ways, John met his match in the Novatian leader Sisinnius, who was intransigent in his doctrinal stance but liberated or relaxed in his style of life. When asked why he had two baths a day (unlike John), he replied jokingly, "Because it is inconvenient to bathe thrice."[30] In some ways, he was like the renowned Roman Catholic chaplain of Cambridge, Monsignor Gilbey (1901–98), who once remarked that "he was socially ecumenical but doctrinally intransigent". John confronted Sisinnius over calling himself Bishop of Constantinople, to which Sisinnius replied in a typical riposte that John was welcome to relieve him of the burden of preaching but, although not bishop to John, he was to his own people.[31] Such wit blunted John's attack and somewhat dented the stridency of his demands.

Beyond his ecumenical relations with the Novatians in Constantinople and his diplomacy with Rome and Alexandria, John made the Goths the main focus of his outreach. The Goths were a people group, both within the borders of the empire and outside, that presented a threat militarily and an opportunity spiritually. They were the barbarians at the gate. It was they who in their various tribes had so comprehensively defeated the Romans at Adrianople in 378. Following that defeat, Theodosius undertook to quell them by force and to woo them with promises, especially promises of land in Thrace. Although the Goths at this point constituted the greatest threat to the empire, and indeed to the West, it was the Visigoths under their King Alaric who would sack Rome in 410, only 20 years later. In 381, Theodosius sought a new accord with the leader of the Thervingian Goths, Athanaric. Hitherto, Athanaric had persecuted Christians remorselessly in his territory, but he was impressed and won over by the military stature of Theodosius. And when Athanaric died in Constantinople, Theodosius gave him a splendid funeral and interred him in a new mausoleum.[32] This treatment of their leader greatly impressed Athanaric's followers.

By 380, the Goths had already been partly evangelized by Ulfilas, a Cappadocian who had been consecrated bishop and commissioned to work among them by the Arian bishop Eusebius of Nicomedia during the reign of Valens. Ulfilas gave the Goths an alphabet and translated some of the Scriptures into this new language, much as Cyril would do years later for the Russians, giving them the Cyrillic script. However, Ulfilas taught an Arian view of the Godhead which persisted among the Goths well into the sixth century, and especially among the Visigoths who came to colonize Spain.[33] Indeed, it was only at the Third Council of Toledo in 589 that the Visigoths gave up their Arian views and fully joined the Catholic Church. It is clear from Sozomen's words, however, that the Goths had come to cherish Ulfilas as their Father in God, since "he had instructed the Goths in the elements of religion, and through him they shared in a gentler mode of life, they placed the most implicit confidence in his directions, and were firmly convinced that he could neither do nor say anything that was evil."[34] That was signal testimony to Ulfilas's character, but despite his evident virtue Ulfilas and the Goths remained Arians, believing that Christ was a created being, and not fully God.

Theodosius had managed to win over Athanaric, who had formerly persecuted Christians. And John, likewise, now carefully handled his mission to the Goths in and around Constantinople, which also bore fruit. He assigned a church to the Goths in central Constantinople, probably the Church of Paul the Confessor, where they worshiped with their Gothic liturgy and their own deacons, priest and readers.[35] John himself preached there at great length and, to our ears, in a very patronizing manner,[36] saying of the Goths to their faces "that they were most barbarous of humans standing alongside the sheep of the church" (by which he meant Roman Christians)! But then he went on to use a handy text: "Had not God made the lamb and the wolf to lie down together?" (see Isaiah 11:6). Furthermore, John recalled all the barbarians whom God had chosen, from Abraham to Moses, noting how he worked through them.[37] Nor did John miss his chance to restate Nicene orthodoxy in order that the Goths might give up their Arian position. All in all, the Goths came to trust John, who had also founded a monastery for them in the city. His plain speaking was more reassuring than any honeyed but superficial welcome, it seems; and this was as well, given the events that lay ahead.

As always with John, his early months as Bishop of Constantinople had been high voltage. Against the odds he had received recognition for his appointment from Rome. He had formed a relationship of sorts with the court and showed himself willing to praise the empress for her display of piety. He had accommodated the Goths spiritually and had developed a respectful *laissez-faire* policy with the Novatians. But bouts of vehemence and his ascetic lifestyle alienated many in his own flock: courtiers and state officials could no longer expect to be entertained by a bishop who ate so sparingly; monks resented being chastised for being in the city and not in their monasteries; and many of his clergy came to dislike him for what they saw as his high-handed ways. Thus, Theodoret wrote, "In public teaching he was powerful in reforming the morals of his auditors; but in private conversation he was frequently thought haughty and assuming by those who did not know him."[38] Theodoret went on to say that after a dispute with a deacon called Serapion, John dismissed several from their posts, and "as it usually happens when persons in office adopt such violent measures, those who were thus expelled by him formed combinations and inveighed against him to the people".[39] It appears from that comment that although John deployed powerful oratory, he did not complement it with persuasive, appealing, personal conversation. The effect of this was to create a pool of discontent that others could more cynically exploit to their ends. Yet the more ordinary citizens of Constantinople, like those in Antioch before, found his preaching and public ministry gripping, especially when set in the night liturgy that John had found so compelling in Antioch and which was now used to great effect in Constantinople, and which would always be associated with him.

There is no doubt that John had a spiritual vision for the city that was both demanding and all encompassing. The issue would be whether he could fulfil it without alienating too many of those who held the levers of power: whether there was enough grace to commend the truths that he brought.

Notes

1. Stephen Williams and Gerard Friell, *Theodosius: The Empire at Bay* (London: Routledge, 1998), p. 134.
2. John Curran, "From Jovian to Theodosius", in Averil Cameron and Peter Garnsey (eds), *The Cambridge Ancient History, Vol. XIII, The Late Empire, AD 337–425* (Cambridge: Cambridge University Press, 1998), p. 102.
3. Curran, "From Jovian to Theodosius", p. 105.
4. Curran, "From Jovian to Theodosius", p. 109.
5. Curran, "From Jovian to Theodosius", p. 107.
6. Williams and Friell, *Theodosius*, p. 119.
7. J. N. D. Kelly, *Golden Mouth: The Story of John Chrysostom, Ascetic, Preacher, Bishop* (Ithaca, NY: Cornell University Press, 1998), p. 105.
8. Sozomen, *Ecclesiastical History* VIII.2.
9. Palladius, *Dialogue* 1.16, Palladius, *Dialogues*, in *Dialogue sur la vie de Jean Chrysostome/Palladios*, ed. and tr. Anne-Marie Malingrey with Philippe Leclercq, SC 341, Vol. 4 (Paris: Les Éditions du Cerf, 1988), p. 321.
10. Kelly, *Golden Mouth*, p. 11.
11. Palladius, *Life of Olympias*, in *Palladios: Dialogue sur la vie de Jean Chrysostome, Lettre à Innocent. Synode du Chêne, index. Tome II*, ed. A.-M. Malingrey (Paris: Les Éditions du Cerf, 1988), pp. 47ff.
12. Kelly, *Golden Mouth*, p. 113.
13. PG 46, pp. 557–8.
14. PG 48, pp. 796–797, Kelly, *Golden Mouth*, p. 115.
15. Sozomen, *Ecclesiastical History* VIII.3, in *Ecclesiastical history: a history of the church in nine books, from A.D. 324 to A.D. 440 by Sozomen*, a new translation from the Greek, with a memoir of the author (London: Bagster, 1846), p. 379.
16. Sozomen, *Ecclesiastical History* VIII.3.
17. Kelly, *Golden Mouth*, p. 118.
18. Palladius, *Dialogue* 12, op. cit., pp. 235ff.
19. *Didache* 11.3.4–6, tr. Bart D. Ehrman, Apostolic Fathers Loeb Classical Series, Vol. 24 (Cambridge, MA: Harvard University Press, 2003), p. 434.
20. Sozomen, *Ecclesiastical History* VIII.9, op. cit., p. 398.
21. See Rowan Williams, *Silence and Honey Cakes: The Wisdom of the Desert* (Oxford: Lion Hudson, 2003), pp. 82ff. and *The Desert Fathers*, ed. Benedicta Ward (Harmondsworth: Penguin Books, 2003), pp. 8ff.

22. Rule of Benedict, 29 and 61.
23. Palladius, *Dialogue* 6, op. cit., p. 131.
24. Sozomen, *Ecclesiastical History* VIII.9, op. cit., p. 389.
25. Kelly, *Golden Mouth*, p. 138.
26. *PG* 50, pp. 699–706.
27. Kelly, *Golden Mouth*, p. 140.
28. *PG* 63, pp. 467–72.
29. Kelly, *Golden Mouth*, p. 11.
30. Socrates, *Ecclesiastical History* VI.22, in *Nicene and Post-Nicene Fathers: Second Series, Vol. II: Socrates, Sozomenus: Church Histories*, ed. Philip Schaff (Grand Rapids, MI: Eerdmans, 1987), p. 152.
31. Socrates, *Ecclesiastical History* VI.22.
32. TCAH Vol. XIII, p. 102.
33. Sozomen, *Ecclesiastical History* VI, op. cit., p. 373.
34. Sozomen, *Ecclesiastical History* VI, op. cit., p. 373.
35. Theodoret, *Ecclesiastical History* V.30.
36. Kelly, *Golden Mouth*, p. 143.
37. *PG* 63, pp. 499–511.
38. Socrates, *Ecclesiastical History* VI.3; op. cit., p. 139.
39. Socrates, *Ecclesiastical History* VI.4, op. cit., p. 139.

8

A city of God

It is evident that John had a vision for a Christian city: a city of God. After all, he served almost his entire ministerial career in two cities of very great consequence in the empire, so the city was the context of his vision. His vision was not of an ancient, classical pagan place devoted to the feasts of the gods, the games, the theatre and the glory of the empire. It was instead a new civic vision of a community or city salted by the Church. In such a city, the themes of Christian marriage, abstinence, contemplative prayer, care of the poor and social contentment would ring out; and all would be made possible by attentive listening to the word preached and the Word worshipped in the liturgy of the Church. Thus, expository preaching linked to night vigils, the celebration of the sacraments and the encouragement of the example of the saints would launch once-pagan cities into a new way of life. The nearest John came to realizing this vision was in Antioch. He was there the longest: as a renowned presbyter from 387–97, and before that as a monk for five years. His time in Constantinople was much shorter, lasting from 397 until his first exile in 403. Six increasingly turbulent years with the complexities of preaching in a place that had more than half an eye on the presence and activities of the emperor were not enough to realize his dream there.

To fulfil this vision, he needed to deal with the great social and personal issues of his day: the creation of enduring Christian marriages and households, the encouragement of singleness of heart and virginity, care of the poor, social contentment even in the midst of slavery, and coexistence with Jewish communities. At the same time, the Theodosian law codes, in part encouraged by his preaching, made sure that paganism, including its pagan temples and worship, was increasingly outlawed, and in many places shrines were abolished or destroyed.

Sex and the city

Many books have been written, all of greater length than this one, about the changing attitudes to sex and marriage in the early centuries of the Church. It was, in fact, an ever-evolving issue. And if people complain that nowadays the Church has sex on the brain, rather than justice, poverty and exploitation, this was doubly the case in the fourth-century Church.

In the later years of the Roman republic and the early years of the empire, before the small communities of Christians began to retill the soil of Roman culture like underground fungi, sexual attitudes were diverse. Roman views on sexuality were understandably contradictory. Although many might think from the wall paintings in Pompeii that phallic art expressed the dominant view of sex, these were graphic symbols rather than illustrative examples of a monochrome culture of sex. Indeed, for the sake of social stability and real estate, marriage and inheritance were firmly tethered to Roman law. Beyond that, the Stoic philosophers, with a Platonic suspicion of human appetites and the exaltation of the soul, had already sowed seeds of abstinence and self-discipline in the classical mind when it came to sex. The Stoic philosopher Epictetus (*c*.80–135) wrote in the second century that to spend your time "in much exercise, in much eating, drinking, evacuating the bowels and much copulating [is quite simply] a lack of refinement".[1] The notion of complete abstinence was rare in the Roman world by the second century, and there was a marked degree of tolerance toward both homosexuality and love affairs, both before and outside marriage.[2]

In Judaism, there were much clearer scriptural guidelines around sexual mores than in the pagan literature of Greece and Rome, although it is true that Jewish kings such as Solomon practised the common eastern habit of having many wives and concubines (1 Kings 11). Indeed, we are told that Solomon had 700 wives of royal birth and 300 concubines (1 Kings 11:3). It is not surprising that such a cornucopia of flesh would "lead him astray". But beside such excess, in later Judaism of the first century there was a growing emphasis on the principle of monogamy as laid down in Genesis 2:24, and this became the norm alongside various views about the difficulty or ease of divorce in Rabbinic teaching (e.g.,

Hillel and Shammai). Besides this growing standard of monogamy, there was also a tradition of abstinence in Judaism, which ranged from the Nazirite vow of abstinence from alcohol, haircuts and contact with dead bodies (Numbers 6:1–21), to the more monastic vows of the Qumran community by the Dead Sea. Documents discovered at Wadi Qumran in 1947 reveal a self-styled community of devout males who wished to establish themselves as "a house of perfection and truth in Israel".[3] It was an eschatological community, which, by its strict ceremonial observance and purity, sought to hasten the coming of the Messiah and the restoration of Israel. What did not exist in Israel, however, was a wholesale commitment to virginity among young women. Instead, young women bore the future and peace of Israel to which the Jewish household and the birth of many children was deemed a blessing (see Psalm 128). This averred tenet of Judaism was a departure from the more neurotic view of third-century Christianity which saw sex, intercourse and birth as a challenge to wholehearted service of God.

Jesus underscored the Jewish concept, and indeed the God-given concept, of marriage found in Genesis 2:24, that "that is why a man leaves his father and mother and is united to his wife, and they become one flesh". Jesus reiterated this foundational text in his response to questions from some Pharisees about divorce, in which he taught that divorce was only permitted in response to man's "hardness of heart", or we might say man's weakness (see Matthew 19:1–12). When confronted by the astonished reaction of his disciples overhearing this most demanding teaching that it might be better *not* to marry, Jesus suggests that rather than marry, some might become "like eunuchs for the Kingdom of God", or in other words take a public or private vow of sexual abstinence. This teaching was later developed by Paul in 1 Corinthians 7, which we shall come to when surveying John Chrysostom's teaching on the subject. Suffice now to say that the seeds of sexual fasting were thus laid down and would germinate and spread from the third and fourth centuries especially.

The early centuries of Christianity gave the Church Paul's teaching on sexuality. It was teaching set in the overarching expectation that the Parousia or the Second Coming of the Messiah was imminent. In the meantime, life must go on, a new Christian community must be built, and marriages, sexual life and Christian service rightly ordered. For this, instruction must be given from the Lord and from the wisdom of the Apostle (see 1 Corinthians 7:25). This instruction consisted in Paul's teaching to the Corinthian church on the issues it faced: sexual fasting in marriage (1 Corinthians 7:1–6); how spouses should conduct themselves towards unbelieving partners (1 Corinthians 7:12–16); Paul's controversial view of homosexuality as disordered humanity (Romans 1:24–7); and several warnings about pursuing sexual relationships outside marriage (see 1 Corinthians 5:11; 1 Corinthians 6:16; Ephesians 5:3; Colossians 3:5). For Paul, the body was weakened by the "flesh"—a self-interested power vulnerable to the devil—which needed conversion by the Spirit and taming by self-discipline (see Romans 7:7–25; 8:13; Galatians 5:16–25). The body and its appetites must be freed from bondage to the Law by the Spirit (Romans 8:2) and be given a new singleness of heart and mind, which would, in the case of sex, find fulfilment in marriage.

Following the apostolic age, which came to an end by the turn of the second century, there were few if any immediate additions to the apostolic teaching. The main contributions came from the book known as the *Shepherd of Hermas* and from peripatetic prophets who gave ecstatic utterances and were frequently committed to a life of abstinence. The *Shepherd of Hermas* was a spiritual work written by a former slave about how to conduct one's life as a Christian. It begins with the author telling of a time when he saw his former owner, Rhoda, arising naked from a swim in the River Tiber and later accusing him in a vision of having impure thoughts.[4] After this graphic beginning, the author is advised by a mature woman, and later a shepherd, on how to live his life and is told which people truly embody the Church.[5] A further sequence of parables and commandments follow, with down-to-earth advice on the need to "hold onto simplicity",[6] "not to slander", to "love the truth",[7] to "guard your holiness"[8] and to be patient.[9] There is teaching to "refrain yourself from some things but not others, in particular refrain from adultery and sexual immorality, from lawless drunkenness, from evil luxury, from an abundance of foods, extravagant wealth, boasting, pride, haughtiness, from lying, slander and hypocrisy, from bearing a grudge and speaking any blasphemy".[10] Finally, Hermas is warned not to entertain "double mindedness"[11] and disappointment, "which wears down the spirit".[12] It became a very popular spiritual work in the Roman church; and indeed, throughout the first four centuries. *The Shepherd* is often found in *codices* with the New Testament Scriptures, as in the case of *Codex Sinaiticus*, and indeed in many other texts and papyruses.

By the third century, the call to singleness of heart, abstinence and indeed the virginal life was only becoming stronger, with more teachers of asceticism in both East and West coming to the fore. In North Africa, and writing in Latin rather than Greek, was the lawyer Tertullian. In Alexandria, first Clement and then Origen, who successively led the theological schools there, became exegetes and teachers of the faith, although Origen was dogged by controversy because of his strongly Platonic inclinations. Tertullian was deeply conservative in his ethics as well as severe, and he believed the leadership of the Church should be left to a "Spirit-filled gerontocracy" unswayed by passions which would have by then died down. In his view, "sexuality was to be rigidly controlled among the marriageable and married young".[13] And unmarried women should be veiled both before and *after* any vow of virginity. He quotes with approval the practice in Arabia of obscuring the whole face with a veil, saying, "Arabia's heathen females will be your judges, who cover not only the head, but the face also, so entirely, that they are content, with one eye free, to enjoy rather half the light than to prostitute the entire face".[14] (This also shows that veiling of women in the Middle East predated Muhammed by at least some 400 years, and was an early form of *hijāb* or even *burqa*). Furthermore, Tertullian wrote *To his Wife*, "Marriage is good, but celibacy is preferable" and the text he used was 1 Corinthians 7:34, "An unmarried woman or virgin is concerned about the Lord's affairs: her aim is to be devoted to the Lord in both body and spirit."[15]

If by the beginning of the third century the teaching on sexuality in the West was moving from singleness of heart to a more demanding abstinence, it was moving in that direction in the eastern Mediterranean also, and in particular in Alexandria. Clement of Alexandria (*c.*150–215) had a deep sense of the transformation that Christ wrought in any soul given to him, more so than any claims made by the Gnostics from their so-called enlightenment or illumination.[16] What Clement gave the Church, in fact, was a handbook on Christian deportment: how to behave at feasts, how to drink water instead of luxurious wine, how to laugh moderately, and how to remain modest even in the bedroom. Thus he writes, "Do not, I pray, put off modesty at the same time you put off your clothes, because it is never right for the just man to divest himself of continence."[17] Indeed, church teachers "tended to speak of the sexual joining of couples as if it were an act from which erotic satisfaction be excluded".[18] And the model Christian person to whom Clement and others aspired in their teaching was one of "awesome serenity",[19] untouched by grief, unsullied by desire and unmoved by burning passion. It was a Christian form of the Stoical *apatheia*: untouched by undisciplined pleasure and unmarked by grief.

Clement was succeeded in his teaching role by Origen, who also wrestled with the right Christian response to desire. Origen was preeminently concerned with the soul in a Platonic tradition. He combined this perception with unrivalled study of the Scriptures, although frequently in the allegorical mode, and a virtuoso book of teaching entitled *On First Principles*. For Origen, marital sexual intercourse took place in a darkened chamber "delineated with a bleak precision as a darkened antithesis to the blazing, light-filled embrace of Christ in the spirit".[20] Virginity came to represent the means whereby heaven is brought to earth, in that the Word chose to be born through a virgin woman. For it was through Mary's body that God joined himself to humanity.[21] In light of this, it is reported that Origen had himself castrated as a young man, the better, he thought, to give himself to his task.[22] Although castration made the recipient infertile, it was not a guarantee of chastity, and later it was forbidden in the canons of Nicaea.

By the beginning of the fourth century, the die was well cast for the future. Clement's handbook for serious Christians, *The Instructor*, which gave precise advice on deportment and sanctification, was rapidly being overtaken by an "aesthetic of virginity".[23] By then, the Church may have numbered throughout the empire some five million souls,[24] but their day-to-day needs were being directed by a cadre of leading bishops who now taught the excellence of virginity and the virtue of abstinence at full throttle against the vivid background of an ascetic movement that was filling the deserts of Egypt, Syria and Palestine. And if no desert was nearby, as in Caesarea, Basil the Great employed the monks in vocational work helping the poor through a hospice in the city.

As already noted, the monastic movement got underway in the desert of Egypt, especially in the early fourth century. It was led by Antony, who first withdrew near his home in lower Egypt from 270, and then at Fayum by the Nile in *c.*280, where he led a solitary life fighting with his desires,[25] fasting, praying, learning Scripture and receiving visitors. Finally, he moved to the eastern desert. Compared to the extreme demands of the desert, the scarcity of food and general privations, sexual abstinence was probably the least of his issues.[26] At root, these ascetics fought to retain their humanity and not be driven by privation to the loss of their senses. Through Athanasius's *Life of Antony*, which became far and away the most popular of his works, the challenge of monasticism pioneered by Antony and Pachomius and birthed in Egypt spread like wildfire throughout the East and soon into the West as well. It seemed the fast lane of Christian discipleship, entailed abstinence, and became a gold standard for so many of the great Christian teachers of the age: notably Athanasius, Basil of Caesarea, Gregory of Nyssa, Ambrose, Basil of Ancyra, Jerome and John Chrysostom. All these were titans in their advocacy of abstinence. They in turn drew on the experience and examples of the saints, none more so than Thecla from Iconium (modern-day Konya), who preserved her virginity against the threat of rape and pagan marriage, was an avid follower of the teaching of Saint Paul, and in the end received a martyr's death in Pisidian Antioch.

John was one of a cohort of church leaders in the mid-to-late fourth century who fully embraced the drive to virginity, but who also extolled the virtues of a faithful and loving household. Among these leaders who may well have influenced John were Basil of Caesarea, Basil of Ancyra and Gregory of Nyssa, none of these places being that far from Constantinople and all well within the eastern part of the empire.

Basil of Ancyra (bishop, *c.*336–64) lived a little earlier than John and was already strongly in pursuit of a celibate lifestyle. He was "a man of recondite learning and singularly unruffled powers of observation conjuring up the facts of sex so as to keep female ascetics of his region at a safe distance from male soulmates".[27] In his book *On the Preservation of Virginity*, Basil observed that as a general rule the male wished to cleave to the female "with an inarticulate intensity that was as mysterious and as inevitable as the pull of a magnet".[28] Wary of this magnetic pull, Basil nevertheless recognized the need in a man for what he intrinsically lacked in himself: sweetness of nature, soft flesh, damp eyes, gliding movements and consoling touch.[29] Thus, he warned, in his work *De Virginitate Tuenda* that because of this latent overflowing sensuality, men should beware a touch, a glance, even a chaste kiss from a relative. Not for him the *subintroductae* (literally, the live-in woman or housekeeper) or the *agapetae* (the love bird); instead, all female company should be eschewed.

If Basil of Ancyra took the line of total-abstinence-through-isolation, Gregory of Nyssa, great Platonist Christian that he was, emphasized the grandeur of the soul over the ephemeral mortal coil of our bodies. Just as in his letters to Theodore, John was able to reduce the beauty of Hermione to a stream of mucus, so Gregory reduced the physicality of reproduction, birth, nursing and raising children to a perpetuation of the race aimed at overcoming the reality of death, something that had the effect of sinking the potential of the soul in the demands of the flesh. In other words, it was a poor second best, but a necessary limitation of our spiritual potential. Thus, Gregory enumerated the negatives of the "garment of skin" as "sexual union, conception, childbirth, dirt, nursing, food, excrement, the gradual growth of the body towards maturity, adulthood, old age, sickness and death".[30] He maintained this state was brought about by the fall of Adam, whereafter his body no longer matched his soul, nor Eve's hers. Nobility had been overtaken by the need to overcome death through birth and all its attendant physical effects. Although to us this may seem a jaundiced and joyless view of bodily life, shorn of countless pleasures of loving sex and the joys of childrearing (without forgetting its labour too), in the fourth century it was nonetheless a powerful apologetic for virginity and an escape route from the demands of bodily life.

Between the extremes of physical isolation and ideological renunciation was Basil of Caesarea's more practical orthopraxy: a renunciation for the sake of service. In about 370, some 30 years before John began preaching in Constantinople, Basil had founded his Basiliad, using his own money to fund a hospice for the poor and sick. It was here that those who had taken vows of abstinence now served the poor of the city. It was a model of monastic service which was to endure, especially in the West, where the Benedictine and Augustinian monks would provide care for the poor and sick from the sixth century onwards. In his discourse on ascetical discipline, Basil encourages the following frame of mind:

> He [the monk] should work with his hands, be ever mindful of his last end, joyful in hope, patient in adversity, unceasingly prayerful, giving thanks in all things, humble toward everyone, hating pride, sober and watchful, keeping his heart from evil thoughts.[31]

Sharing many of the precepts of Basil of Caesarea was John Chrysostom, who, like his contemporaries and those immediately before him, both wrote and preached on the blessings of abstinence and virginity, the calling of marriage, and the Christian household. John envisaged a city moulded by these callings in which most Christian city dwellers would share. Indeed, the "the themes of marriage, of the household, and of sexuality bulk so large in his sermons because it was through such themes that John wished to express a new view of the civic community".[32] The opportunity to preach as continuously in Constantinople as he had had in Antioch was simply not forthcoming. He had preached in Antioch for 11 years; in Constantinople he would only have six years before his exiles, and these were punctuated with grave events in the city which at times preoccupied him. He would complete a long, but not so satisfactory, series on Acts, as well as others on the Pauline epistles, including Colossians, Philippians and 1 and 2 Thessalonians.

Drawing on Colossians in Constantinople and on 1 Corinthians 7 in Antioch, John extolled marriage as the natural and only place for sexual intercourse, as a bulwark against the temptations of the brothel,[33] and as *the* relationship from which a fundamental Christian community might be forged. Like Tertullian before him, John was not afraid of being explicit in his teaching. Tertullian opined on the formation of a person in which the soul and body were forged in these terms:

> For although we shall allow that there are two kinds of seed—that of the body and that of the soul—we still declare that they are

inseparable, and therefore contemporaneous and simultaneous in origin. Now let no one take offence or feel ashamed at an interpretation of the processes of nature which is rendered necessary by the defence of the truth. Nature should be to us an object of reverence, not of blushes. It is lust, not natural usage, which has brought shame on the intercourse of the sexes. It is the excess, not the normal state, which is immodest and unchaste: the normal condition has received a blessing from God, and is blest by him: "Be fruitful and multiply, and replenish the earth". Excess however, has he cursed: in adulteries, in wantonness, and chambering (*lupanaria*). Well, now, in this usual function of the sexes which brings together, the male and female in their common intercourse, we know that both the soul and the flesh discharge a duty together: the soul supplies the desire, the flesh contributes the gratification of it; the soul furnishes the instigation, the flesh affords the realization. The entire man being excited by the one effort of both natures, his seminal substance is discharged, deriving its fluidity from the body, and its warmth from the soul.[34]

Nor was John bashful about discussing the sexual relationship between men and women, and the reproductive process as he understood it, at the same time telling his congregation, like Tertullian, not to be embarrassed by his explicitness and to honour marriage by having modest marriage celebrations. Thus, in his twelfth homily on Colossians, John describes sexual union in almost poetic terms:

> How do they become one flesh? As if she were gold receiving the purest of gold, the woman receives the man's seed with rich pleasure, and within her it is nourished, cherished and refined. It is mingled with her own substance and then she returns it as a child! The child is a bridge connecting mother to father, so the three become one flesh, as when cities divided by a river are joined by a bridge. And here the bridge is formed from the substance of each!

But suppose, he goes on to ask, "there is no child: do they remain and not one? No; their intercourse effects the joining of their bodies, and they are made one, just as when perfume is mixed with ointment."[35]

Most of John's teaching on marriage is found in his expositions of 1 Corinthians 7. Indeed, this chapter of Paul's first letter to the Corinthians covering sexual relations in marriage, extolling virginity and the state of singleness in view of the difficulties of the times and the expectation of the Parousia, became seminal to the age. In fact, looking across the teaching of the fourth-century Church Fathers it would not be an exaggeration to say that 1 Corinthians 7 was as determinative for them as the first five chapters of Paul's Epistle to the Romans were to the Reformers of the sixteenth century. While John touches on the beauty of sexual intercourse to a point where he may have embarrassed his hearers, by far the larger part of his teaching on sex is about the married relationship and what each partner contributes to the other. Sex could not be neglected or brushed over in marriage, however. And perhaps going where few pagan teachers were willing to go, first Paul and now John outline this aspect of the relationship with real frankness. Echoing Paul's injunction, John says, "Do not deprive each another [sexually] except perhaps by mutual consent" (1 Corinthians 7:5). By this "Paul is saying that the wife should not abstain without the husband's consent, and vice versa. Why? Because great evils—adultery, fornication and broken homes among them—have often resulted from this kind of abstinence." And then with the unanswerable logic of realism John argues from experience: "If men fornicate even when they have the consolation of their wives, what do you expect will happen if they are deprived of this."[36] This was typical of John's down-to-earth and realistic preaching. Furthermore, and following Paul's teaching, John says marriage should be honoured even where a partner is not a Christian. But if a person is gifted to abstain from marriage in the first place, then they do well to remain single.

If 1 Corinthians 7 highlights sex, singleness and marriage to unbelieving partners, in its classic teaching, Ephesians (5:21–33) highlights the relationship between husband and wife and the nature of their calling as a married couple. There is no doubt that for John, Christian marriage is to be the cornerstone of society. Thus, in Homily 20 on Ephesians he says, "The love of husband and wife is the force that welds society together."³⁷ For John, marriage was the means of tethering sexual feelings to a single spouse, and hence combating promiscuity or fornication.³⁸ In this way, the potential anarchy of sex in a city would be tamed, and the Christian household made the cornerstone of the community.

In his teaching on marriage, John shows his perceptive knowledge of the challenges of living peacefully and effectively together, and of the necessity for collaboration.³⁹ The husband must be willing to sacrifice himself for his wife. He goes on to say that "even if you see her belittling you [the husband], or despising and mocking you, still you will be able to subject her to yourself, through affection, kindness, and your great regard for her".⁴⁰ In choosing a wife, a man is to look for affection, gentleness and humility: these are the tokens of beauty. He "must not seek lovely physical features, nor reproach her for lacking things over which she has no control". The husband and wife are "not to seek wealth or high social position but true nobility of soul".⁴¹ As for the woman or wife, John shows that he is a man of his times with a limited view of women and their abilities. He considers "the female sex is rather weak and needs a lot of support and condescension".⁴² A wife's calling is not to nag her husband, egging on his ambition by saying, "You lazy coward, you have no ambition! Look at our relatives and neighbours—they have plenty of money. Let no wife say any such thing; she is her husband's body, and it is not for her to dictate to her head, but submit and obey."⁴³ Nor is she to desire jewels and fine clothing especially. Thus, John says, perhaps a little unrealistically, "Beginning on their wedding night, let him be an example of gentleness, temperance, and self-control: and she will be likewise. He should advise her not to decorate herself with golden earrings, necklaces, or other jewellery, or to accumulate expensive clothes. Instead, her appearance should be dignified, and dignity is never served by theatrical excess."⁴⁴

Despite John's continuous, unremitting and explicit teaching about the role of sex, its dangers and its joys in a married relationship, as well as the simultaneous call to abstinence and virginity, we would be wrong to think that Antioch or Constantinople adopted this teaching and practice wholesale. With it being only some 80 years since the adoption of Christianity as the religion of the empire (dated from the Edict of Milan in 313) and with much of that time filled with the Arian Controversy (*c.*310–90), it is not surprising that many civic and pagan ceremonies relating to marriage were still current and active. These involved elaborate wedding feasts to which John objected and characterized as "pageants or theatrical performance(s)".⁴⁵ He wanted no "disorderly uproar" at weddings and even questioned whether virgins should attend in case they were seduced by the event. Instead of drunkenness there should be an abundance of spiritual joy, for "when Christ is present at a wedding, he brings cheerfulness, pleasure, moderation, modesty, sobriety and health: but Satan brings anxiety, pain, excessive expense, indecency, envy, and drunkenness".⁴⁶ As ever, John did not mince his words. Nevertheless, as Peter Brown points out, "to hope that an Eastern Mediterranean city (like Constantinople) would shed its profane traditions by becoming little more than an assemblage of pious Christian households involved a fatal underestimation of the power of the classical sense of the civic community".⁴⁷ It would take generations for doctrine to become custom among a majority of citizens and for there to be irreversible change. In the meantime, John preached not only the blessings of marriage as well as of abstinence, but also our obligations to the poor. Indeed, this was his greatest and overriding concern. John's "deepest concern and his poignant legacy [was] his insistence on solidarity with the shared bodies of the poor".⁴⁸ Indeed, it was through both John's sermons and the later Byzantine liturgy of the *kontakion*, composed by Romanos the Melodist, that compassion for the poor was inspired and instilled in the worshipper.

Rich and poor in the city

Throughout his teaching John laid great emphasis on the duties and obligations of the rich, as well as on the needs and opportunities of the poor. There can be no doubt that one of the striking features of these great cities of Antioch and Constantinople was their great diversity of wealth and poverty. In an important sermon series on the Acts of the Apostles, preached in Constantinople in *c.*398, John comes to an important passage about the *koinonia* or the sharing in the Early Church. Luke recorded in Acts that in the Church of Jerusalem, "All the believers were one in heart and mind. No one claimed that any of their possessions was their own, *but they shared everything they had*" (Acts 4:32, current author's emphasis). This must have been an important text for John, who applies much of his preaching to the virtue of relieving poverty. As he preaches, he surmises that if all the wealth of the congregation of Hagia Sophia in Constantinople were pooled into a common fund for the poor, there would be "ten hundred thousand pounds of gold".[49] It would be enough to sustain a ministry to the poor. Indeed, he thought that in the city of Constantinople, which had a population then of c.300,000, there were approximately 100,000 Christians, with the remainder being pagan Greeks, Goths and Jews. And amongst them he estimated there were some 50,000 in need of daily food and some shelter. The best way of meeting the needs of the poor, he said, would be to have communal feeding centres and communal lodgings, and he was all for creating "a plan" whereby this might come about.[50]

Throughout his ministry in Antioch John chastised the rich for any display of wealth. Indeed, his biblical expositions or commentaries are remarkable for "his indignation against conspicuous affluence and the selfishness of the rich, and his passionate championship of the poor, the exploited and the helpless".[51] In much of his exposition, whether of the Gospel of Matthew or of Paul's Epistles, John frequently turns to castigating the rich and upholding the needs of the poor. In sustained teaching on the Resurrection in Homily 40 on 1 Corinthians, he warns the rich about their desire to flaunt their wealth in the public square and asks pointedly, "Why has thou so many servants [slaves].... It is only for your self-indulgence. Why must the way be cleared before you in the marketplace? Why must thou have slaves carrying fasces [Roman symbols of authority] before you?"[52] He contemptuously scorned all self-aggrandisement, all display of wealth, all pomposity and arrogance. A man's true glory consists instead in humility, gentleness and costly charity—while exotically carpeted floors, cohorts of gold-liveried eunuchs, marbled and pillared houses made for easy targets of John's vaunting rhetoric and were gifts for his ready invective. Commending the needs of the poor and castigating the ostentation of the rich were exactly where John's heart and oratorical gifts lay.

His most sustained attack on the wealthy can be found in a series of seven sermons preached on Jesus's parable of Dives and Lazarus (Luke 16:19–31). The series must have begun in Antioch the day after a feast in the city: not a pagan festival, which was now banned, but some other kind of civic event, for John commends his congregation, probably in the Great Church, for not having taken part in what he calls "The Feast Day of Satan". Instead, they had grown "drunk" on the teaching of the Apostle Paul. "They had danced in the chorus of Paul."[53]

He commends the congregation in a pastoral manner, saying:

> In this way a double benefit came to you, because you kept free of the disorderly dance of drunkards and you revelled in well-ordered spiritual dances. You shared a drinking bowl that did not pour out undiluted wine but was filled with spiritual instruction. You became a flute and a lyre for the Holy Spirit. While others danced for the devil, you prepared yourselves by your occupation here to be spiritual instruments and vessels. You allowed the Holy Spirit to play on your souls and to breathe grace into your hearts. Thus, you sounded a harmonious melody to delight not only mankind but even the powers of heaven.[54]

In this first sermon, John characterizes both Dives, the rich man, and Lazarus, explaining there is potential for virtue in being rich and in being poor, while making especially plain both the snare of wealth and the possibilities for charity, and the virtue there is in enduring poverty. It is typical of John, as we shall see when we come to consider the issue of slavery, that he looks for the spiritual blessings in situations which are of themselves evil. Neither abject poverty, entailing hunger and homelessness, nor slavery can ever be considered a "good"; indeed John calls them "dreadful".[55] He is nevertheless quick to see if some spiritual virtue may be found in exercising faith in the midst of either situation. Thus, the rich man's main fault is his failure to give alms and the way he keeps his wealth for himself and uses it on unnecessary luxuries. He lives sumptuously every day, but whenever he goes out, he passes the beggar in abject poverty at his gate, covered in sores. By doing nothing, he condemns his soul. For John, Dives is worse than an animal, surpassing "the cruelty and inhumanity of any beast in his behaviour".[56] His luxury leads to forgetfulness of others' needs and failure to pray. John warns his hearers, "If you sit at table, remember that from table you must go to prayer. Fill your belly so moderately that you may not become too heavy to bend your knees and call upon your God."[57] For John, food is given in order that we might pray, read the Scriptures and do works of service, especially almsgiving. To live as he does, the rich man must quell the accusations coming from "the imperial throne of his conscience".[58] And while Lazarus is outwardly destitute, inwardly his soul is strengthened and burnished. Thus, in anticipation of a reversal of circumstances after death, John says that although outwardly sumptuous, the rich man is inwardly famished and covered with the sores, while Lazarus, although outwardly full of sores and hungry, is inwardly covered in splendour and finery.

In his second sermon on this parable, John praises his congregation for their attentiveness and commends their reaction to the teaching: they are appalled at the callousness of the rich man and are aware of the virtue of Lazarus. Death is the moment that reveals who is really rich, and who is really poor.[59] Bearing this in mind, we should see the rich on earth as poor, and the poor as potentially rich. Having dealt with the erroneous view that those who die a violent death are subject to demons, John encourages his congregation to make the most of their time on earth, using a quotation from Sirach in the Apocrypha, "In all you do, remember the end of your life and then you will never sin" (Sirach 7:36). Furthermore, we must never be taken in by superficial appearances. Long before Shakespeare, John sees men as hiding behind masks, each one making their exits and entrances:[60]

> In the same way even here, sitting in this world as if in theatre and looking at the players on the stage, when you see many rich people, do not think they are truly rich, but that they are wearing masks of rich people.[61]

Hence, a Christian is to have a right perception of rich and poor, and resolve, if rich, to use that wealth to benefit others. John concludes his sermon by saying:

> I beg of you remember this without fail, that not to spare our own wealth with the poor is theft from the poor and deprivation of their means of life: we do not possess our own wealth but theirs. If we have this attitude, we will certainly offer our money: and by nourishing Christ in poverty here and laying up great profit hereafter, we will be able to attain the good things that are to come, by the grace and kindness of our Lord Jesus Christ.[62]

The remaining sermons in the series of seven address issues relating to present suffering or prosperity and future salvation. In many ways, these themes pick up the issues raised by the book of Job. Imbued with both Stoic philosophy and Christian theology, John seems to suggest that suffering borne well in this life necessarily gains greater reward in the next. Thus, suffering is almost redemptive in itself. John says, "If there are two righteous men, of whom one has endured greater tribulation, the other less, he who endures the greater tribulation is more fortunate since 'he will reward each according to his works.'"[63] The reverse is also true, in that one who has enjoyed great prosperity and failed to relieve the needs of the poor will be like Dives, separated by a great gulf from Lazarus in the bosom of Abraham (paradise). He will be unable to quench his own suffering (see Luke 16:24–6), but also unable to warn his brother on earth of the consequences of neglecting the poor. John often emphasizes that it is better to bear the punishment of suffering *now* if it leads to repentance and faith, than to enjoy prosperity *now* without repentance, and suffer eternal punishment later. Therefore

> we need great wisdom and perseverance, to keep sober and watchful in prayer, not to desire others' property, but to distribute our goods to the needy, to reject and repudiate all luxury, whether of clothing or table, to avoid avarice, drunkenness, and slander, to control our tongue and keep from disorderly clamour and to abstain from shameful and witty talk.[64]

In other words, John says we must be like Job, and not drawn into sin by suffering.[65] Punishments in this life, whether through poverty or natural catastrophes like earthquakes, floods or famine, are beneficial in restraining sinfulness. However brutal this form of theology, it is of a piece with John's general view of hardship as a school for virtue. Those in want, loss and mayhem, or suffering the effects of natural disasters, are being punished now, but in these things have an avenue of repentance open to them through which eternal felicity might be found. So, he pleads:

> Let [such a person] seek a penalty for his sins by self-condemnation, by complete repentance, by tears, by confession, by fasting and almsgiving, by self-control and charity, so that in every way we may become able to put aside all our sins in this life and to depart to the next in full confidence.[66]

On its own, this encouragement appears a rather Stoic form of spirituality, with John making our repentance and tears the basis of our hope rather than Christ alone. However, he adds at the very end, "May we all attain this, by the grace and love of our Lord Jesus Christ with whom to the Father, together with the Holy Spirit, be glory for ages of ages. Amen."[67]

There is no doubt that relieving the poor is central to John's idea of a city of God, a godly city salted by the presence of the Church. The Church is to be the instrument of God through which the needs of the poor for food, clothing, shelter and hope will be met. And the Church is to care in this way from its own resources. But John makes plain the rich in particular are called to share from their abundance to relieve the lack amongst the poor. Besides the poor, there is a specific group whose interests cannot be ignored in any city of God, and this is the slaves.

Slaves in the city

Many among the congregations in the Great Church or Old Church in Antioch and the congregation of the imperial churches of Hagia Sophia and Hagia Eirene in Constantinople, where John preached and ministered as a bishop, were slave owners. Slavery was still very much part of Roman society in the New Rome (Constantinople) in the fifth century.

Following victories in the West at Milvian Bridge on 28 October 312, and later in the East so as to claim the entire empire as emperor, Constantine quickly showed that he was both a highly effective soldier and an administrator, ready to give attention to detail.[68] From the imperial rescripts or orders in relation to slavery from this period, we glean that Constantine (Christian although he was) and his successors in West and East, were not going to rush to deconstruct a society and empire that had been built on the institution of slavery. Although in general terms Constantine wanted to protect the weak in society from persecution by the powerful, "his attitude to slavery was deeply ambivalent".[69]

> He abhorred the possibility that a person could be unfairly condemned to that status, a sentence that he saw as an emblematic act of a tyrant. In seeking to prevent people from being unfairly enslaved, he asserted the importance of a person's birth in determining his status as an adult. On the other hand, he did little to alleviate the condition of those who were already slaves, and deplored the notion that a free person could associate with a slave on an equal basis. In all of this, Constantine's attitudes are harsher than those of earlier generations and probably reflect changes in the course of the third century.[70]

We would be wrong to think that because he was a Christian emperor, slavery was about to end. If anything, society was more stratified into slave and free, and one was not to be confused with the other whether by marriage or by any other partnerships.

There were many forms of slavery in late Roman society, since slavery was far from monochrome. As usual, Roman military victory meant enslavement of vanquished peoples, and in Constantinople this meant the Goths. When Constantine founded Constantinople in 324, large numbers of Goths were used as slave labour to help build this great new city with its walls, imperial palaces, churches and impressive spaces like the Hippodrome. In addition, there were the slaves who helped in agriculture and those who worked in the households. Household slaves probably made up the largest contingent of slaves in the city. These included midwives, wet nurses, nannies, teachers, pedagogues (literally personal tutors),[71] accountants, scribes, cooks, general staff and managers. In fact, in a large Roman household, slaves attended to almost all household and family duties. These household slaves were still owned by the master or mistress, but from Constantine onwards, there were now more relaxed societal rules about "free women" marrying "higher value" slaves.[72]

In the countryside, many estates were managed and tended by slave labour. Senator Symmachus (340–402) wrote frequently about his fears of a slave revolt on his estates in Italy. And the noble and very rich Melania (distinct from the equally wealthy ascetics Melania the Elder and Younger) liberated 8,000 slaves from her estates in Sicily, Italy, Africa, Mauretania and Britain.[73] It was quite common for senators to have as many as ten or 20 estates of between 1,000 and 2,000 hectares each, and a wealth of 10,000 to 15,000 pounds of gold in annual income.[74] There is no doubt that John Chrysostom would have found in his congregations in Antioch or Constantinople many rich citizens with many slaves. What would John have said to such slave-owning men and women in his church?

It is clear that for the most part John did not especially call for the end of the institution of slavery in his teaching and preaching, although he did recognize that in origin men and women were born free and only enslaved by others. He looked instead for curtailment of the evils of slavery. In his *Homily on Genesis 4*, John regards slavery as "not a natural but an unnatural phenomenon".[75] He sees it as a product of the sin which impaired the capacity of our ancestors to act with any true moral freedom (*autexousia*). In effect, sin disrupts the harmony of human relationships and leads to the domination and subjection of others, whether in the marriage relationship, in relations between parents and children and other family members, or in the enslavement of others to serve the desires of their masters. Nevertheless, John says that at the outset, beside humanity's rule or stewardship over creation, "God made only one form of government, placing man over woman but after our race ran aground into much disorder, other forms of rule appeared, that of slaveholders and of secular governors".[76] And later, in his commentary on Ephesians concerning household relationships between children and parents and slaves and masters, he says:

> Slavery is the result of greed, of degradation, of brutality, since Noah, we know had no slave, nor Abel, nor Seth, nor those who came after them. The institution was the fruit of sin.[77]

We have already seen that John had a vision of a Christian household as "a little church", and also the means of seasoning the whole city with the salt of Christianity. He makes the influence of the household clear by saying that it is like "a small city".[78] Just as fidelity and chastity are to be the mark of Christian marriage, so true fellowship and respect are to mark out the relationship between slave and master: the one is faithfully to obey, the other to treat the slave with respect (Ephesians 6:3–9). The vision of a Christian household or villa in which slaves are present is best described by the Apostle Paul in his letter to Philemon. There he talks about how to treat the runaway slave, and now Christian, Onesimus. Runaway slave though he is, Onesimus is to be welcomed back and treated as "a dear brother" (v. 16). In other words, the bonds of service are to be seasoned with brotherly love.

Furthermore, in the Christian household, Scriptures should be read, hymns and songs sung, homilies given and prayers made. It is here that the sick might be prayed for, alms given in a poor box, and relationships guided.[79] For Chrysostom the household was a monarchy with the husband as king and his wife as the vice regent.[80] But it is not necessarily an emollient rule: for Chrysostom fear of punishment is a necessary constraint in the good ordering of the household, both with regard to slaves and, if needed, with children too, although they are not to be whipped.[81] And for Chrysostom, the direction of travel for a truly Christian household is to reduce the number of slaves in the house from the so-called "strategic" large-scale household or estate to something smaller, more manageable and "tactical". This is in part to be achieved through manumission. Manumission, or the granting of liberty to a slave comes about through the direction of the slave-owner, often when the slave is old and has lost physical condition after long service. Or frequently it can be simply the will of the owner, something which John encourages.[82]

If Chrysostom did not seek to abolish slavery in an empire still very committed to, and dependent on it, he attempted within his own overarching moral framework to limit its evils, which included physical violence, especially whipping and the sexual abuse of pederasty or the penetration of slave boys and the seduction of slave girls or women.

Indeed, Chrysostom was concerned in an almost Stoic manner to see the growth of virtue in the household as a whole, and for this advance he laid especial responsibility on the master of the house, who should be concerned not just for their service but also for the moral improvement of the slave.[83] For John, "wicked men treat their slaves with derision, while the virtuous man will be gentle to his wife, children and slaves".[84] The inculcation of virtue in the slave-owning Christian was also a means of restricting the evils of slavery. At the same time, Chrysostom, no stranger to pain and abstinence himself, finds it natural that a slave should fear his master, suffer pain for virtue's sake, and recognize that "masters can resort to violent punitive measures to teach their slaves virtue".[85] Furthermore, Chrysostom recommends depriving a licentious slave woman of her freedom and securing her in chains to protect her own modesty.[86] It is only through quarantine, seclusion and solitary confinement that an unchaste female slave can be trained in sexual modesty in his view. Indeed, John believed that disobedient slaves should be punished, for, as with God, punishment shows an underlying care (see Hebrews 12). Chrysostom's attitude to slaves is clear in his commentary on 1 Timothy, where he says, "Slaves are satisfied to receive no more than they need and often less; with straw for their bed, and only bread for their food, they do not complain or murmur at their hard life, but because of their fear of us are restrained from impatience."[87] One wonders if John ever asked any household slaves what would truly satisfy them.

Chrysostom's wholehearted embrace of the need for physical punishment for disobedience seems some way from Paul's warm instruction to Philemon to cherish the runaway slave Onesimus "as a dear brother" (Philemon 16). Still, John's advocacy of punishment or whipping when deserved is matched by warning masters not to indulge in unjust cruelty. Even if the courts would not recognize such treatment as unjust, God would, he says. And just because a slave has an inferior status in Roman law, there is no reason to neglect God's law of "loving our neighbour as ourselves", for by observation of that law we shall all ultimately be judged. Nevertheless, there is a balance to be struck in Christian teaching to masters and slaves which Chrysostom seeks. Masters or mistresses (for they too were capable of humiliating their female slaves out of anger by forcing them to strip) should control their anger, gain the admiration of their husbands, and act judiciously and calmly.[88] If Christian slaves suffered unjustly, they were to remember and draw strength from Christ, who likewise suffered unjustly, and follow him.[89]

The final way slaves suffered was through sexual exploitation, which, quite apart from its inherent immorality and abuse of power, carried all kinds of risks. In Roman society, marriage was "the most important form of social regulation in the Roman world".[90] It was through marriage that families might enter into advantageous alliances; it was only in marriage that heirs might be legitimately born or adopted; and lastly, marriage provided overall social cohesion to Roman society and values, not least in the transference of property. Legislation was often brought forward in the reign of Augustus and subsequently, to bolster marriage and to encourage the birth of children by fining families that did not produce heirs through either natural birth or adoption. Thus, marriage was the means whereby Roman society and leadership would continue in successive generations. The presence of female slaves was a threat to this, and yet these women fulfilled vital roles in Roman households as nurses, governesses, ladies' maids and general servants. If marriage was to be supported, and slaves or even servants (i.e., free slaves) were to be an integral part of society, as they would be in Europe thereafter, how did Chrysostom deal with the temptations for men in his congregation with young female staff under their sway?

The answer is that Chrysostom writes and preaches about this evident temptation with his characteristic plain speaking or *parrhesia*. Far from overlooking this risk to marriage, he deals with it squarely. For John, promiscuity or fornication is an ever-present reality, for which marriage is the solution. Thus, he argues in *Concerning Virginity*:

> So marriage was granted for the sake of procreation, but an even greater reason was to quench the fiery passion of our nature . . . At the beginning, as I said, marriage had these two purposes but now, after the earth and sea and all the world has been inhabited,

only one reason remains for it: the suppression of licentiousness and debauchery.[91]

The slave girl herself is to preserve or seek virginity, meaning not just actual virginity, for which there were tests, and indeed upon which a higher value was set, but a modest lifestyle as well. Husbands and wives were to avoid time alone with slaves of the opposite sex.[92] Furthermore, the threat to a woman whose husband admired a slave girl more than he did her was not lost on Chrysostom:

> So whenever a slave girl happens to stand out, if she captures her master's fancy and puts him under her spell or has more influence over him beyond being admired, the distress felt by the mistress of the house is the same: she has been surpassed, if not in love, at least in youthfulness and admiration.[93]

Once again, the unmarried Chrysostom shows that he both knows and can articulate the almost inevitable tensions created by male and female slaves for both spouses. The answer for John is both to acknowledge the issues and commit to a chastity of mind and heart. Furthermore, he is not slow to call out the sexual exploitation of a slave, however complicit she or he might be, as adultery, which is both a sin and a crime.[94] (John appears to make Abraham a special case, for he says that in his case neither lust nor jealousy was involved, he simply wanted an heir!)

The final type of sexual corruption that slaves might become enmeshed in was prostitution. Many slaves became prostitutes, and as such were available to their owners. Chrysostom makes clear Paul's teaching on the nature and reality of prostitution from 1 Corinthians (6:12–20). Men are to flee sexual relations with prostitutes: "Do you not know that your bodies are members of Christ himself? Shall I take then the members of Christ and unite them with a prostitute? Never!" To the tempted, John pleads for the self-discipline of chastity and fidelity to a wife. After all, the *materfamilias* is the embodiment of virtue and chastity and of *dignitas* and *pudicitia* (modesty). He continues, saying that a wife offers at the same time pleasure and security, joy, honour, order and a good conscience,[95] while a relationship with a prostitute risks the birth of an illegitimate child, brings disgrace to the household, and the risk of death, poverty and perpetual shame to the illegitimate child.[96] John's advice to the prostitute is, if possible, to find a husband in order to leave her illicit lifestyle. To put it simply, for John, sex with a slave was a crime and an act of adultery or fornication, even though it might be permitted in Roman law. He was basically redefining the sexual mores of a Christian society in opposition to the pagan world: no small task.

In these various ways, John deals with the evils and the results of slavery. As we have seen, it becomes a question of diminishing slavery's effects rather than running a campaign to abolish the institution wholesale, even though he recognizes the practice was never something that had the blessing of God. He seeks to restrain, if not abolish, slavery and as such his teaching may have had more direct impact on the daily life of his congregation than most other theological topics.[97] There can be little doubt that in accommodating the institution of slavery, although reducing its parameters, he supported the Roman construct of *paterfamilias*, which enforced a masculine or patriarchal role model and the submission of male and female slave bodies to the will of the owner. This, in turn, involved submission of slaves to education, punishment, sexual regulation and training in virtue. And because slavery was frequently used as a model of our relationship with Christ (see 1 Corinthians 7:22), in which we find freedom in becoming Christ's servant or slave, there is a danger of spiritualizing the reality of slavery and making it seem less harsh than it actually was. Indeed, John shows more concern about those who are slaves to sin (see John 8:34 and Romans 6:20) than for those enslaved to a human master. De Wet goes as far as saying, "Institutional slavery informed the [scriptural] metaphor, and the metaphor sustained the institution."[98] Familiarity with the spiritual metaphor about slavery-under-Christ potentially allowed owners to become blasé about the real consequences of slavery.

Nevertheless, Chrysostom did have a vision that the household should become a "little church", in which the father of the house has almost priestlike duties: reflecting on sermons, leading prayers and worship, administering Christian discipline on children and slaves alike and, where possible, making arrangements for the manumission of slaves. It was a grand vision, although how often it was fulfilled, we cannot truly know. Yet the overall verdict must be that although the application of Christian virtue to the institution of slavery may in some cases have ameliorated it, the institution itself prevented human flourishing, and despite the otherwise powerful presence of the Church in society, would not be outlawed in Christian states until the mid- or late-nineteenth century: for instance, in Britain (1838), the United States (1865), and Russia (1861). It was a long process of change which was essentially giving up power over another which was written into laws.

Jews in the city

The issues Chrysostom found himself dealing with in late fourth-century Antioch and Constantinople are undeniably perennial. Indeed, they have been centre stage in human history ever since. How should men and women conduct their sexual relationships? How should children be taught and safeguarded? How should we deal with the history of slavery in empires? And now, as a microcosm of race relations, how should the Church respond to the history and presence of the Jews?

Jews have emigrated to other societies perhaps more than any other people group. By the first century AD, there were Jewish communities across the Mediterranean. As recorded in the New Testament, all the principal cities of the empire had lively Jewish communities, whether in Tarsus, Ephesus, Corinth, Rome, Thessalonica, Galatia or Alexandria. The emigration of Jews to the Mediterranean and further afield was accelerated by the failure of the Jewish Revolt in 66–70, the destruction of Jerusalem by the armies of Vespasian and Titus, and then, finally, by the catastrophic defeat of the Jewish Bar Kokhba revolt by the Emperor Hadrian in 132–6. Hadrian's suppression of the Jewish population in Jerusalem and Judea, together with the banishment of the Jews from Jerusalem, except for specified festivals, must have only hastened the emigration of Jews to the Diaspora. As Christianity expanded further afield in Europe to Kyiv, Russe and Eastern Europe, Jews frequently followed. We have already seen that there was a large Jewish population in Alexandria from the third century BC, and also a significant centre of Jewish studies there. Antioch was no different. We know from the Acts of the Apostles and Paul's letter to the Galatians that there was a further significant community there (see Acts 11:19–29; Galatians 2:11–16), and, reading between the lines in Galatians, that there was tension between the Jewish and Gentile Christians as to how much of the Law (Torah) it was necessary to keep, including the food laws.

There is no doubt that Chrysostom saw the presence of the Jews in Antioch and in Constantinople as a threat to the faithfulness of his own congregation. While still a relatively new presbyter in Antioch, in 386 John preached two full-length sermons or addresses on the Jews, quite probably in the Great Church. With their give-away title, *Against the Jews*, these addresses take the form of a rhetorical device called the *psogos* (sustained invective) against a particular person or group which is the exact opposite of an *encomium* (praise). John uses the *psogos* against various groups of people and activities: fashionable women and their extravagant living or dressing,[99] men, and their propensity to display wealth and indulge in reckless or self-indulgent pastimes, and the crowds who loved attending the theatre and the hippodrome (particularly Homily 7, delivered in Constantinople in 399). In his sermons against the Jews, however, he unleashes a burst of unrestrained invective in the strongest possible terms, which, given the history of anti-Semitism, is shocking for us today.

At the outset of his first sermon (of eight), John makes it clear that he wants to end the practice of Christians attending Jewish festivals. The Jews, he says, are no better than the Arians, since both disregard the divinity of Christ. The Jews do not think Jesus is the Messiah or the Son of God, and likewise the Arians do not think he is the same substance as the Father. In reality, the Jews and the Arians are the same: unwilling to recognize the full divinity of Christ. For John, the Jews are wretched: "For truly they are wretched and miserable since they spurned the numerous blessings which came into their hands from heaven, and they took great pains to throw them away."[100] John goes on to say that the Jews fail to observe the Law. They are obstinate and stiff-necked. They are beset by gluttony, drunkenness and lust, and their synagogues, "far from being holy places are places to be despised".[101] Since they conspired to kill the Messiah, they should be treated no better than murderers. John adds: "If someone killed your son, could you bear to lay eyes on them? Could you bear to listen to their greeting? Wouldn't you avoid them as you would an evil spirit, as the devil himself? The Jews killed your Master's Son—do you have the effrontery to go with them to the same place."[102] For these reasons, there should be no visiting of synagogues to sample their feasts, no requests for healing prayer from their Rabbis, or taking oaths in their ceremonies, and, most importantly of all, no joint celebration of the Passover with the Jews, which had begun as a practice in the Syrian Church on the Sunday following 14 Nisan, but which was later outlawed by the Council of Nicaea.[103] What a difference there might have been to Jewish–Christian relations if such a practice had been maintained!

John's eight addresses vary in the intensity of their vituperative content, but the general object remains the same: to sever the connection between Christians and Jews. John maintains that the Jews should observe their festivals in Jerusalem, but this of course was practically impossible, especially after the destruction of the Temple in 70. He also maintains that Jesus had been emphatically upheld as the Messiah through the fulfilment of his predictions of the destruction of the Temple and the city, and that, at root, Jews remained idolaters, as they always had been.[104] In a word, rather than seeking harmony between the two great religions of the Bible, John wanted separation, and for the Church in the city to be notably distinct from pagans, Christian heretics such as the Arians, and others, especially the Jews.

Thus, in these early years after the acceptance of Christianity in the empire by Constantine, John wanted the Church to have the field cleared of religious competitors, that it might be seen as the true instrument of God's providence on earth: an ark of salvation, a place of transformation, and a spiritual and physical hospital for the sick and needy in the city.

In summary, John had an integrated vision for the role of the Church in the city, with practices of Scripture reading, preaching, Easter baptisms of catechumenates, observation of festivals and saints' days, prayer (especially overnight vigils), and an increasingly ornate liturgy, attributed to John himself, as the centrepiece of weekly worship. All this was intended to equip the "little church" of the Christian household. It was in the household that Christianity would take root and spread. The *paterfamilias* in the household would now take on a supremely Christian role in contrast to his pagan counterpart. He would lead

Bible study and prayer. He would reflect on the sermons preached in the city church. He would personally commit to a life of chastity and purity. He would practise almsgiving. He and his wife would regulate the lives of their servants or slaves, reducing dependence upon them. His daughters would increasingly consider a life of abstinence and virginity. Marriages would be conducted with the utmost sobriety. Widows would, if possible, forswear a second marriage, and if wealthy, give their estate to the Church to use in almsgiving. The sons of the household would have an education centred more on the Bible than on the classics, and monks would take over from pagan pedagogues. Taken as a whole, this was a revolution in household management, education and family values. It was this that John was driving at in Antioch and again in Constantinople. Extraneous matters would intervene to prevent its fulfilment, however: bitter ecclesiastical rivalries, a stand-off with the imperial household and especially the empress, and the circumstances of life. But these brickbats were worsened by the fact that through his vehemence in pursuing his goals, John had failed to win sufficient allies outside the ordinary people of the city. His hospitality had been too sparse, his criticism of the imperial court had not been sufficiently balanced by a close pastoral relationship, and he appeared to have overreached himself in laying down church discipline, giving him few powerful allies nearby, and an increasing number of enemies. But much of this lay in the future, even if the seeds were already being sown in the exceptional style of his ministry.

Notes

1. Epictetus, *Enchiridion 41*, cited by Peter Brown, *Body and Society: Men, Women, and Sexual Renunciation in Early Christianity* (London: Faber and Faber, 1988), p. 27.
2. Brown, *The Body and Society*, p. 29.
3. G. Vermes, *Dead Sea Scrolls in English Community Rule 5* (Harmondsworth: Penguin, 1968), p. 85.
4. *Shepherd of Hermas* 25, Loeb Classical Series, Apostolic Fathers II (Cambridge, MA: Harvard University Press, 2005), p. 175.
5. *Shepherd of Hermas* 25.5, op. cit., p. 235.
6. *Shepherd of Hermas* 27.2, op. cit., p. 239.
7. *Shepherd of Hermas* 28.3, op. cit., p. 241.
8. *Shepherd of Hermas* 28.3, op. cit., p. 241.
9. *Shepherd of Hermas* 33.1, op. cit., p. 255.
10. *Shepherd of Hermas* 39.9, op. cit., p. 275.
11. *Shepherd of Hermas* 39.9, op. cit., p. 275.
12. *Shepherd of Hermas* 40.1, op. cit., p. 276.
13. Brown, *The Body and Society*, p. 79.
14. Tertullian, *On the Veiling of Virgins* XVII, in *The Ante-Nicene Fathers: The Writings of the Fathers Down to A.D. 325 Volume IV Fathers of the Third Century: Tertullian Part 4*, ed. Alexander Roberts, James Donaldson and Arthur Cleveland Coxe (New York: Cosimo, 2007), p. 37.
15. Tertullian, *To His Wife*, in *The Ante-Nicene Fathers: The Writings of the Fathers Down to A.D. 325 Volume IV Fathers of the Third Century: Tertullian Part 4*, ed. Alexander Roberts, James Donaldson and Arthur Cleveland Coxe (New York: Cosimo, 2007), p, 40.
16. Brown, *The Body and Society*, pp. 124–5.
17. Clement, *The Pedagogue or Instructor* II.10 (Fairfield, NY: Lighthouse Publishing, 2014), p. 131.
18. Brown, *The Body and Society*, p. 132.
19. Brown, *The Body and Society*, p. 133.
20. Brown, *The Body and Society*, p, 174.
21. Origen, *Contra Celsum* I.35.
22. Eusebius, *Ecclesiastical History* VI.8.2.
23. Brown, *The Body and Society*, pp. 138–9.

24 Ramsay MacMullen, *Christianizing the Roman Empire: A.D. 100–400* (New Haven, CT: Yale University Press, 1984), p. 32, pp. 135–6.
25 Athanasius, *Life of Antony, PG* 26, p. 848.
26 Brown, *The Body and Society*, p. 219.
27 Brown, *The Body and Society*, p. 276.
28 Basil, *De Virginitate Tuenda 3*, ed. and tr. A. Vaillant (Paris: *Institute des études slaves*, 1943); *PG* 30, pp. 669–810.
29 Basil, *De Virginitate Tuenda 3, PG* 30.676C.
30 Gregory of Nyssa, *On the Soul and Resurrection, PG* 46.148C–159A.
31 St Basil, *Ascetical Works: A Discourse on the Ascetical Discipline*, Fathers of the Church, Vol. 9, tr. Sister Monica Wagner (New York: Catholic University of America, 1950), p. 33.
32 Brown, *The Body and Society*, p. 306.
33 Brown, *The Body and Society*, pp. 308–9.
34 Tertullian, *A Treatise on the Soul* XXVII, op. cit., p. 208.
35 John Chrysostom, *Colossians, Homily 12: On Marriage and the Family*, Popular Patristics, No. 7, tr. Roth and Anderson (Crestwood, NY: St Vladimir's Seminary Press, 1986), pp.77ff.
36 Chrysostom, *I Corinthians, Homily 19*, op. cit., p. 27.
37 Chrysostom, *Ephesians, Homily 20*, op. cit., p. 44.
38 Brown, *The Body and Society*, pp. 307–8.
39 Brown, *The Body and Society*, p. 312.
40 Chrysostom, *Ephesians, Homily 20*, op. cit., p. 46.
41 Chrysostom, *Ephesians, Homily 20*, op. cit., p. 49.
42 Chrysostom, *Ephesians, Homily 20*, op. cit., p. 56.
43 Chrysostom, *Ephesians, Homily 20*, op. cit., p. 59.
44 Chrysostom, *Ephesians, Homily 20*, op. cit., p. 60.
45 Chrysostom, *Colossians, Homily 12*, op. cit., pp. 79ff.
46 Chrysostom, *Colossians, Homily 12*, op. cit., p. 80.
47 Brown, *The Body and Society*, p. 319.
48 Brown, *The Body and Society*, p. 321.
49 Chrysostom, *Acts of the Apostles, Homily XI*, NAPNF, Vol. XI, First Series (Grand Rapids, MI: Eerdmans, 1975), p. 74.
50 Chrysostom, *Acts of the Apostles, Homily XI*, op. cit., p. 74.
51 Kelly, *Golden Mouth*, p. 97.

52. Chrysostom, *I Corinthians*, Homily 40.6, NAPNF, Vol. XII, First Series (New York: Cosimo Reprint, 2007), p. 248.
53. Chrysostom, *First Sermon: On Lazarus and the Rich Man, On Wealth and Poverty* (Crestwood, NY: St Vladimir's Press, 2020), p. 21.
54. Chrysostom, *First Sermon*, op. cit., p. 21.
55. Chrysostom, *First Sermon*, op. cit., p. 30.
56. Chrysostom, *First Sermon*, op. cit., p. 24.
57. Chrysostom, *First Sermon*, op. cit., p. 28.
58. Chrysostom, *First Sermon*, op. cit., p. 34.
59. Chrysostom, *Second Sermon*, op. cit., p. 40.
60. William Shakespeare, *As you Like it*, Act 2 Scene 7.
61. Chrysostom, *First Sermon*, op. cit., p. 46.
62. Chrysostom, *First Sermon*, op. cit., p. 53.
63. Chrysostom, *Third Sermon*, op. cit., p. 63.
64. Chrysostom, *Third Sermon*, op. cit., p. 64.
65. Chrysostom, *Third Sermon*, op. cit., p. 65.
66. Chrysostom, *Fourth Sermon*, op. cit., p. 90.
67. Chrysostom, *Fourth Sermon*, op. cit., p. 90.
68. David Potter, *Constantine the Emperor* (Oxford: Oxford University Press, 2013), p. 183.
69. Potter, *Constantine the Emperor*, p. 187.
70. Potter, *Constantine the Emperor*, p. 187.
71. De Wet, Chris L., *Preaching Bondage: John Chrysostom and the Discourse of Slavery in Early Christianity* (Berkeley, CA: University of California Press, 2015), pp. 142–8.
72. Potter, *Constantine the Emperor*, p. 177.
73. C. R. Whittaker and P. Garnsey, "Rural life in the later Roman Empire", in A. Cameron and P. Garnsey (eds), *The Cambridge Ancient History, Vol. XIII* (Cambridge: Cambridge University Press, 1998), p. 294.
74. Whittaker and Garnsey, "Rural life in the later Roman Empire", p. 300.
75. De Wet, *Preaching Bondage*, p. 53.
76. Chrysostom, Chris L., *Homily 34.7, I Corinthians*, NAPNF, Vol. XII (New York: Cosimo, 2007), p. 205.
77. Chrysostom, *Ephesians*, Homily 22.1, op. cit., p. 159.
78. Chrysostom, *Ephesians*, Homily 22, op. cit., p. 159.
79. Chrysostom, *Homily Genesis 6*, op. cit., p. 93.

80 Chrysostom, *Homily Genesis 6*, op. cit., pp. 97–8.
81 Chrysostom, *Homily Genesis 6*, op. cit., p. 103.
82 Chrysostom, *Homily Genesis 6*, op. cit., p. 22.
83 Chrysostom, *Homily Titus 4.1*, op. cit., p. 179.
84 Chrysostom, *Homily Hebrews 24.7*, F7.274–5, cited in De Wet, *Preaching Bondage*, p. 180.
85 Chrysostom, *Homily Hebrews 24.7*, F7.274–5, cited in De Wet, *Preaching Bondage*, p. 191.
86 Chrysostom, *Adv. Jud 2.124*, PG 48, p. 942, cited in De Wet, *Preaching Bondage*, p. 191.
87 Chrysostom, *Homily 1 Timothy 16:2*, F6.144, cited in De Wet, *Preaching Bondage*, p. 205.
88 Chrysostom, *Homily 1 Timothy 16:2*, cited in De Wet, *Preaching Bondage*, pp. 212–13.
89 See Chrysostom, *Homily 1 Peter 2:18–25* and *Ephesians, Homily 22.1*, op. cit., p. 158.
90 Chrysostom, *Homily, 1 Timothy, Homily 16:2*, cited in De Wet, *Preaching Bondage*, p. 222.
91 Ambrose, *de Virginitate*, 19.1.2–3, 11–13, in *Jean Chrysostome: La Virginité*, ed. H. Musurillo and B. Grillet, SC 125 (Paris: Les Éditions du Cerf, 1966), pp. 156–8, cited De Wet, *Preaching Bondage*, p. 225.
92 Ambrose, *de Virginitate*, 60.17–9, op. cit., pp. 240–2.
93 Ambrose, *de Virginitate*, 67.9–14.
94 Chrysostom, *Homily 1 Timothy, 16:2*, cited in De Wet, *Preaching Bondage* pp. 233–6.
95 *Propt. fornic 5*, PG 51.217.6–8, cited in De Wet, *Preaching Bondage* p. 241.
96 Chrysostom, *Romans, Homily 24*, NAPNF Vol. XI, First Series (Grand Rapids, MI: Eerdmans, 1976), p. 520.
97 *Propt. fornic 5*, De Wet, *Preaching Bondage,* p. 271.
98 *Propt. fornic 5*, De Wet, *Preaching Bondage,* p. 272.
99 Chrysostom, *Colossians, Homily 7*, op. cit., pp. 288ff.
100 Wendy Mayer and Pauline Allen, *Against the Jews I, in John Chrysostom* (London: Routledge, 2000), p. 151.
101 Mayer and Allen, *Against the Jews*, p. 158.
102 Mayer and Allen, *Against the Jews*, p. 163.
103 Kelly, *Golden Mouth*, pp. 63–4.

104 Kelly, *Golden Mouth*, p. 65.

9

A eunuch, a Gothic commander and the empress

It was William Shakespeare who wrote that "when sorrows come, they come not as single spies, but in battalions",¹ and this was to be true of Chrysostom also during the years 400–7: one sorrow or difficulty came fast upon another. These crises, ever more personal in character, were increasingly launched from quarters that made them difficult to rebut, and they also prevented John from realizing his vision of a Christian transformation of the city. The first crisis, more political than personal in nature, but nonetheless requiring careful handling so as not to imperil his own position, came from the court: literally yards away from his own residence.

The eunuch: Eutropius

By 399, the Emperor Arcadius had been in power for five years since the death of his powerful father Theodosius I in 395. Although declared *augustus* when just five years old, Arcadius only assumed the full powers of emperor in the East following the death of his father. For much of the early part of his reign, Arcadius was dependent on his court chamberlain, Eutropius, who was a eunuch, and thus unlikely to challenge Arcadius's authority. It was Eutropius who had encouraged Arcadius's marriage to his beautiful but mercurial wife, Eudoxia, and who had overseen the appointment of John Chrysostom to Constantinople. He grew too confident of his abilities, however, and fatally underestimated the growing authority and independence of mind of the empress. Eunuchs also had an uncertain position in the popular thinking of the Roman Empire. Eastern in origin, and frequently found in the courts of Persia, Babylon and further east, eunuchs seemed to represent an effeminate expression of power that sat ill with the martial, masculine and patriarchal rendering of Roman authority.

Castration could come about in various ways in the late empire, but it became increasingly common in Constantinople at the court through the influence of the East. It occurred either naturally, through underdeveloped or injured genitalia; by force, particularly against household slaves who might be in constant contact with female members of the household; or by the free choice of individuals, possibly to enhance their employability by powerful rulers. This last option was also sometimes practised by Christians seeking control of their sexual urges as part of their rule of life, in the hope that castration would reduce or destroy their sexual desires or lusts at a stroke. However, although the removal of the testes by strangulation of the scrotum destroyed fertility, it did not necessarily destroy sexual urges.[2] According to Eusebius, Origen had famously castrated himself (although this account, supported by Peter Brown, is disputed by Henry Chadwick). Such action was condemned by the Council of Nicaea, however. Of the 20 canons promulgated by the Council, the first, and least known one was the prohibition against clergy castrating themselves. Such were the times of the Council of Nicaea that, at one and the same time, it established the outline of a Trinitarian Creed, and it regulated the practice of castration among the clergy.

Eutropius was the chief official and favourite at the court of Arcadius and, as such, in a very powerful position. But inevitably he had many opponents, some equally powerful. Claudian the poet, an Alexandrian (c.360–404), poked fun at Eutropius, writing:

> It was indeed a beautiful sight when Eutropius stretched out his etiolated limbs burdened by his belt of office and the weight of his toga ... He was like an ape which for a joke a boy dressed up in costly eastern silks, leaving both his back and buttocks bare to amuse the dinner-guests.[3]

Claudian's lampooning of Eutropius had as much to do with Claudian's support of Stilicho (c.359–408)—Eutropius's rival—the army commander under Theodosius and then of Honorius in the West, as it did with his contempt for the eunuch. However, Eutropius had less to fear from the mocking verse of Claudian than from the manoeuvrings of Gainas, another powerful army commander who was nearer to home, in Constantinople.

Gainas had successfully led the campaign against the Goths and now moved against Eutropius. Loathed and feared by the military establishment, Eutropius was also despised by the senatorial aristocracy as a eunuch.[4] In a word, he had acquired too much wealth, enjoyed too much imperial patronage, had statues of himself placed in the city, and commanded a virtual private army. He had set himself up as a military commander but was despised by the professional soldiers and officers. He was, as far as they were concerned, riding for a fall, which came abruptly in late July 499. That was when he lost the favour of the imperial family, and in particular of Eudoxia, whom he boasted he could have removed from the court because she had been his choice for empress in the first place. He prided himself too much on his management of the emperor, but times had changed. His was another case of a too-powerful official like Cardinal Wolsey, thinking himself untouchable but finding that he had feet of clay, and that he owed everything to the emperor who now, under his wife's influence, turned against him.

When the trap against Eutropius was fully sprung, he literally fled the palace to the church of Hagia Sophia down the road and sought sanctuary there, hiding under the altar. It was both a shrewd and ironic move. It was ironic because he had previously sought to curtail the right of sanctuary in churches for political refugees or asylum seekers, but now needed it himself. He had sought to limit the powers of the Church in the State, but now he was in need of its intercession and help in his own life-threatening predicament.[5] The move was also shrewd, because he judged that if anyone would protect him from imperial reach, it would be John, who jealously guarded the rights of the Church. Eutropius therefore flung himself at the base of the altar, but now "when government officers arrived to arrest him John refused to yield to their demands".[6] Soldiers assembled outside the palace, demanding Eutropius's end, until eventually Emperor Arcadius himself came out to address the troops and called for mercy towards his once-trusted favourite, whom he pleaded for, even with tears. At this point on a Saturday in late July, the baying mob disassembled with the promise that John would preach the following day in Hagia Sophia while Eutropius continued to cling to the altar overnight in his desperate bid for asylum.

The following day the church was completely full, as if for Easter, in the next act in an unfolding political drama. Eutropius continued to cling to the altar but was veiled by the altar cloth under which he crouched. This was then pulled back to reveal the unfortunate man who John now used as an object lesson in his preaching. For John, it was an occasion of which to make much. His experience in Antioch of preaching in the political crisis of the statues had prepared him for another political crisis in the capital with the emperor and empress standing by. Ignoring the specific issues that had caused Eutropius's downfall, John concentrated on broader biblical issues, notably the ephemeral nature of human power and position. He began, "Where now are the splendid trappings of the consulship. Where are the gleaming torches? Where are the outbursts of applause and the choruses and the festivities and the public holidays? Where are the crowns and banners?" Of course, all such things pass, as the Preacher of Ecclesiastes said, "Vanity of vanities, all is vanity" (Ecclesiastes 1:2, RSV), and this was the text for his sermon. And in the light of Eutropius's fall from grace, John goes on with the rhetorical questions:

> Where are the drinking parties and the dinners? Where the swarms of hangers-on, and the undiluted wine that filled glasses all day long, and the valued arts of the chefs, and the cultivators of power who would do anything to please him? They were all night and a dream and, when day came, they vanished.[7]

Having developed this theme of the transitory nature of human fame, earthly honours and power, John turned to address Eutropius more personally. Whereas he may have paid scant attention to the Church and sought to reduce its standing, he was now in need of its protection:

> Indeed, the church that you made war against has opened its arms and taken you in, while the theatre on which you lavished care and, on whose behalf, you were often angry with us has betrayed and destroyed you.[8]

John continued, saying he had no wish to hit a man when he was down even if that was what it looked like. He sought instead to draw out the lessons from Eutropius's fall for all:

> Do you see how each person receives medicine and departs from here after being treated by this sight alone? Have I softened your passion and cast out your anger? Have I quenched your inhumanity? Have I drawn you into sympathy? I very much think so—the faces indicate it and the fountains of tears. Let's ask God, who loves humankind, to soften the rage of the emperor and make his heart gentle so that he'll grant our favour in its entirety.[9]

Finally, having acknowledged the emperor's efforts to mollify the crowds the previous day, John urged mercy be shown: "It isn't the time for the lawcourt", he pleaded,

> but for mercy. It isn't the time for demanding an account, but for generosity, not for interrogation but for concession, not for a ballot and a penalty, but for pity and grace. So then let no-one get heated or upset, but rather let's ask God, who loves humankind, to grant this person an extension of life and snatch away the threatened slaughter so that he might shed his misdeeds.[10]

John then concluded with a reminder that God forgives, that he loves "mercy rather than sacrifice", that this was an opportunity for Constantinople to become known worldwide for its clemency and forgiving love, so that "the ends of the earth will marvel at the humanity and gentleness of the city and, when they learn what's happened, people all over the world will cry out our name".[11]

In the event, Eutropius was persuaded to give himself up. He was exiled to Cyprus, having been given an assurance in Constantinople that his life would be spared.¹² But in the end the wheels of Roman retribution ground on, now in the hands of a new Prefect, Aurelianus, and the army commander and *magister militum*, Count Gainas, an implacable enemy of Eutropius. Later Eutropius was hauled back to Constantinople for a trial, stripped of all his property and titles, condemned to death and duly executed for high treason on a trumped-up charge. No mercy was shown.¹³ Constantinople's reputation was hardly burnished by mercy. As for John, he had shown once again that he could rise to a political occasion with great eloquence. Without being drawn into the details of the controversy, he had elaborated great biblical themes in a time of heightened passion: namely the ephemeral nature of human power and position, the requirement for forgiveness and mercy, and the principle of humility in public life and relations. But if John had temporarily saved Eutropius's life, he was equally criticized by Gainas and Aurelianus, the new power brokers in Constantinople, for his lack of deference and for his outspokenness (*parrhesia*) in an affair they considered political and hence beyond John's remit, a far from unfamiliar gibe by politicians of church leaders.¹⁴ But for John, even the political must be subject to the theological; power must always be exercised in a godly manner, and the Church was there to see it done.

The Gothic commander: Gainas

With the removal of one overmighty subject, a new rift appeared; this time between the Roman Prefect Aurelianus and the Gothic army commander, Gainas. Both had been involved in the removal of Eutropius, but now, as so often happens with the removal of that which unites, they had come to see each other as rivals. By 400, Gainas was positioning himself for a full-scale acquisition of the levers of power in Constantinople. He saw himself occupying the same role in the East as Stilicho in the West, where the latter was in effect the enforcer of the Western Emperor Honorius, the brother of Arcadius. Like many of the barbarian army commanders (i.e., ethnically non-Roman), they both wanted unrivalled power, but at the same time sought to uphold the Roman system that gave them their position, and furthermore they respected the emperor. Emperors and their generals needed each other: the latter-day emperors because they were no soldiers and these barbarian generals because they were genuinely committed to the imperial system and cherished the legitimacy that system gave them. At this point, they did not wish to overthrow it.

Nonetheless, they wanted all rivals removed. To this end, Gainas entered into a pact with the Gothic leader Tribigild.[15] Far from suppressing Tribigild, who was laying waste to Phrygia, Gainas in fact joined him so as to threaten Constantinople and bend the city and the government to his will.[16] From his headquarters at the Church of Euphemia, which later hosted the Council of Chalcedon in 451, Gainas made his demands of Arcadius, at which point "the emperor [Arcadius] declared that he was ready to be favourable to him in every point, and sent to Gainas to offer him whatever he might demand".[17] Gainas's demand was that his chief rivals should be handed over to him as hostages: they included Aurelianus, the high-ranking general Saturninos, and Count John, Eudoxia's favourite, and according to some, her lover also. The emperor was in no position to refuse and also acceded to further demands that Gainas be appointed overall commander of the imperial troops (*magister utriusque militae*) and that his troops, including Goths from Tribigild's forces, be billeted in Constantinople.

It was into this crisis that the imperial family sent John Chrysostom as a mediator. His interest in the Goths was well known, and his standing as a persuasive advocate was high. There were ensuing negotiations with Caesarius, a newly appointed Prefect in place of Aurelianus, who was also the brother of Gainas. Despite Caesarius's desire to see the hostages executed, Gainas was persuaded to do otherwise, and John, who was quite used to preaching on topical issues that filled his church, gave a sermon on the predicament of Aurelianus and Saturninus. If this sermon was really about the predicament of these two hostages, which is disputed by some scholars,[18] it nonetheless followed a growing pattern of John's dealings with these political crises on his doorstep. He raised awareness of the issues through candid preaching, explained his own involvement in them and his own use of time, and applied biblical teaching of restraint and mercy to obtain a solution. It is quite possible that in 401 he was dissuaded from going on a tour of churches in the region where issues had come to light in order to help the imperial family in their tortuous power struggle.

There was, however, a third hostage, the empress's favourite Count John, whose life was still at risk. On the fate of Count John, there does appear to be some genuine uncertainty. It appears he went into hiding, and that in some way John Chrysostom gave away his whereabouts, given a charge which was later brought against him that he had deliberately betrayed the Count's sanctuary. A sermon preached in 401,[19] and often misapplied to Eutropius, could very well have centred on this rumour. In this sermon, Chrysostom says he had no reason to betray Count John and nor was he "afraid of the wrath" of the rampaging Gothic troops in the city. Nor did Count John's purple diadem (a sign of imperial favour) help the count at all.

Although the count was found and arrested, he was not harmed.[20] Nonetheless, the affair of the hostages did not redound to Chrysostom's credit in the imperial household, despite his success in defusing the crisis and the eventual release of all three men unharmed. But a more serious crisis developed in Constantinople in 400 when the Gothic army sought both billets and sanctuary in the city, swamping the city's amenities and demanding a church to worship in. The problem was that they were Arians.

The Gothic army numbered 35,000 troops, and they sought shelter in Constantinople. To have an army of foreign (non-Roman) troops residing in the imperial city was a threat, however much Gainas may have respected the emperor. The size and presence of the army left Gainas in effective control of the government. And it was on this basis that Gainas approached Arcadius for a church in which the Goths could worship, albeit according to their Arian lights. As we have already noticed, the Goths were evangelized by Bishop Ulfilas (c.311–83), whom they much respected and who subscribed to an Arian creed in which only the Father, and not the Son or the Spirit, was deemed uncreated.[21] When John was approached by the emperor and by Gainas to allocate a church for their worship, a storm broke out. In the presence of both the emperor and the army commander, Chrysostom spoke at great length, reproaching Gainas for not acknowledging that Theodosius I had elevated him, and adding it was Theodosius who had made the law that no church in the city could be given over to heretical (heterodox) worship. In response, Gainas threatened the city, and in particular its bankers and commercial district.[22] John stood his ground, reminding Gainas that previously he had been "a rough-clad, penniless barbarian, whereas he was now a commander-in-chief worthy of the Consul's robe of office".[23] He had freely sworn allegiance to Theodosius. Was he now to turn his back on his oath of allegiance to the former emperor? Word got round the city that John had emphatically rebuked Gainas with his powerful invective. At this point, in July 400, Gainas made the unlikely excuse that he was possessed of an evil spirit and needed to go to a church outside the city for deliverance.[24] He set out for the Church of John the Baptist at Hebdomon on the Via Egnatia, some seven miles west of the city, but the city was suspicious of his intentions.

If Gainas had intended that his army be quietly withdrawn from Constantinople westwards, that is not what happened. The city was already in a high state of alert and anxiety about the troops, and news had circulated about Chrysostom's confrontation with Gainas. Commands had no doubt been misunderstood or badly communicated and the troops did not withdraw quietly and instead began to attack their billets.[25] Violence escalated among the exasperated residents and a panicky army. In effect, there was a popular uprising against the Goths, the city gates were shut, and thousands of Goths took sanctuary in a city church close to the palace. In an equally panicky response, the emperor ordered the destruction of the Goths and the church was set alight. On 12 July 400, the church was torched and thousands perished inside in a terrible holocaust. It was not the result that John had wanted or prayed for. If John had opposed Gainas and his demand for Arian worship, he had neither sought nor connived at this terrible destruction. He wanted their salvation, not their destruction, but a combination of mass panic and imperial haste had produced an awful result. Even the pagan historian Zosimus took the view that Christians would have been horrified at this desecration of a church,[26] and John would surely have been equally shocked by this violation of the important principle of sanctuary he had upheld earlier to protect Eutropius.

The aftermath of this event was no less shocking. With a large section of the army he commanded still intact, Gainas marched into Thrace, burning, pillaging and ravaging as he went. Punishment was inflicted on an innocent population in the name of revenge. Meanwhile, despite Arcadius garnering popular support at the destruction of the Goths, his administration, led by Caesarius, dithered. They were opposed by Eudoxia, and by the previous administration led by Aurelianus, the brother and political foe of Caesarius, who had been deposed by Gainas earlier in the year. Once again, the fearless John was despatched as a negotiator between the court and Gainas, who had by this time been declared a public enemy by the emperor.[27] What followed was an extraordinary meeting. Gainas came out from his camp to meet John, and such was his regard for the man of God, he asked John to bless him and pray for his children. Although the specific outcome of this meeting and talks are unknown, it seems that the emperor wanted Gainas to return as the commander of the army, however unpalatable that might be, in exchange for Aurelianus being reappointed prefect.

John's diplomacy on this occasion failed. Gainas could not be induced to return and continued laying waste to Thrace. But in due course a new army was assembled by the emperor and led by another barbarian general, Flavita, who defeated Gainas as he tried to cross the Hellespont into Asia. Prevented from getting into Asia, Gainas escaped north into upper Thrace, where he was confronted by the Hunnic chieftain Uldin, based in present-day eastern Romania, and finally defeated.[28] Despite John's failure to bring about a negotiated settlement in almost impossible conditions, through his supreme detachment from the purely political struggle of his day, he had shown his ability to act trenchantly in the wider interests of the orthodoxy and orthopraxy of the Church.[29] While in late 400 his stock had never been higher in the city and at court, he was to make a fatal enemy of the rising power at court, the empress, by resisting her favourites and criticizing her way of life.

The empress: Aelia Eudoxia

It must be something of a truism that leaving their place of work for a long period of time renders leaders vulnerable to a diminution of influence at best, and loss of position at worst. At the invitation of the churches in Asia, which needed support and resolution of inner conflicts at the time, John had left Constantinople for three months at the start of 402. The intricacies and intrigues of this tour we shall return to shortly, but the upshot of his absence was a weakened position at court, and particularly with the empress, whose voice was becoming increasingly important both at court and in the government generally.

The Empress Eudoxia had married Arcadius, the second son of Theodosius I, in April 395, three months after the death of her father-in-law from an oedema on 17 January that year. It seems that Aelia Eudoxia's own father, one Flavius Bauto of Romano-Frankish descent, who was the *magister militum* (head of the army) in the West, had died some years before her marriage, and Eudoxia had been brought up in the household of Promotus, the equivalent *magister militum* in the Eastern empire. It was there that she would have come to know the future Emperor Arcadius and also Eutropius, the chief official and chamberlain at the court. It was Eutropius who proposed the marriage between Eudoxia and Arcadius, rather than have her marry into the family of Rufinus, the ambitious Prefect of the East. Rufinus would come to an untimely end at the hands of the Praetorian Guard on suspicion of imperial ambition and of whipping up the Huns to invade the empire.[30] Eudoxia and Arcadius were both about 18 years old at the time of their marriage and, according to the historian Zosimus, Arcadius was entranced by her beauty.[31] Of the two, Eudoxia was the stronger character and soon came to influence her husband, especially after the fall of Eutropius.

By the end of 400, Eudoxia's influence was on the rise. She had weathered the threat of Gainas and seen the return to court of Aurelianus, her preferred choice for Prefect. "Eudoxia and her allies [now] dominated the government of the East for the next four years."[32] These would be tempestuous years for John and the court, not least with Eudoxia herself. In the same period, Eudoxia would give birth to four of her five surviving children including Pulcheria (399–453), who would herself become *augusta* during the minority of Theodosius II (401–50).

Whatever else may be said of Eudoxia, her children would show remarkable loyalty and commitment to the Church and its teaching in the half century ahead, especially in the controversy over the person of Christ that led to the Council of Chalcedon. Pulcheria would remain committed to the life of a virgin, as would her sisters, and even though as an empress or *augusta* she married Marcion, who by virtue of their marriage became emperor. She insisted, aged 50, on remaining celibate. Equally, Theodosius II, Eudoxia's son, became one of the greatest Byzantine rulers. What they must have inherited from their mother was a steely determination, mixed in her case with a degree of hauteur and fieriness which led to the tragic clash with Chrysostom. Eudoxia was in that line of empresses who greatly influenced Roman rule in the fourth and fifth centuries. Her half-sister-in-law, Galla Placidia, whose tomb resides in a remarkably decorated mausoleum in Ravenna, was, in her words, a "blood-sister" of her half-brother Emperor Honorius of the West. Galla Placidia likewise saw her status as entitling her to intervene in the affairs of the Church, although to a much greater and more beneficial effect.[33] Eudoxia's interventions in church matters in Constantinople fatefully occurred when John took himself off for nearly four months on his ecclesiastical mission to Asia Minor.

This tour was opposed on other grounds (as we shall see), but in appointing as his deputy a popular Syrian bishop named Severian, who was especially liked by Eudoxia, John opened up the possibility for a new area of tension between himself and the empress. What made matters worse was that Severian was appointed to a public role involving preaching and presiding at the Eucharist, but the levers of power in the diocese were left with Serapion, an unordained archdeacon with a great deal of dislike for Severian, who managed affairs in John's absence and reported to him. This combination of circumstances and personalities laid the basis for a conflagration over an incident, trivial in itself, but which, given this background, was blown up out of all proportion.[34] To an English reader, the incident has a positively Trollopian feel to it, but its effect was all too real.

The historian Socrates records the incident in two of his works: once in a fragment of the first edition of his *History,* which is now almost entirely lost, and again in a second, later, revised edition.[35] Both records agree about the substance of the rift. One day when Serapion was seated, Severian walked past him, and Serapion conspicuously failed to rise, "indicating" according to Socrates "how little Serapion cared for [Severian's] presence".[36] Insulted by this lack of respect, Severian is reported to have said, "If Serapion should die a Christian, Christ has not become incarnate."[37] Serapion then twisted these words in his report to John, making out that Severian had simply said, "Christ had not become incarnate." He then charged Severian as a heretic interested only in making money out of the churches of Constantinople. In one of his accounts, Socrates made out that, on his return to Constantinople, John held an enquiry which upheld the charge of heresy and Severian was sent packing back to Syria. It is more likely that Severian was simply asked to leave, but when the empress heard about this she strongly objected, having taken a liking to Severian's demeanour and preaching, and kept him at court.

Although sent back to his diocese in Syria by John, Severian had not gone far and was staying with Bishop Cyrinus, who was to become an implacable opponent of John's in the near future.[38] John had to agree to Eudoxia's instruction countermanding his own and was forced to invite Severian to return. The affair did not end there. Given to theatrical and emotional gestures, and not wanting to alienate John, Eudoxia sought him out in the Church of the Holy Apostles, placed her son, the future Theodosius II, in his lap, and implored him to be reconciled to Severian in a public act of reconciliation to demonstrate to the people their accord.

A service was arranged in the Great Church to enact a public reconciliation, as the rift between the two men had become so public that it was deemed necessary to publicly assuage the feelings of the populace. "A spectacular liturgical celebration lasting two days was arranged", in which the two bishops pledged themselves to unity and harmony.[39] In his opening address, Severian describes John and himself as two brothers or magistrates, who, although physically separate, are bound together by the female figure of Concordia (presumably the empress herself) standing between them.[40] Indeed, this very idea of harmony was modelled by the two emperors, Arcadius and Honorius, who ruled harmoniously over the empire, East and West. In this comparison, Severian intimates that John and himself are merely following the example of the august co-emperors, who have chosen to rule jointly and amicably. John himself also preached on the first day, but in a rather begrudging and cool manner, clearly impelled by Eudoxia, but in his heart still harbouring deep reservations about Severian and his ambition. Nevertheless, in his peroration John called on the congregation to set aside any excited feelings, to put a curb on their indignation at any presumption on Severian's part, and to continue to give obedience and devotion to himself, their bishop.[41] Describing himself as an ambassador seeking peace, he called upon the congregation to receive Severian back, concluding: "If then I have prepared your minds to accept my petition as an ambassador, receive back our brother Severian." At this point, there was a burst of applause. John continued: "Even as I spoke, you expelled all your anger from your minds. So, receive him back with full hearts and open minds. Overlook and forget the wretched events of the past: when the moment of peace has arrived, there should be no remembrance of divisions."[42] Severian then responded with his usual eloquence, comparing this altercation with John to the difference between Paul and Barnabas described in Acts (15:36–41), drawing out the point that such conflict had existed between those two also, great though they were. On occasions in his sermon, Severian refers to John as "our common father", and presumably with reference to his undoubted oratorical skill, as "the divine trumpet". But in general, it was a lengthy and well-constructed call to peace, reminding the congregation that Christ "himself is our peace, who has made the two groups one" (Ephesians 2:14). Any dissension that had come between them was, he said, the work of the devil, and if it was acknowledged and resisted, peace would reign.

Although John had reluctantly agreed to stage this public act of reconciliation for the empress's sake, their hearts remained at odds. Socrates tells us:

> In this manner then these two men were outwardly reconciled, but they nevertheless continued cherishing a rancorous feeling

toward each other, such was the origin of the animosity of John against Severian.[43]

John was now entering turbulent waters. Severian would remain in Constantinople as a thorn in his side (see 2 Corinthians 12:7). Severian was on terms with the imperial court. His eloquence won him admirers. He was confident of his position. He became a key figure and the focus for all the intrigues and plots against John. Furthermore, John had opened himself up to wider criticism through his intervention in church affairs in Asia Minor. Indeed, while John was away for the first few months of 402, ironically it was Severian who had been appointed to look after the diocese of Constantinople. John's appointee turned out to be his adversary, and the intervention in Asia also turned out to further inflame church leaders in the region and beyond in Alexandria. The empress was an increasingly powerful influence at court, at best nurtured and listened to, but given her sex, her youth, her sway over the emperor, her admiration of Severian, the much older and more experienced John might have chosen to deflect her passions or gain her ear. Instead, it appears that John made an enemy of her. In the context of Roman politics, this was foolhardy at best; at worst it was tragic. It was always unlikely that the emperor would isolate or criticize his wife. Thus, John's position and vision for the Church was being rapidly undermined by poor human management and a hectoring style that worked against the very things he hoped to achieve. Things would only get worse.

Notes

1   William Shakespeare, *Hamlet*, Act 4, Scene 1.
2   *Propt. fornic* 5, cited in De Wet, Chris L., *Preaching Bondage: John Chrysostom and the Discourse of Slavery in Early Christianity* (Berkeley, CA: University of California Press, 2015), pp. 256–60.
3   *In Eutropium* 1.299–307, cited by Christopher Kelly, "Emperors, government and bureaucracy", in A. Cameron and P. Garnsey (eds), *The Cambridge Ancient History, Vol. XIII* (Cambridge: Cambridge University Press, 1998), p. 176.
4   J. N. D. Kelly, *Golden Mouth: The Story of John Chrysostom, Ascetic, Preacher, Bishop* (Ithaca, NY: Cornell University Press, 1998), p. 146.
5   Socrates, *Ecclesiastical History* VI.5, in *Nicene and Post-Nicene Fathers: Second Series, Vol. II: Socrates, Sozomenus: Church Histories*, ed. Philip Schaff (Grand Rapids, MI: Eerdmans, 1987), p. 140.
6   Kelly, *Golden Mouth*, p. 147.
7   Wendy Mayer and Pauline Allen, *Against the Jews* I, in *John Chrysostom* (London: Routledge, 2000), pp. 132–3.
8   Mayer and Allen, *Chrysostom*, p. 134.
9   Mayer and Allen, *Chrysostom*, p. 137.
10 Mayer and Allen, *Chrysostom*, p. 138.
11 Mayer and Allen, *Chrysostom*, pp. 138–9.
12 Zosimus, *Historia Nova*, ed. I. Bekker, *Corpus Scriptorium Historiae Byzantinae* (Bonn, 1837), p. 269.
13 Kelly, *Golden Mouth*, pp. 149–50.
14 Socrates, *Ecclesiastical History* VI.5.5, op. cit., p. 140.
15 Kelly, *Golden Mouth*, p. 152.
16 Socrates, *Ecclesiastical History* VI.5, op. cit., p. 141.
17 Sozomen, *Ecclesiastical History* VIII.4, in *Nicene and Post-Nicene Fathers: Second Series, Vol. II: Socrates, Sozomenus: Church Histories*, ed. Philip Schaff (Grand Rapids, MI: Eerdmans, 1987), p. 401.
18 Kelly, *Golden Mouth*, p. 154.
19 Chrysostom, *De capto Eutropio*, PG 52, pp. 395–414.
20 Kelly, *Golden Mouth*, p. 155.
21 Sozomen, *Ecclesiastical History* VI.37, op. cit., p. 373, and VIII.4, op. cit., p. 401.
22 Sozomen, *Ecclesiastical History* VIII.4, op. cit., p. 403.
23 Kelly, *Golden Mouth*, p. 158.

24. Sozomen, VIII.4, op. cit., p. 401.
25. Kelly, *Golden Mouth*, p. 159.
26. Zosimus, *Historia Nova* 5.19.5, op. cit., p. 272.
27. Socrates, *Ecclesiastical History* VI.6, op. cit., p. 142.
28. Socrates, *Ecclesiastical History* VIII.4, op. cit., p. 402.
29. Kelly, *Golden Mouth*, p. 162.
30. Socrates, *Ecclesiastical History* VI.1, op. cit., p. 138.
31. Zosimus, *Historia Nova* 5.1, op. cit., pp. 246ff.
32. R. C. Blockley, "The dynasty of Theodosius", in A. Cameron and P. Garnsey (eds), *The Cambridge Ancient History, Vol. XIII* (Cambridge: Cambridge University Press, 1998), p. 117.
33. Hagith Savin, *Galla Placidia: The Last Roman Empress* (Oxford: Oxford University Press, 2011), p. 76.
34. Kelly, *Golden Mouth*, p. 184.
35. Kelly, *Golden Mouth*, p. 184 and *PG* 67, pp. 696–700.
36. Socrates, *Ecclesiastical History* VI.11, op. cit., p. 146.
37. Socrates, *Ecclesiastical History* VI.12, op. cit., p. 146.
38. Kelly, *Golden Mouth*, p. 185.
39. Kelly, *Golden Mouth*, p. 186.
40. *PG* 52, pp. 426–7.
41. *PG* 52, pp. 425–8.
42. *PG* 52, pp. 428ff.
43. Socrates, *Ecclesiastical History* VI.11, op. cit., p. 147.

10

Ecclesiastical politics

Constantinople's precedence in ecclesiastical politics was growing but contested. The city, after all, had only been formally founded by Constantine in 330 and had grown to a position of eminence largely because of imperial patronage. It rapidly became a large city of over 200,000 inhabitants; its buildings spoke of imperial power; its churches would become some of the most prestigious in Christendom; and its reach extended east to Persia and west to Greece. And now, with the Eastern emperor residing there, it was bound to attract leaders from both within and without the Church. In fact, even before John's appointment as bishop, church leaders gravitated towards the new capital, which would overtake Antioch in significance, surpass Ephesus, the ancient centre of the Church from Apostolic times (see Acts 19:1–41), and vie with Alexandria for precedence in the eastern Mediterranean.

The see of Alexandria was conscious of this, and whenever a vacancy occurred in the bishopric of Constantinople, sought to suggest or impose its own candidate to the office. This happened at the time of Gregory of Nazianzus, before the final appointment of Nectarius (bishop 381–97) when it forcefully and slyly proposed Maximus. Likewise, when John succeeded Nectarius, Alexandria had promoted its own candidate, Isidore, at an informal synod held by the young Emperor Arcadius.[1] Although Theophilus had opposed John's selection, he was coerced by Eutropius to accept this decision with the threat of some treasonable correspondence that had fallen into Eutropius's hands being made public.[2] Because of these deeply embarrassing revelations, Theophilus withdrew his candidacy of Isidore and supported John. Having suffered this humiliation, however, Theophilus would look for an opportunity in the future to unsettle John, and reimpose a candidate promoted by Alexandria.

At the same time as Constantinople's rise to political eminence, it also became an ecclesiastical centre, at first informally by virtue of the presence of imperial power, and by 451, more formally, with its establishment as a Patriarchate at the Council of Chalcedon. It was in Constantinople that the Nicene Creed of 325 was both affirmed and expanded at a council in 381, becoming the Niceno-Constantinopolitan Creed. While Chalcedon would recognize *de jure* the creation of the archdiocese of the see of Constantinople in its 28th Canon,[3] from the accession of Theodosius in 379 onwards, this was already *de facto* the case. Something of an informal synod would meet in Constantinople whenever there were problems in the region.[4] This was composed of the bishops from outlying dioceses in the East, temporarily resident in Constantinople to seek the emperor's help in resolving various issues. Needless to say, these supplicant bishops were generally referred to the Bishop of Constantinople. As Anatolius, a later Bishop of Constantinople, said, "It is a time-honoured custom that the reverend bishops visiting our famous city should meet together when occasion demands to resolve ecclesiastical disputes and causes, and to give answers to petitioners".[5] It was one such fateful petition in April 400, soon after resolving the conflict with Gainas and the Goths, that drew John into an affair that largely shaped his future for his remaining years.

A call to wider pastoral supervision

One Sunday morning, probably in April 400, John was about to begin the liturgy in the Great Church, later Hagia Sophia, when he was accosted by a number of bishops seeking resolution of an issue.[6] The bishops, Palladius tells us, included three elderly metropolitans from Ephesus, Scythia and Thrace, respectively. One of the suffragan bishops, Eusebius, Bishop of Valentinopolis, proceeded to make violent protestations against the behaviour of his own diocesan bishop, Antoninus of Ephesus, one of the oldest sees in Asia. John asked him to desist from such intemperate attacks on a senior pastor. This was unseemly, especially before the celebration of the liturgy in the Great Church. Eusebius brought seven charges against his bishop, some of them quite bizarre. The second charge was that he had used some of the marble from the baptistery for his own bathroom. Likewise, in the third charge, he was accused of stealing columns from the church and putting them in his own dining-room![7] Furthermore, one of his slaves, it was alleged, had committed a murder, but was still retained on the bishop's staff! And lastly, he had taken back the wife from whom he had separated when made a bishop and resumed sexual relations with her. But perhaps worst of all to his colleagues, he had sold holy orders. Palladius tells us that John asked Eusebius to stop making these serious accusations, particularly just before the liturgy. But Eusebius was not so easily silenced and choosing his moment carefully for effect, interrupted the liturgy and "adjured John with terrible menaces"[8] to take these charges further. John was so taken aback and shocked that he excused himself from taking the liturgy and asked the Bishop of Pisidia to celebrate instead. Clearly something needed to be done.

Initially, John sought to contain the dispute. He asked another bishop, Paul of Heraklion, to investigate the charges. But then, on the advice of other bishops present in Constantinople for an informal synod, it was agreed to look into those charges that could be most swiftly dealt with, in particular the charge that Antoninus had sold bishoprics to some of the bishops present. Of course, they denied it, and Eusebius was unable to bring forward any incontrovertible evidence that money had changed hands. At this point, and perhaps tempted by the prospect of a wider sphere of influence than Constantinople and its environs, John announced that he would leave the city, and conduct an investigation himself. This was not to be, however. He was needed in Constantinople by the emperor for the crisis with Gainas and the Goths, and in particular for negotiating with Gainas to end the crisis. In John's place, three senior clerics were sent to investigate the claims. These were Synkletius of Thrace, Hesychius of the Hellespont, and John's biographer Palladius of Bithynia. They were to undertake interrogations in a town between Ephesus and Sardis, with the procedure resembling the sort of imperial investigation that had happened in Antioch following the toppling of the statues of the imperial family. Failure to show up within two months of being called to the enquiry would result in excommunication.

The enquiry soon began to unravel, and for all its good intentions was frustrated by a number of events. One of the commissioners, Hesychius, a friend of Antoninus, dropped out, and none of the witnesses appeared. Eusebius was bought off by Antoninus. In the meantime, the remaining two commissioners gave Eusebius more time to appear with witnesses, but he failed to do so and was excommunicated. Wearied by the heat and the process, the two commissioners returned to Constantinople empty-handed.[9] If nothing else, the saga gives the observer of fourth-century church life the impression of how open to abuse it was and how hard it was to ascertain the truth. It seemed like something of an ecclesiastical "wild west".

The second stage of this bizarre affair was about to begin, drawing John further into its orbit, and with fateful repercussions. At some point in the ensuing months of 400, Antoninus died, and a further request came to John to intervene and settle the issues that had arisen in the Church in Ephesus and Asia. John may have left the capital either at Epiphany on 6 January 401 or, according to Palladius, more probably a year later, in the winter of 402, in order to take up the call of overseeing the Church in Asia.[10] Indeed, there is evidence that John was present in Constantinople at the birth of Eudoxia and Arcadius's only son, the future Theodosius II, on 10 April 401, so his trip must have started after that. Furthermore, it seems that John most likely set off soon after 6 January 402, when the emperor's son, later Theodosius II, was baptized in the Great Church and almost certainly by John. The baptism would have been a state and religious occasion of awesome magnificence. In a later message to John at the start of his first exile (from which she excuses herself), Eudoxia recalls it, describing John as the respected baptizer of her children.[11] If these dates are right, then John only had from early January until soon after Easter 402 to undertake his enquiry and settle the affairs of the province of Asia, and the Church in Ephesus in particular. Whatever the precise date of John's departure, he appointed Severian as his deputizing bishop, overseen (or reported on) by Archdeacon Serapion, who was given administrative control of the diocese. This was to be a fateful step, as we have seen, and indeed John's absence from Constantinople from January to late April 402 allowed opposition to emerge against him, as so often happens when controversial leaders leave their posts.

John probably then set sail from Constantinople on or around 7 January 402, despite his bad health and the winter season, in order to tend to affairs in the "province of Asia", whose health was still worse than his own.[12] Never well at the best of times, recent events and the earlier neglect of his own body had made John vulnerable to disease. Because of the wintry time of year, a violent north wind blew up and made them shelter by the island of Proconese, although two days later they were able to reach Apamea, where they were met by Palladius, the bishop of nearby Helenopolis, Cyrinus, bishop of Chalcedon, and Paul, bishop of Heraklea. Together they formed a commission of enquiry and travelled on by road to Ephesus.[13]

The main business in Ephesus was to elect a new bishop in place of Antoninus, who had been so roundly accused of corruption by his suffragan, Eusebius. To this end John summoned a council of bishops from the provinces of Lydia, Phrygia and Caria in the Roman civil diocese of Asia. Among these bishops were some who had no right to elect a new bishop of Ephesus and were simply there to listen to the wisdom of John. In fact, no consensus emerged and the council ended in deadlock. John suggested the appointment of Herakleides, a Cypriot who had spent some years with Evagrius Ponticus (345–99) in the Egyptian desert and who had been his own assistant in Constantinople. Although the new bishop was settled, the appointment was problematic for three reasons.

Firstly, Herakleides was deeply influenced by Origen through the teaching of his mentor, Evagrius, an associate of Rufinus and Melania in Jerusalem who had later retreated to the Egyptian desert. Evagrius was one of the foremost scholars of his age and an ascetic. He was, however, also a follower of Origen, himself increasingly suspect in the Church because of his Platonism. And while Evagrius was a brilliant scholar and an eloquent speaker, his commitment to Basil of Caesarea and Gregory of Nazianzus, two of the Cappadocian Fathers, did not mask his underlying Origenism and this made him mistrusted in Ephesus.

Secondly, an appointment by John extended the influence of the Bishop of Constantinople into the Province of Asia, something eyed with deep suspicion by the see of Alexandria. And lastly, the appointment was not popular in Ephesus itself. Indeed, while Palladius, always a staunch supporter of John, passes over the appointment in silence, in a fragment of his history not included in the final edition of that work, Socrates writes of rioting in the streets of Ephesus at news of Herakleides's appointment.[14] Any high-handedness on the part of John was compounded by his deposition of other bishops, including an influential but erratic man, Gerontius, who had been blackballed by Ambrose, Bishop of Milan. John now deposed him along with 13 other bishops in the region.[15] While there were good reasons for doing so (probably for simony, cf. Acts 8:18–19), John's right to depose anyone at all came under question.

Much as when John came to Constantinople from Antioch as the harbinger of change in 399, so too he aimed to bring a new broom and clear out corruption in the province of Asia. Once again, although such action was in a sense unexceptional, the question had to do with his authority for acting in this way. The answer is probably that he came with the emperor's support and at the invitation of the churches, and in particularly Eusebius, who had laid serious charges against the former bishop, Antoninus. Having made the appointment of the new bishop of Ephesus, however unpopular he proved to be, and having deposed other bishops for corruption, John now moved to the main purpose of his visit, which was to investigate the charge of simony made by Eusebius against several bishops in the area. Antoninus had already died and the accusations that he had embellished his house at the expense of the church and lived with a woman who had once been his wife had died with him.[16]

John's investigation of corruption

Alongside the appointment of Herakleides as the new Bishop of Ephesus, and the appointments of at least six new bishops in place of the 13 who had been deposed for simony, John now had to instigate an enquiry into the charges Eusebius had levelled against the bishop of Ephesus and the church there. Although Antoninus had died, and his replacement, however unpopular, had been appointed, there were still outstanding charges to be answered, particularly those of further simony in the western part of the civil diocese of Asia (or Asiana).[17] At this reconvening of the Council of Enquiry, which was made up of 70 church leaders, including Eusebius, the instigator of the charges, and which included some of the accused, witnesses this time came forward. The witnesses were able to supply information about the dates, places and sums of money given by men for their appointments. Although at first those accused denied complicity, in light of the precise evidence given by witnesses they caved in, pleading they had sought to become bishops to avoid the taxes imposed on minor officials and councillors in their communities—for bishops were exempt from tax in view of their responsibilities. Constantine had exempted bishops from such payments, but this had created an opportunity for the less scrupulous clergy and officials to seek episcopacy for their own advantage.[18] It was, in other words, a kind of tax avoidance, in which payment of a single sum to become a bishop vitiated the requirement to pay municipal taxes. This practice seems to have become widespread. It seems that Antonius did indeed run a racket from Ephesus and took numerous lump sums from candidates in exchange for bishoprics. But now, if their appointments were to be rescinded, they demanded the return of the money they had paid, including any jewellery or personal belongings of their wives which had also been handed over to Antoninus!

In the event, John was not too severe towards the culprits. They were stripped of office but were allowed to remain in the sanctuary of the church, where the senior clergy sat during the liturgy. Furthermore, John even interceded with the emperor to see if those who had committed simony might still be exempted municipal taxes. While this seems unusually clement of John, he may have thought that this more lenient approach would encourage others guilty of simony to come forward in confession, and in this way excise this canker from the higher echelons of the Church. Six new bishops were consecrated as a result of the enquiry, which meant that together with the other 13 appointments made in the civil diocese of Asiana, John's actions had been cathartic, cleansing and comprehensive.

John now made his way back to Constantinople by road, since the sea voyage was not recommended in March. However, Socrates tells us that before he began that journey he closed down many churches belonging to the Novatians and Quartodecimans.[19] The Novatians were a sect, who, in following their founder Novatian, an antipope in the third century, took an uncompromising line towards any "lapsed" Christians (i.e., those who had burnt incense to the gods or called the emperor a god) and refused them membership of the Church. The Quartodecimans celebrated Good Friday on the same day as the Passover (14 Nisan), regardless of whether or not Easter day fell on a Sunday. Both communities were harshly treated by John, and in the case of the Novatians, who had been given special privileges by Theodosius I, doing so only built up resentment back in Constantinople where, as we have seen, the Novatians under Bishop Sisinnius had been given privileges by the emperor.[20] Furthermore, on the way back to Constantinople, John deposed the popular but highly erratic Bishop Gerontius of Nicomedia, previously exiled by Ambrose from Milan, and replaced him with Pansophius, an irenic and scholarly friend of the empress. Pansophius did not appeal to the populace of Nicomedia, however, who then rioted and complained to the emperor. Nonetheless, John was seen to have taken decisive action in the best interests of the Church.

When John reached Constantinople soon after Easter 402, he probably felt the tour had been a success. He had responded to the request that he intervene in the Church's affairs in Asia and had sought to remedy the effects of abuses of power, and in particular the creeping corruption of simony. Many bishops had been deposed, but without bitter recriminations and with a degree of clemency. Appointments had also been made, not least in Ephesus, which caused more lasting resentment. If John had not been acting in isolation, but with the backing of the emperor, he might well have spread the authority of his see over the regions south of the city and in the emperor's nearby bailiwick. But ecclesiastical politics were complicated. John appeared to be gaining authority and this was resented, not by Antioch, the oldest archbishopric in the region, but by Alexandria. Under Athanasius, Alexandria had led the charge to maintain the orthodoxy of the Church against the incursions of Arianism and had maintained and helped redefine the doctrine of the Trinity. But now a new enemy had been identified in the Eastern Church, and that was Origen. Origen, brilliant, deeply philosophical, greatly influenced by Platonism, and an adherent of the spiritualizing of Scripture, had become a bête noire of the Alexandrian school in the time of Bishop Theophilus. Origen's teaching was increasingly, and tragically, seen as a poisoned well in the formulations of orthodoxy. By promoting a new bishop of Ephesus who was more than sympathetic to Origen, John was in danger of sailing into a new theological storm. Not only this, but his position in Constantinople had been weakened by his treatment of the Novatians, his three-month absence, the growing court influence of Bishop Severian, and the coalescence of those he had offended with his reforms in the city.

Provided he still had the wholehearted support of the emperor his reforms and tenure were viable; but should the empress throw herself in with his opponents, his position would become precarious. In other words, by allowing himself to be cast as an opponent of Eastern orthodoxy through his indirect support of Origen, he had imperilled the great vision he had for the city based on thoroughgoing biblical teaching and the use of an inspiring liturgy. In less than two years he would be exiled, and in five he would be dead, aged 58. He was about to sense a gathering storm, the danger of which he was as yet barely aware of. So focused was he on delivering what he perceived to be true, that he was almost naively unaware of the machinations of others against him. He was treading the path of a storm, with no idea where it would eventually lead.

Notes

1. J. N. D. Kelly, *Golden Mouth: The Story of John Chrysostom, Ascetic, Preacher, Bishop* (Ithaca, NY: Cornell University Press, 1998), p. 106.
2. See Socrates VI.2 for an account of this background to the election of John.
3. ACO II.1.388–9.
4. Kelly, *Golden Mouth*, p. 128.
5. Kelly, *Golden Mouth*, p. 129, and citing A. Grillmeier and H. Bacht, *Das Konzil von Chalkedon* II (Würzburg: Echter, 1953), pp. 472–4.
6. Palladius, *Dialogues*, in *Dialogue sur la vie de Jean Chrysostome/Palladios*, ed. and tr. Anne-Marie Malingrey with Philippe Leclercq, *SC* 341, Vol. 4 (Paris: Les Éditions du Cerf, 1988), p. 275.
7. Palladius, op. cit., p. 275.
8. Palladius, op. cit., p. 279.
9. Palladius, op. cit., p. 285.
10. Kelly, *Golden Mouth*, p. 166.
11. Sozomen, *Ecclesiastical History* VIII.18, *Nicene and Post-Nicene Fathers: Second Series, Vol. II: Socrates, Sozomenus: Church Histories*, ed. Philip Schaff (Grand Rapids, MI: Eerdmans, 1987), p. 411.
12. Palladius, op. cit., p. 288.
13. Palladius, op. cit., p. 288.
14. Kelly, *Golden Mouth*, p. 175.
15. Sozomen, *Ecclesiastical History* VIII.4, op. cit., p. 403.
16. Palladius, op. cit., p. 277.
17. Kelly, *Golden Mouth*, p. 174.
18. Theodosian Code 16:2, 21 October 319.
19. Socrates, *Ecclesiastical History* VI.19, op. cit., p. 151.
20. Socrates, *Ecclesiastical History* VI.22, op. cit., p. 152.

11

The gathering storm

It is worth reminding ourselves that the fourth and fifth centuries were quite unlike our own times. The holy men of the period had concerns about diet, sleep and sexual intercourse that are strange to our minds. The authority of leaders meant either a gateway to life or a door to effective isolation. Power was respected and feared. Emperors had almost untrammelled authority, provided they had the character and skill to project it militarily or through existing institutions. At their best, bishops combined a world-denying spirituality with expectations of total obedience; many of them were in heart and in reality monks. And yet this spiritual and political edifice was precarious. Only recently in 378 in the East, Roman arms had been comprehensively defeated by Goths at Adrianople before Theodosius re-established power and installed his family as the last dynasty of the Roman Empire. But even that was to be short-lived in the West, as Rome would fall to another invasion by the Visigoths under Alaric in 410.

Just eight years earlier, a strange group of monks called the Tall Brothers had turned up on the streets of Constantinople like some early-day asylum seekers. They were fleeing the dictates of an imperious bishop of Alexandria called Theophilus (whose name means "lover of God") and were looking for material and spiritual help from the emperor in the face of persecution for unlikely causes.

The Tall Brothers (literally *makroi adelphoi*), so named because of their height, were part of the upsurge of Egyptian monasticism. This form of monasticism had started at the very end of the third century during Diocletian's Great Persecution and had resulted in various types of withdrawal into the Egyptian desert. The seeds were sown by two people of totally different religious views: Plotinus, the Neo-Platonist philosopher, and Antony, the monk, and the movement would go on to shape Christian Egyptian asceticism, and much of monasticism in both East and West.[1]

The Tall Brothers, who were part of this fourth-century monastic movement, had settled in the southwest of the Nile Delta at Kellia of Wadi Natrun (the Cells) and had become a prominent part of the group led by Evagrius Ponticus (345–99), himself one of the founders of monastic mysticism.[2] Elsewhere, monks and church leaders in both Syria and Cappadocia followed a similar path, not least Gregory of Nyssa, who expressed this type of devotional spirituality in his own profound work on the Song of Songs, a seminal text in Christian mysticism. Likewise, the Tall Brothers had become followers of Origen in terms of their understanding of God, and for this some of them were excommunicated by Theophilus, the Patriarch of Alexandria.[3] At this stage, it does not appear that Theophilus was completely opposed to Origen, but he had nevertheless sided with the more literalistic monks in Egypt, those who believed in an anthropomorphized God with the corporeal attributes of a human being: eyes, hands, ears and mouth. This view hardly sits well with the biblical revelation (John 4:24). The reason for Theophilus's support of these monks may have been political, not theological. In other words, he wanted them on his side and was prepared to indulge their theological eccentricities to do so. He may well have dressed up his objections to the Tall Brothers theologically, in order to use their mild Origenist tendencies against them.

There was by now a movement against Origen spreading through the Church, and there were good theological reasons for this. Put simply, Origen was part biblical scholar and part Platonist. Because of his Platonism, Origen did not believe that God created the universe *ex nihilo*, but that instead he used a substance already in existence. Furthermore, he attributed souls to almost all creatures and entities, including the heavenly bodies such as the moon and the stars. He believed that there was an outer superficial significance to Scripture, but also an inner mystical sense with a more profound meaning (a soul principle). Origen thus always looked for the inner spiritual meaning of biblical texts, even when it was something as simple as a place name or historical fact.[4] It was Origen's eschatology, however, that provided the greatest challenge to Christian orthodoxy. He taught that in the end everything would be reconciled, and that all things would be returned to how they were at the beginning. In other words, he professed what came to called "universalism", where evil was not judged and excluded, but redeemed and reconciled. This seemed quite contrary to Christian apocalyptic teaching as set out in the book of Revelation. For these reasons, those who in their teaching or spirituality followed Origen, as very many did—because of his inspiring example (he was probably martyred); because of his rigorous asceticism (including his self-castration); and because of his scholarship, biblical teaching and devotion to the Bible (being proficient in Greek, Hebrew and Syriac and translating the Jewish Scriptures)—became suspect. Among them were the Tall Brothers.

While Theophilus gave the impression that his objection to the Tall Brothers was due to their Origenism, in fact his reason for pursuing them had murkier causes. But in pinpointing and advertising their Origenism, Theophilus gained wider support in his campaign against them.

The Tall Brothers were headed by Dioskorus, who had been the Bishop of Hermopolis (Damanshir), a small area southeast of Alexandria, and by Ammonius, Eusebius and Euthymius. These four were the leaders of this community,[5] but more than that, as Socrates, the historian, tells us: "They were distinguished both by the sanctity of their lives, and the extent of their erudition, and for these very reasons their reputation was very high in Alexandria."[6] A trigger for their dispute with Theophilus was the decision by Eusebius and Euthymius to leave Theophilus's service and return to the desert.

It transpired, however, that there was a deeper reason for their departure, which subsequently came to light and which Socrates sees as Theophilus's "devotion to gain and greedy intent of the acquisition of wealth".[7] Indeed, Socrates says, no stone was left unturned in the pursuit of money-making schemes by Theophilus. It had reached the point where the Tall Brothers feared that this desire infected even their very own souls. When Theophilus discovered their reason for leaving and learnt of their criticism of him he began a full-scale campaign against them. He did this by attacking their Origenist tendencies, and in particular their view that God the Father lacked the human attributes of hands, eyes, ears and mouth. In making this his main disagreement with them,

Theophilus masked the true nature of the rift and gave the impression that at root it was a theological dispute. Monastic communities that held to this anthropomorphic view of God then closed their doors to the Tall Brothers as heretics, and they became vagrants.

Theophilus then broke fellowship with his guest-master Isidore—who had been his trusted colleague and who Theophilus had nominated as bishop of Constantinople before John's appointment—for even more squalid reasons. Ordained by Athanasius, Isidore was the godliest of men.[8] According to Palladius, Isidore had been entrusted by a rich widow with 1,000 gold staters to give to the poor. She insisted that Theophilus was not to know about this gift in case he siphoned off the money for his building projects, for which he was notorious. Nevertheless, Theophilus got to hear about the gift, was very annoyed that he had been kept in the dark and set about trying to ruin Isidore's reputation. To this end, he published an unsubstantiated account given to him 18 years earlier of Isidore committing buggery with a young sailor and went so far as to circulate it in a pastoral letter to the bishops of Palestine and Cyprus.[9] The now octogenarian Isidore left his post in Alexandria and fled to the Nitrian desert where he found his way to the same monastery as the Tall Brothers. For his part, Theophilus refused the biblical injunction that all revenge belongs to the Lord (see James 4:11,12; Romans 12:19) and conceived instead a cunning way of isolating and judging both the Tall Brothers and Isidore.

It involved using theology as a smokescreen for retribution and settling scores. Knowing that there was a general move in the Church against Origen, and that the Tall Brothers and Isidore could be smeared as Origenistic, Theophilus now made a *volte face* in his prior support of Origen and declared "a holy war on all Origenism and its adherents".[10] He thus began a purge, expelling any abbot or church leader who was in any way an advocate of Origen. When some went to Alexandria to seek clarification about their misdemeanours or complain, they were attacked. Indeed, Theophilus seized Ammonius by the throat, struck him on his face causing his nose to bleed, and shouted in his face, "Anathematize Origen, you heretic!"[11] Palladius said Theophilus had the eyes of an enraged bull. Soon after this Theophilus called a synod in Alexandria to try and formalize his break with all who followed or promoted Origen.

At this event, the Tall Brothers were formally excommunicated and branded as impostors, although until recently they had been highly regarded by him. Yet even this vilification, assault and condemnation of theological views which had recently been his own, was not enough for the archbishop. Theophilus wanted nothing less than the removal and exile of these men from Egypt. To this end he went even further, and called on the authority of the civil power, the Roman prefect of the province of Egypt.

The next step in this vendetta is scarcely believable and is completely removed from the model of leadership held up by Jesus and Paul in the New Testament (see John 13:12–16 or 1 Timothy 3:1–7). Having asked the prefect for military aid in the spring of 400, Theophilus supervised a night attack on the monasteries, using troops and a drunken rabble to drive the Tall Brothers and their supporters from the monasteries. The Tall Brothers were ejected and Theophilus wrote to the bishops saying they were not to entertain or give succour to these heretics, high on Origen.[12] At first, some 300 monks made their way from the Nitrian desert to Jerusalem, a distance of about 700 kilometres. So effective was Theophilus's campaign against them that wherever they went, doors were slammed in their faces, and they could find no permanent, or even semi-permanent lodging or food. At last, the Tall Brothers decided to leave Palestine and sail to Constantinople and submit their case to the emperor.[13] In the meantime, Theophilus had sent requests to the emperor asking that the Tall Brothers be excommunicated, whilst John, agreeing with their orthodox views about the nature of the Godhead, allowed them to pray in his churches, although they were not to participate in the liturgy or receive the sacrament. He himself wrote to Theophilus but received no reply.[14] For his part, Theophilus now wondered how he might remove John from office because of his reported support (some of it much exaggerated by Theophilus's agents) for the Tall Brothers and Isidore.

The dispute moves to Constantinople

The dispute with the Tall Brothers moved now to Constantinople, probably in the autumn or winter of 401, and before John's tour of the churches of Asia to settle the complaints which had been brought to his attention by Eusebius and others. John gave a cautious welcome to the Tall Brothers. Although supportive of their doctrine of God, he was well aware of the danger that Theophilus posed in his deep antipathy towards them. He knew also of the campaign against them from Theophilus's pastoral letters to Cyprus and Palestine. For John, this incipient controversy had at least three principal aspects: the Tall Brothers seeking recognition and justice in the face of overbearing animosity from Theophilus; Theophilus himself, with his growing campaign against them; and the teaching and influence of Origen and the imperial household. When he returned to Constantinople in April 402 where the Tall Brothers had already been waiting several months for a fair hearing of their case, John knew that time was not on his side.

At this point, John's own relations with the court and the empress were more fragile than they had been for some time. While he was away on his Asia tour, as we have seen, Bishop Severian had inveigled himself into the good graces of the empress. More than that, the empress herself had become deeply enmeshed in the attempt to reconcile the two men after John's return and the attempt to send Severian packing. When John had sent Severian back to his diocese in Syria, Eudoxia had sharply rebuked him and had called for a reconciliation between the two men.[15] The two-day liturgy of reconciliation that followed at Eudoxia's request, in which both rivals preached and superficially embraced each other, may have calmed the city and been some kind of victory for Eudoxia, but it did not produce a real rapprochement. Indeed, relations had already worsened between John and the court because of John's earlier accusation that the empress was a latter-day Jezebel! The accusation arose from some shadowy event in which Eudoxia was supposed to have sequestered a widow's field,[16] in much the same way that Jezebel took Naboth's vineyard for King Ahab (see 1 Kings 21:5–16).

It was against this backdrop of a weakening relationship between John and the court that the empress and emperor summoned Theophilus to Constantinople to answer the charges laid against him by the Tall Brothers. In the intervening period Theophilus had come up with a plan to turn the tables on the Brothers and on John also. Theophilus was not a man to be content with half measures. It was he who had led the attack in Alexandria on all its pagan sites. He had incited the destruction of the Serapeum and any remnants of the great Alexandrian library there.[17] Earlier, when threatened with violence by the anthropomorphizing monks who believed God had human features, he was prepared to change his mind to gain their support. He now instigated a full-scale attack on Origen, whose theology had been discredited both by the extreme monks and also by others in the eastern Mediterranean, in particular Epiphanius of Cyprus. This attack on Origen was the precursor of a campaign against Chrysostom, who had interfered in Alexandrian church matters by apparently giving support to the Tall Brothers.

In his campaign against Origen, Theophilus enlisted the support of Epiphanius of Salamis, in Cyprus, an inveterate heresy hunter and a staunch supporter of Athanasius in the torrid days of the Arian controversy. In the first instance, he asked Epiphanius to call a synod of the bishops of Cyprus to condemn Origen and his teachings. Epiphanius was flattered at being asked to take a leading role and glad that Theophilus had come round to his point of view about the godhead. For Theophilus, it was a superficial conversion, however, which he seemingly only embraced to hound the Tall Brothers. The bishops of Cyprus were particularly asked to condemn the anti-anthropomorphic view of the godhead. Once they passed this resolution, they were to send the minutes of the meeting to both Chrysostom and Theophilus. In this way, both would see that the teaching of the Tall Brothers was "erroneously" following Origen and should, therefore, be condemned.[18]

While this was the first theological salvo in the campaign against the Tall Brothers, more was to follow, and Chrysostom himself would soon come into Theophilus's sights. For his part, John wanted to defuse the potential conflict, and on his return from his Asian tour in April 402, sought to put this strategy into practice. To this end, he sought to dissuade the Tall Brothers from asking the emperor for a full-scale enquiry into the conduct of Theophilus. But this attempt at deflecting a confrontation with Theophilus was in vain. So John sought to forewarn

Theophilus, writing to him a second time, enclosing a copy of the indictment lodged with the emperor and begging him "to respond to it as he judged best".[19] Theophilus responded in the way he knew best: with explosive anger. He excommunicated Bishop Dioskorus, the senior Tall Brother, and reproached John for interfering in his diocesan affairs, and for thus breaching the Nicene canons which prohibited interference in the diocese of another. Palladius records that Theophilus was "enflamed by febrile anger".[20] All the while, the Tall Brothers waited to get a hearing for their complaints, feeling certain of the justice of their cause. By June 402, and running out of patience, the Tall Brothers approached the court directly, for they now believed that little help would come from John Chrysostom.

An opportunity to approach the imperial couple came on the Feast Day of John the Baptist on 24 June 402, when, according to Palladius, the Tall Brothers appealed directly to the empress for her support, and for a hearing of their case.[21] She was literally travelling in her carriage to the shrine of the Baptist when this happened. She already knew something of their case and was willing to at least listen and, if possible, to help. Now they went further and asked that Theophilus himself should stand trial for his misdemeanours in a court presided over by John. Apparently, the empress responded to the request with the words: "Pray for the emperor, for me and for our children and for the empire. For my part, I shall shortly cause a council to be convened to which Theophilus shall be summoned."[22]

Eudoxia was as good as her word, and on behalf of the refugee monks, requested that their case be heard. She approached "the master of the offices" and an imperial order or rescript was taken to Alexandria by the chief of the imperial couriers commanding Theophilus to come to the court in Constantinople and answer charges laid against him. At the same time, Theophilus's agents in Constantinople were arrested and asked to substantiate in court the charges made against the Tall Brothers, or face penalties for slander.

Although Theophilus was not best pleased to receive an imperial summons which must be obeyed, his bravado and "hauteur" were probably mixed with a modicum of fear. After all, he could be deposed or exiled, as many bishops in the fourth century were if an emperor disliked their religious policies. The Church was very much the fiefdom of the emperor. Theophilus was not without a strategy for managing the situation as best he could, however. In effect he played for time, hoping to galvanize all those who were opposed to Chrysostom, now portrayed as the protector of these excommunicated refugee monks. John became a focus for opposition, since he was to be the presiding judge at the court of enquiry.

Rather than taking the sea voyage across the eastern Mediterranean, Theophilus plumped for the land journey through Palestine and present-day Turkey in order to delay his arrival in Constantinople. While the sea journey took up to 20 days, the land journey would probably take at least two months, with teaching and preaching diversions along the way at important centres of the Church, such as Jerusalem and Ephesus. There were also opportunities to gather support, smear the names of the Tall Brothers and Chrysostom, and winkle out any incipient opposition to any or all of them. Palladius tells us that Theophilus began to dig for any dirt on Chrysostom particularly, even as far back as his time in Antioch.[23] Old opponents of John, including Acacius, Antiochus, Severian and the monk Isaac, were only too ready to give evidence against Chrysostom if required. Theophilus went further in whipping up support by appealing to Epiphanius of Cyprus to go beyond his earlier condemnation of Origenism in general and launch an all-out assault on Chrysostom who, according to Theophilus, was in danger of leading the Church astray, along with the Tall Brothers. Fanciful although this was, Epiphanius was always quick to see dangers to orthodoxy lurking under any episcopal bed. He determined now to go to Constantinople himself and nip the incipient Origenism in the bud.

We are told by Socrates that Epiphanius went to Constantinople following the synod in Cyprus, carrying a document that condemned the writings of Origen. He refused to accept hospitality from John and instead lodged in his own rented apartment in the city.[24] He then convened a meeting of bishops living in Constantinople with the express purpose of condemning Origen. Having assembled these bishops, Epiphanius proceeded to read out his Synod's condemnation of Origen's works and sought the support of the meeting. Many did support Epiphanius, but others, indeed a majority, such as Theotimus, Bishop of Scythia, saw no reason to condemn Origen, whom previous generations had not condemned and who had died a martyr for his faith in Christ.[25] Furthermore, Theotimus read out some of his writings, which appeared entirely orthodox.

Epiphanius had by now already violated normal courtesies. He had ordained a priest without permission. He had preached in the Church of John the Baptist at Hebdomon in the diocese, the very church where Eudoxia had heard the grievances of the Tall Brothers some months before and promised them a hearing. He had refused John's offer of hospitality. From the outset Epiphanius's actions were high-handed and disrespectful. He did not seek John's blessing on his arrival. All of this was tantamount to disrespecting, ignoring or, even worse, repudiating John's episcopacy. For his part, John had been the model of restraint, seeking to honour this much-respected and older bishop who had stood for Nicene orthodoxy when others deserted the cause. But far from retreating after his rebuke by Theotimus, Epiphanius now sought a more dramatic condemnation of Origen at the Church of the Holy Apostles in the very heart of the city.

The day following Epiphanius's decision publicly to condemn Origen in the diocese of another without any recourse to a church council, John decided he had had enough. He sent his former archdeacon, Serapion to confront Epiphanius and point out the ways in which he had ridden roughshod over canon law: he had ordained a priest without permission; he had not informed John either of his preaching or of his presence in the diocese; he had come without invitation (when he had been invited before); and he had condemned out of hand an eminent figure in the Church. Finally, John said that he could not guarantee his safety from the mob.[26] Epiphanius left the church and returned home but died on the voyage to Cyprus on 12 May 403. All of this had happened over the course of a few weeks. A bitter exchange was later attributed to the pair which is probably not true. Epiphanius is held to have said: "I hope you will not still be a bishop when you die." And the riposte from John: "I hope you will not set foot in your city (Salamis in Cyprus) again." It was a legend born of their known conflict and probably untrue, but it would nevertheless be used against John in the forthcoming enquiry into the fate of the Tall Brothers.

As far as the imperial court was concerned, it appears that Epiphanius's visit kicked up mud in relation to the empress and John, some of which stuck. Socrates tells us that an unnamed person had spread a rumour that the empress had herself put Epiphanius up to attack John.[27] This seems wide of the mark, however, especially since Sozomen tells us that Eudoxia's son, Theodosius, was badly ill at the time, and that normally Eudoxia would have asked anyone with gifts of healing or authority (and especially her bishop), to pray for him. According to Sozomen, Epiphanius attempted to use the illness of young Theodosius to wrest from Eudoxia a promise that she would not support the Tall Brothers in their case, and in return he would pray for the young heir.[28] This manipulation only enraged Eudoxia, who replied that if his powers of healing were so certain, his own valued archdeacon would not have died. Nevertheless, it seems that Epiphanius *did* meet the Tall Brothers at the instigation of the empress and was asked whether he had read their works. When he replied he had not, but still condemned them, they replied that they had often defended Epiphanius, whose works they had read, so how could he attack them when he did not know the content of their writings? Epiphanius had no answer to that, or, as Sozomen circumspectly puts it, "He was measurably convinced and dismissed them." Soon afterwards, Epiphanius left for Cyprus, and, as we have heard, died on the voyage home (hence fulfilling John's words, if they were ever spoken).[29]

But this was merely the first act in this developing and depressing saga, with its unexpected twists and turns. Almost one year after his summons by the emperor, Theophilus arrived, having taken the most time-consuming route and working up a campaign against the Tall Brothers, Origen and John, who was cast as their unprincipled protector. Theophilus was about to reach Constantinople in August 403, having taken the better part of a year to arrive. The trouble was that John had already, by then, laid the groundwork for his own fall, by alienating the very people who might have defended him against Theophilus's unwarranted attack. This occurred when the often-outspoken Chrysostom vented his wrath, for no justifiable reason, against women in a sermon in the old Hagia Sophia in May 403. Sozomen simply tells us that "John when preaching in the church as usual, chanced to inveigh against the vices to which females are peculiarly prone".[30] Although we don't have a record of the sermon, it appears that his remarks may not have been especially directed against the court or the empress in particular, but this was quickly supposed to be the underlying reason. Since John failed to dispel this rumour, it was widely held to be true in the court, causing great consternation, and it may have been then that the court determined to turn the tables on John by supporting Theophilus's case against him.[31] It was to be a tragic twist.

Meanwhile Theophilus's journey from Egypt had reached a climax. He had come overland. He had collected an entourage as he went, many of whom were bishops John had deposed in Asia. He arrived at Chalcedon on the Asian side of the Bosphorus where he was welcomed by Bishop Cyrinus, himself an Egyptian and a relative of Theophilus, but who then suffered a fatal accident when his leg was injured, operated on, and became infected.[32] Nevertheless, recovering from this blow, Theophilus was taken by ship, recently arrived from Egypt, to the great port of Eleutherius in Constantinople where the grain fleet from Alexandria was already unloading. He was hailed by the Alexandrian sailors as their Patriarch, and hence suitably supported, he arrived with a great fanfare in the New Rome, Constantinople.[33] From there he proceeded to the Golden Horn, the finger of water heading north from the Bosphorus and which would eventually divide the expanding city. Here Theophilus disembarked in the port of Prosphorianus, just a kilometre from the heart of the imperial city. It was an impressive arrival, and one that boded ill for John.

As with Epiphanius, John offered hospitality to his fellow bishop and Metropolitan of Alexandria. Once again, the offer was turned down. Theophilus spurned that fraternal offer, even though a welcome party had been sent by John, and he did not go into any of the churches as custom dictated. Later, in an explanation of the feud to Pope Innocent I (pope 401–17), John wrote, "[Theophilus] paid me no call, but rejected all conversation with me, and declined to take part in prayer or communion with me."[34] Things were only going to get worse, for Theophilus was in fact accorded hospitality by the Empress Eudoxia in her palace of the Platinum Placidianum, assigned to the reigning *augusta*. It was here, and in another house lent by a rich widow, Eugraphia, that over the next three weeks Theophilus would meet with all the malcontents who had been either deposed, criticized or overlooked by John. These included rich women who had felt the lash of his tongue and strictures, bishops whose simony or corruption had been found out, and monks who hitherto had free rein but now were under demanding discipline. Nor was Theophilus above offering a little financial incentive to potential witnesses to speak out against John.

Meanwhile, alarmed at the turn of events and the increasing backing of Theophilus by the ruling classes and elite in the city, the Tall Brothers sought reassurance from Emperor Arcadius that their case would be heard. At this point, the emperor summoned John to the palace of Rufinianai near Chalcedon, which had once belonged to the praetorian prefect Rufinus until his fall. When called upon to put in motion the trial of Theophilus for the grievances lodged with the court by the Tall Brothers, John refused. This was very surprising, given all that was at stake. Explaining his reasoning to Pope Innocent I in a later letter, John said that he refused to try a judicial case which arose outside of his territory. Indeed, he went on, "I refused to act as his judge, indeed I rejected the proposal with the utmost vehemence."[35] This almost otherworldly refusal to take up the case against Theophilus at the eleventh hour sealed his own fate. While John was reluctant to act as judge, Theophilus had no such scruples. While John refused to act on grievances which arose outside his diocese, Theophilus gathered any number of grievances in Asia and Constantinople and used them against John. If there was one law for John, there was quite another for Theophilus. Instead of John sitting in judgement on Theophilus, a new plan was circulating in the court: the trial of John by Theophilus. The momentum for this came not only from Theophilus's almost perpetual lobbying of the disaffected and the powerful, but from a mood in the palace which Eudoxia shared: a mood of disenchantment with John himself.

Theophilus now turned the screw on John. Using the complaints of Isaac, the monk whom John had disciplined, and two deacons whom John had earlier sacked, a charge sheet against John was drawn up.[36] Not only that, but the emperor gave permission for proceedings to be opened against John, and for the court to assemble for that purpose in a suburb of Chalcedon called The Oak (Drus).[37] Before any proceedings began, the empress probably insisted that Theophilus achieve some measure of reconciliation with the Tall Brothers. This most probably happened before the opening of proceedings at The Oak.[38] Clearly seeing the way the wind was blowing and their seeming desertion by John, the Tall Brothers made peace with Theophilus, their Egyptian Pharaoh. By this time, one of the Tall Brothers, Dioscorus, had died and another, Ammonius, was gravely ill. Absolution was quickly given by a magnanimous-in-victory Theophilus, as a larger prize was now in view. Furthermore, Theophilus dropped all criticism of Origen, seeing that his strategy of condemning Origen had failed and had wider ramifications, which could now wait. The sole object in view was the deposition of John, and to this end Theophilus sought to intimidate John's clergy and prise them away from their bishop.

Some time in late September 403 what became known as the Synod of the Oak met, with the sole intention of making John answer charges brought against him. Paul, Bishop of Heraklea, was the official president of the synod, with Theophilus, Antiochus, Severian and Cyrinus as co-adjutors. In fact, Theophilus was in control of the proceedings and the agenda. A charge sheet which included 29 charges against John was drawn up by the two deacons whom John had earlier sacked, but whom Theophilus now promised to reinstate. A further 17 charges were added by Isaac later. When summoned, John objected that Theophilus, although not the president, was nevertheless interfering in a diocese not his own, and was thus contravening Canon 5 of Nicaea. And given that the Synod or court was packed with enemies, John refused to appear. The emperor himself commanded John to attend and a further four citations were sent by the court in a single day. John steadfastly refused to appear, however, giving again his earlier objections.[39] John's refusal to attend only strengthened the emperor and empress's growing support of Theophilus and his own equally growing isolation.

The charges were a ragbag of complaints. Some alluded to John's Origenist teaching and the welcome he had given to the Tall Brothers. Others accused him of behaving with unfettered power, imprisoning the accusers of the Tall Brothers, hitting one Menon in the face before the divine liturgy, ordaining clergy illegally (charges 2, 10, 13, 14, 18, 24), suspending clergy unjustly and accusing or exiling others.[40] Moreover, on a more personal level, he was accused of showing insufficient hospitality by eating alone, and of receiving women whilst alone (charges 15, 23, 25). These comprised the earlier 25 charges to which Isaac added his even more bizarre 17, some of which still baffle scholars. For instance, John was charged with giving asylum to pagans even when they had persecuted Christians, and with promising forgiveness of sins-repeatedly-committed without seeking the discipline of penance (for by then there was a thoroughgoing tariff of penances for sins).[41] It is true that John was often imperious and authoritarian in his ways, but little more so than other bishops of any large diocese of his day.

These charges were heard by the Synod of the Oak, and in his absence, John was found guilty. As Socrates tells it, the synod deposed him without assigning any other cause for his deposition other than that he refused to obey the summons.[42] Sozomen gives the same reason.[43] Some 45 voted in favour of deposition; none dared to counter the will of Theophilus. A further biography of John, alongside that of Palladius, was by Martyrius, which we only have in piecemeal form.[44] This noted that the synod worked in great haste and possibly over a matter of days. Emperor Arcadius was immediately informed of the synod's decision, with the expectation that John be immediately deposed, and if need be, sent into exile. The report of the synod's findings was further spiced up by the inclusion of John's defamatory remarks about the empress, in which he compared her to Jezebel.[45] Such a reminder would have only strengthened the palace's desire to be rid of him.

Meanwhile John waited up to three days for his arrest and dismissal and, being John, on the second day preached in his cathedral to a packed and very agitated congregation. For if the palace and the synod had conspired to depose him, the people of Constantinople were very much on his side. It was a sermon designed to prepare his congregation for the worst: his own dismissal and exile. "He dwelt eloquently on his own readiness to face whatever disasters were in store, on the invincibility of the Church so often demonstrated in history, on the bond between bishop and flock which, like that between husband and wife, makes them inseparable."[46] Allusions were made to Theophilus being like Potiphar in seeking to ensnare Joseph, and the need for Arcadius (although not mentioned by name) to become like King David, who had upheld true religion. With the words of Jesus, "Lo, I am with you always" (Matthew 28:20, RSV), ringing in his ears, what had John to fear? But the congregation, enraged by his deposition, fearful of the future without him, and stirred by his preaching, were more than ready to make their feelings known.

Knowing well the volatility of the crowd, John did not want to create any dangerous disturbances in the city. So, the next day, in that autumn of 403, he left the city quietly. As Sozomen tells us, "John made his escape from the church at noon, three days after his deposition."[47] When Severian claimed that John's deposition was necessary because of his pride, the crowd were infuriated. "The people ran to the churches, to the marketplaces, and even to the palace of the emperor, and with howls and groans demanded the recall of John." This exile would prove short-lived, but John's troubles and full tragedy were yet to be played out.

Notes

1. Peter Brown, *The World of Late Antiquity* (London: Thames & Hudson, 1971), pp. 96ff.
2. Socrates, *Ecclesiastical History* VI.22, in *Nicene and Post-Nicene Fathers: Second Series, Vol. II: Socrates, Sozomenus, Church Histories*, ed. Philip Schaff (Grand Rapids, MI: Eerdmans, 1987), p. 152.
3. J. N. D. Kelly, *Golden Mouth: The Story of John Chrysostom, Ascetic, Preacher, Bishop* (Ithaca, NY: Cornell University Press, 1998), p. 191.
4. Origen, *On First Principles* 4.3.5, cited by Ronald E Heine, *Origen: Scholarship in the Service of the Church* (Oxford: Oxford University Press, 2009), pp. 135ff.
5. Kelly, *Golden Mouth*, p. 191.
6. Socrates, *Ecclesiastical History* VI.7, op. cit., p. 143.
7. Socrates, *Ecclesiastical History* VI.7, op. cit., p. 143.
8. Palladius, *Dialogues*, in *Dialogue sur la vie de Jean Chrysostome/Palladios*, ed. and tr. Anne-Marie Malingrey with Philippe Leclercq, SC 341, Vol. 4 (Paris: Les Éditions du Cerf, 1988), p. 131.
9. See Kelly's footnote 14, based on Jerome's Epistles no. 92.3 CSEL 55: 150–1, p. 193.
10. Kelly, *Golden Mouth*, p. 193.
11. Palladius, *Dialogue* 6, op. cit., p. 138.
12. Palladius, *Dialogue* 7, op. cit., pp. 141–3.
13. Socrates, *Ecclesiastical History* VI and VII, op. cit., p. 144.
14. Sozomen, *Ecclesiastical History* VIII.13, *Nicene and Post-Nicene Fathers: Second Series, Vol. II: Socrates, Sozomenus: Church Histories*, ed. Philip Schaff (Grand Rapids, MI: Eerdmans, 1987), p. 407.
15. Kelly, *Golden Mouth*, pp. 185–6.
16. Palladius, op. cit., p. 179.
17. Stephen J, Davis, *The Early Coptic Papacy: The Egyptian Church and its Leadership in Late Antiquity* (Cairo: American University of Cairo Press, 2004), p. 64.
18. Socrates, *Ecclesiastical History* VI:10, op. cit., p. 145.
19. Kelly, *Golden Mouth*, p. 199.
20. Palladius, Dial. 7, op. cit., p. 155.
21. Palladius, Dial. 8, op. cit., p. 157.

22 Sozomen, *Ecclesiastical History* VIII.13, op. cit., p. 407.
23 Palladius, *Dialogue* 6, op. cit., p. 129.
24 Socrates, *Ecclesiastical History* VI.12, op. cit., p. 147.
25 Socrates, *Ecclesiastical History* VI.12, op. cit., p. 147.
26 Socrates, *Ecclesiastical History* VI.14, op. cit., p. 148.
27 Socrates, *Ecclesiastical History* VI1.4, op. cit., p. 148.
28 Sozomen, *Ecclesiastical History* VIII.11, op. cit., p. 409.
29 Sozomen, *Ecclesiastical History* VIII.15, op. cit., p. 408.
30 Sozomen, *Ecclesiastical History* VIII.16, op. cit., p. 409.
31 Kelly, *Golden Mouth*, pp. 211–12.
32 Sozomen, *Ecclesiastical History* VIII.16, p. 409.
33 Palladius, *Dialogue* 8, op. cit., p. 161.
34 Chrysostom, Ep. I *ad Innocentium*, SC 342.70-2.
35 Chrysostom, Ep. I *ad Innocentium*, SC 342.72.
36 Palladius, *Dialogue* 8, op. cit., p. 163.
37 Kelly, *Golden Mouth*, p. 217.
38 Sozomen, *Ecclesiastical History* VIII.17, op. cit., p. 410.
39 Socrates, *Ecclesiastical History* VI.15, op. cit., p. 149.
40 Kelly, *Golden Mouth*, p. 221.
41 Basil of Caesarea, Letter 119.
42 Socrates, *Ecclesiastical History* VI.17, op. cit., p. 149.
43 Sozomen, *Ecclesiastical History* VIII.17.
44 Palladius, SC 342.112.
45 Palladius, *Dialogue* 8.230–52, op. cit., p. 179.
46 Kelly, *Golden Mouth*, p. 230.
47 Sozomen, *Ecclesiastical History* VIII.19, op. cit., p. 411.

12

The last exile

Somewhat like the Apostle Paul, wrongly imprisoned in Philippi and released by his gaoler after an earthquake (Acts 16:25ff.), a further metaphorical and actual earthquake came to John's aid, although in a different set of circumstances.

Everything had happened so quickly and unexpectedly: Theophilus turning the tables on John; the rapid condemnation by the Synod of the Oak; the order to depose him, and his departure from the city after a memorable, defiant sermon and three days of emotional turbulence among the population. The day after he left, John had only reached Praenetos, a small market town in Bithynia, and across the Sea of Marmara from Constantinople. He had been taken by military escort to his ship surrounded by a large and emotional crowd. But, as fast as John left, he returned. The unease in the palace at so swiftly deposing him was compounded in their superstitious minds when an earthquake hit the vicinity.[1] Then came the more immediate and very personal setback for the imperial family of the sudden death of Eudoxia's daughter, Flacilla, possibly through a miscarriage.[2] These two events undermined the palace's confidence in their decision to exile John, and strengthened a niggling suspicion that God's favour rested on their uncompromising bishop. They therefore sought to reverse the decision to exile him. To get him back, a eunuch called Brison, a great admirer of John, was sent with a handwritten note from the empress in which she disowned any part in his exile and pledged her support to him as the man who had baptized her children.[3]

At this point, John played hard to get, and for some days the emissaries from the palace could not find him. It could well be that he went into hiding, and when found, like the Apostle Paul in Philippi, did not want to return by the back door without a proper overturning of the charges brought against him at the Oak. He wanted his reputation exonerated, his enemies exposed for who they were, and his authority re-established. Eventually he agreed to return, and when he arrived at the mouth of the Bosphorus, there was a flotilla of small craft waiting to escort him into the harbour. But he still made it plain, from a villa in the outskirts of the city provided by Eudoxia, that he would only return if the charges against him were squashed, and indeed entirely overturned. But eventually the desire of the people, the reality of rampaging monks doing yet more damage to the churches in the city (as some already had), and the promise of a synod to re-examine the charges against him prevailed, and John was escorted back to his church and house in the city by a great crowd.

At first, he was accompanied by 30 bishops to the Church of the Holy Apostles where he gave a short extempore sermon based on a text from Job. A week later, on a Sunday, he was persuaded to sit in the bishop's chair in Hagia Sophia and offer the prayer of peace from the throne and preach.[4] John did not hold back. He compared Theophilus to the Pharaoh who had desired Abraham's wife Sarah only to find that she brought illness to Pharaoh's household (Genesis 12:10–20).[5] After condemning his adversary, John praised the emperor and empress and was drowned out with applause.[6] Such harmony between bishop and palace was not to last, however, for when it came to handling his sovereigns, John was his own worst enemy.

By now his accusers, and principally Theophilus, who were in the sights of the crowd, had left the vicinity. Theophilus returned to Alexandria and was as deliberately fast in leaving as he had been slow in coming. He came by land but returned by ship. And Severian, who had taken such an important role in the proceedings of the Oak left also (although he would soon return), but not before he had preached that should all the charges against John be proven false, he should still be deposed for his haughty spirit.[7] Although summoned back to Constantinople, on this occasion Theophilus remained in Alexandria. Meanwhile the palace had called for a general council of bishops, but in the meantime, and in deference to John, 60 bishops had been summoned to consider the proceedings of the Oak and John's deposition. Sozomen reports that some 60 bishops did meet to reverse the decisions of the Oak and the deposition of John.⁸ It looked as though all was set fair until the empress exalted herself, and John, unable to contain his criticism, caused a final breach with the palace.

John's relationship with the imperial family had always been complex, and particularly so with the empress. There is no doubt that he had an inordinate respect for Theodosius, the father of the present Emperor Arcadius. In squashing the Arian tendencies of many church leaders, Theodosius had been the saviour of Nicene Orthodoxy. Arcadius was included in John's respect, not especially because of his own merits, which were few, but because his father had saved the Church from heresy and the city of Constantinople from the Goths. John's relationship with Eudoxia was less straightforward, however. He had praised her devotion when she walked like a simple pilgrim to the church outside Constantinople where the bones of martyrs were interred. He had baptized her children. He had yielded to her pleas to be reconciled with Severian. Her family would turn out to be remarkably committed to a life of dedicated service and abstinence. But his underlying suspicion of women as snares to godliness easily subverted any respect. He was too quick to believe the worst of women, and consequently the biblical figures of Jezebel and Herodias readily sprang to his mind as types in his own day. Furthermore, he simply could not resist deploying his eloquence against women in general and the empress in particular.⁹ This had been clearly seen in his sermon shortly before his first exile, where the inference was drawn that he was condemning the empress. And now there were fresh grounds for the same suspicions.

Some time in mid-November 404, Simplicius, the city prefect, erected a silver statue of Eudoxia arrayed in the distinctive garb of an *augusta* in front of the Senate House and close by Hagia Sophia. "It stood resplendent on a column of porphyry",¹⁰ and on its plinth there was an inscription in Greek hexameters with a Latin translation. On its own, the statue might have been overlooked by John, but when it was unveiled on a Sunday with dancing and music, the celebrations interrupted John, who was preaching and performing the liturgy in nearby Hagia Sophia. He castigated the cause of this interruption to the congregation and the statue of the empress in particular. Sozomen tells us that John "added fuel to her indignation by still more openly declaiming against her in church".

From his experience in Antioch, John of all people should have known the sensitivities surrounding imperial statues. To denigrate them was to denigrate the one they depicted. Imperial statues were commonplace: they were not idols so much as reminders of the sovereigns' rule. What is more, John's eloquence got the better of him, and in a later sermon, after the initial furore, he poured petrol on the fire by saying, "Herodias is again enraged; again she (or her daughter Salome) dances; again she (Herodias) seeks the head of John in the basin."[11] It was all too clear that in his own mind he was John the Baptist and the empress was Herodias, although there is no evidence that she ever wanted him executed! The fragile relations between John and the palace after the Oak and his first exile were now completely shattered.

By Christmas 403, the breach between John and the palace became official. This new fissure between bishop and emperor allowed some of the original accusers to return to the city in the hope of another synod which would uphold the earlier condemnation of John. Palladius also recalls a weakening of the resolve of some of the bishops who had come to the city to support John.[12] But John still had, he said, 42 bishops in support, and the congregations in Hagia Sophia were as large and as devoted to him as ever. In the midst of this melee, word came from Alexandria that there might be a simpler and subtler way of getting rid of John. The Dedication Council held in Antioch in May 341 had ruled in its canons that for a bishop to resume his office after censure by a synod, a further synod must be held at which he must be formally reinstated. No such synod had as yet been held, although there were plenty of bishops milling around Constantinople ready to attend. The irony of this was that this canon from the Council of Antioch had originally been devised by the Arian contingent to keep Athanasius out of office, but now one of his successors, Theophilus, was using it to keep a thoroughly orthodox bishop from resuming his ministry. Such were the contortions of church life. Some informal gathering of bishops took place, said to be a synod, which upheld the Synod of the Oak. At this point, the emperor refused to attend the liturgy with John presiding, which in effect put John under an interdict.[13] By Easter 404, John was a prisoner in his own palace and not allowed to leave it. In his letter to Innocent I, John recalls that "I was expelled from my own church, but worse was to follow that Easter".[14]

John was now under a kind of house arrest in his own palace, close by Hagia Sophia. Following the advice of Theophilus and the majority of bishops present in Constantinople, the findings of the Synod of the Oak stood, since no further council or synod was forthcoming to overturn the condemnation. This uneasy situation, confirmed by Emperor Arcadius, only grew worse the closer Easter 404 came. Easter, rather than Christmas, was the main festival of the Church. Here baptism of the catechumens would take place during a dramatic Easter eve vigil over which the bishop was expected to preside. But Arcadius added further pain to John by forbidding him the use of Hagia Sophia. It was in this sense that John was expelled from his church. He typically responded that no human power had given him Hagia Sophia but God alone, and no human power had the right to take it away from him. But despite the intercession of 40 bishops loyal to John, his ban from Hagia Sophia continued.[15]

With this stand-off between bishop and palace continuing, Holy Week moved towards its climax on Easter Eve, the time when catechumens were traditionally baptized. Services were held by clergy loyal to John in Hagia Sophia and Hagia Eirene, but the imperial authorities in the person of the Master of Offices were directed by others, most probably encouraged by Bishops Severian, Acacius of Aleppo, Antiochus of Ptolomeias and Cyrinus of Chalcedon, who were falsely advising the emperor. On Easter Eve, 400 troops under a young officer called Lucius were sent into the churches and baptisteries to disperse the worshippers:

> There followed extraordinary scenes of brutality and sacrilege, with officiating clergy being driven out with cudgels, women catechumens who had undressed in preparation for immersion fleeing half naked, the water in the fonts turned red with blood of the wounded, and unbelieving soldiers forcibly entering the place where the holy sacrament was kept and desecrating its contents.[16]

The devout historian Sozomen could not bring himself to describe the scene in case he gave reason to unbelievers to attack the Church for its divisions and its behaviour.[17]

Not wishing to be overcome by the brutality of the imperial troops, the loss of life and the terror, the clergy refused to put off the baptisms, and the following day, Easter Day itself, the congregation reassembled in the Baths of Constantinius. The Church of Hagia Sophia, where Arcadius was due to worship, remained virtually empty, and so the emperor was forced to cancel his attendance. The worshippers in the Baths were once again attacked by troops and dispersed to a place called Pempton, in an area outside the city walls designed by Constantine for horse racing. The emperor came across this now-bedraggled group later in the day while riding through the area. But from that date those loyal to John began to worship separately from other city congregations.

This sudden outbreak of violence and the ensuing shock both to people and palace left all in a state of almost paralysed disbelief. John remained confined in his palace. At one point, he was under threat of assassination from the slave of a priest called Elpidius, who had himself testified against John at the Oak.[18] Another man, "possessed of a devil", sought to kill John, but was prevented by the people. He was arrested and taken to the Prefect for interrogation, but John sought to free him before he could be detained and tortured. Elsewhere in the city, some of John's supporters worshipped separately from the other churches.[19] But despite these one-off events, an uncertain gloom hovered over the city, and John's fate seemed to be hanging by an imperial thread.

It was during this time between Easter and Pentecost, and quite possibly on 7 June, that John took the important step of writing to Pope Innocent, as well as to the Bishops of Milan and Aquileia (near Venice), to give them an account of his troubles and warn of the machinations of Theophilus. In a long letter detailing his treatment, John makes his recipients aware of the vendetta that has been pursued against him.[20] Although John may not have regarded Innocent of Rome as having the final say in adjudicating his case, he nevertheless sought to inform him of developments. Beyond that, John may have hoped that Honorius, the emperor in the West, would encourage his brother Arcadius to support him in the dispute with Theophilus and the other bishops. But Honorius had his hands full contending with the successive invasions of Goths, Alans and Suebi from the northeast. Indeed, the Western empire had only years to continue.

The stalemate between John and his opponents dragged on. Severian and the others were anxious to see the back of him and put pressure on Arcadius to this effect. On 20 June, the imperial lawyer, Patrikios, informed John that he must leave the city and go into exile. John gathered the loyal bishops and went into the Church of Hagia Sophia and held a last meeting and service there. At the same time, he was told that a detachment of soldiers under the command of Lucius, the same officer who had invaded Hagia Sophia and the Baths of Constantius at Easter, stood ready to force him to leave the city if he did not go willingly.[21] John objected that his case had not been reheard and that he had not been given a fair trial. But with the population being so much on his side, and because there was much tension and a risk of riot in the city,[22] he slipped out of a side door of the church and surrendered to his captors. He tried to leave quietly by a ship heading for Bithynia, but news of his eviction and exile leaked out and "great confusion ensued".[23] Some ran to the shore as if to follow him, and others were trapped in Hagia Sophia, whose doors had been forcibly closed from the outside. But soon the doors were shattered by stones hurled by the crowd; and then, starting from the bishop's throne the church caught fire, and soon Hagia Sophia was engulfed in flames, as was the neighbouring grand senatorial council room. Each side blamed the other for starting the fire. It continued from the afternoon until the following morning, and the imperial guard sought to arrest all those among the clergy who had supported John, believing them to be the culprits. They were arrested, and on pain of torture, forced to anathematize John before being released.[24] The Johnites (as they were now called) were to be persecuted for years, and indeed the campaign against John spread to his native city of Antioch, where, when Bishop Flavian died, Severian and friends appointed the anti-Johnite, Porphyrius. This unpopular action simply created a further schism in Antioch, which had been plagued with disunity for years: for no one could have been more respected in that city than Flavian and John.

Meanwhile John's captors took him to Cucusos, a city in Armenia. He would never see Constantinople again. Having been put down on the Bithynian coast he travelled by land southeast to Nicaea (Iznik). Meanwhile, in less than a week, a successor to John was appointed: an ineffectual octogenarian and brother of Bishop Nectarius (John's predecessor) called Arsacius. He was given the epithet by Palladius of being "as dumb as a fish, and as inactive as a frog".[25] He was only to survive or croak for 14 months.

Exile and correspondent

While John waited at Nicaea, where only 80 years before the Emperor Constantine and the bishops had thrashed out the Nicene Creed, he hoped for news of his final destination, and of the aftermath of his departure from Constantinople. He must have quickly realized that there was a continuing campaign against him. His successor in Constantinople was an octogenarian placeman who had been appointed quickly, and many of his supporters in Constantinople were in gaol, charged with starting the fire in Hagia Sophia. His reputation in Antioch was under threat, and a successor to Flavian had been found from amongst the cabal of bishops led by Severian and Theophilus. Furthermore, many of his appointments, such as Herakleides in Ephesus, had been brutally deposed. John must have realized his exile was intended to remove him from the cockpit of church life and also diminish the growing influence of the see of Constantinople. There was also a good deal of plain personal animosity towards him from the likes of Count John, a favourite of Eudoxia and now the finance minister of the imperial government. In the meantime, John wrote letters such as those to the prisoners in gaol in Chalcedon, bracing them for their ordeal, and extolling the crown of suffering which they nobly wore upon their heads.[26]

John had hoped that he would be moved to a large and important provincial town such as Sebasteia (Sivas), capital of Armenia Prima near Cappadocia, and where a wealthy friend, Arabius, was prepared to give him a fine house.[27] Instead, he was deliberately sent to a complete backwater, a place called Cucusos in Armenia Secunda, where a previous bishop of Constantinople, Paul, had been sent into exile in 351 during the Arian controversy. There he had been strangled by his guards. The omens were not good. John was deeply disappointed. He wrote of his disappointment in a letter to friends, complaining that the climate, housing and lack of opportunities would be detrimental to his health and a barrier to his usefulness.[28]

On 4 July 404, John began the long journey from Nicaea to Cucusos. It was about 1,000 kilometres from Nicaea. The route went through two principal cities: Ankara and Caesarea. John was travelling in a litter attached to a mule, and in the hottest time of the year. In one letter he writes reproachfully of the filthy water, the mouldy bread, poor food, and, surprisingly for one who had virtually given up bathing in the earlier part of his ministry, the lack of baths.[29] In Ankara, Bishop Leontius had been opposed to John and was one of those who believed that the Antioch canons could be used against him. He was thus given no welcome. Sometimes inhabitants from roadside villages came out to greet him, giving him a much-needed boost. But equally, later in the journey, he was sometimes in danger of attack by Isaurian tribesmen, the land-pirates of southern Anatolia.

In Caesarea, former home of the great Basil (c.329–79), the leading Cappadocian Father, John had higher hopes of a welcome. With his help of the poor, his enlightening teaching and his struggle for the Nicene faith, Basil would still have been affectionately remembered by the population, and many thought that Basil, had he lived that long, would have been a natural ally of John's. However, although Bishop Pharetrius sent messages of welcome and set aside lodgings, unlike so many of the civic, military and ecclesial leaders, he barely turned out to greet John. Indeed, John remembers in a letter that in the heat of the ecclesiastical battle in Constantinople, Pharetrius had not come in person to support him even then and had only sent lukewarm letters of support. It seems that he had been intimidated by the opposition led by Theophilus. Indeed, Palladius says that he was filled with "excessive fear".[30] But things grew much nastier in Caesarea when a group of berserk monks attacked the very lodgings where John was staying, threatening to burn the place down unless he left the city immediately. By then, John had become ill and was hardly able to move. Nevertheless, despite appeals by the civilian governor that John be given time to recover his fitness, he was driven out by a renewed assault from the monks, whereupon he travelled only a short distance with some sympathetic clergy to stay at the fortified dwelling of a rich lady called Seleukeia. But even she was threatened by the bishop, and John was turned out in the middle of the night. It proved one of the most dramatic occasions in an eventful life, which John records in one of his many letters of the period.[31] Although John had been accorded reasonable treatment by his guards and the escort he had been given by the emperor and also had freedom to socialize, a kind of fanaticism seems to have taken hold of these more provincial leaders, and a growing resentment towards John had turned into an implacable enmity which was neither worthy of the gospel they served, nor proportionate to the reasons that caused it.

After this gruelling and eventful journey, John eventually arrived at the out-of-the-way town of Cucusos (Goksun) around 20 September, having taken over two months to get there. It was a mountainous region southeast of present-day Kayseri (Caesarea) and about 170 kilometres north of Tarsus. There the Taurus Mountains were ranged over by the Isaurians, who posed a continual threat to the small villages in the region. John was to reside there for almost three years, before a final, fatal move and his untimely and premature death. As for anyone of his intellectual energy and leadership experience, having hitherto had great influence over a city and with opportunities to preach to large crowds, this small remote place must have felt like a restrictive backwater. What made matters worse was his almost continuous ill health and the regular attacks by the Isaurians, whose marauding was almost ceaseless. Such was the cold in the winter that John lay in bed covered with blankets, frequently suffering headaches and stomach upsets. There was also a shortage of medical care and medicines. Furthermore, the Isaurians attacked often, unexpectedly and brutally, much like the Viking raiders on Britain. In one letter John recalls "the butchery, wild confusion, bloodshed and blazing buildings... ravaging with sword and fire".[32] At one point, their attacks became so bad that John and his entourage moved to another town, Arabissos (Afsin), about 70 kilometres east of Cucusos, beyond a nearby lake.

However, between the raids of the Isaurians and his own weakness and illness, John enjoyed times of real peace, both while recovering from the journey there and at other times, as in 406 after a stay in Arabissos. He made friends with some local men such as Orietris, the bishop of Arabissos, and was able to entertain the occasional friendly visitor. But with his epistolary and communicative genius, his chief occupation was writing to his many contacts, friends and co-adjutors, and chiefly, as we shall see, to his soulmate Olympias, from whom he gained emotional sustenance and the satisfaction of being her spiritual director, at a time when most such possibilities had fallen away.

It was a wide correspondence. Some 240 letters from John's exile have survived, although many others would have been lost. These letters were addressed to over a hundred individuals, both in Constantinople and elsewhere. Very few of them contain anything remotely personal. Some have descriptions of his life and whereabouts, but many are imbued with a great sense of his loneliness and inactivity in such a remote spot, far removed from the activity of city, church and imperial life, all of which he had grown very accustomed to.[33] In many ways, this was the hardest burden: the isolation. He longed for news and for letters in return, or even better, for visits from old acquaintances. Some colleagues did make the journey and found a man isolated, but nevertheless still pastorally involved, using some of the money settled on him by Olympias to ransom slaves and others captured by the Isaurian raiders.[34]

Other letters have more than a touch of a bishop seeking to direct and console his diocese and supporters from a place of exile. He praises those who resisted the pressure put on them for being his supporters. One such was his faithful deaconess, Pentadia, who had courageously resisted brutal interrogation and calls to remain at her post in Constantinople rather than visit him so many miles away.[35] In other letters, he rebukes priests for neglecting their preaching duties or deserting their posts. He encourages still others to continue their support of him in the face of opposition, employing the Pauline perspective that present difficulties are storing up for them an eternal weight of glory (2 Corinthians 4:17). Beyond the Church, he writes to people he would have known within the imperial administration. Among them is Anthemius, Master of Offices during the attack on Hagia Sophia and the Baths at Easter 404. Anthemius had tried to be a restraining influence then but had failed to be so; now he was to be appointed consul for the East and praetorian prefect, and as such the virtual ruler of the Eastern provinces and the overseer of John's fate. John congratulates him and hopes he and others badly affected by the purge will be dealt with fairly. John may even have cherished some hopes of being rehabilitated, but this was far from being a real possibility.[36]

John's correspondence ranged even further afield. He wrote, for example, to Christians in important social positions in Rome. Writing between 404 and 407, just a few years before the sack of Rome by the Visigoths in 410, John had no idea what awaited these people. He wrote to one Candidianus, a high-ranking general, and his Christian wife, Vasianalla. He also wrote to Proba, the wealthy widow of S. Claudius Probus, who had been praetorian prefect four times, and to Juliana, the wife of a consul, Olybrius. These were elite women, part of the well-to-do Christian community, and from whom John gained support, both emotional, and, quite possibly, financial. After all, Pope Innocent I was solidly behind John in his struggle with Theophilus of Alexandria, as was the Roman Church, and Innocent would work tirelessly for John's rehabilitation.

Although on good terms with these high-value individuals, John did not confine himself to the rich and powerful, but also had a special interest in evangelism and mission among the Goths and in the Levant. As for the Goths, he hoped a suitable successor would be found to succeed Ufila, bishop to the Goths, based in the northwest coastal area of the Black Sea.[37] Likewise he hoped that progress would be made in the missions to modern-day Lebanon and in Mesopotamia.[38] In other words, his correspondence shows that although removed from the centre, which was Constantinople, John continued his prayers for, encouragement of, and influence on missions that looked to Constantinople for support and leadership. He was not one to fall silent, and in his correspondence he sought to encourage, sometimes to direct, and also to draw attention to his plight. But of all his correspondence during these years, his most important correspondent was Olympias, giving her guidance, while at the same deriving emotional support from doing so.

Correspondence with Olympias

John's exile produced a rich and moving correspondence between two resolute but vulnerable characters. He and Olympias would find in their correspondence much comfort in more than testing times. While we have all 17 letters of John written over 32 months of exile, Olympias's letters have been lost, and we can only guess at their content from John's replies.

There is no doubt that much comfort and consolation is to be derived from simply telling another person of the conditions and challenges of one's life. To do this with a person who is a soulmate, and a sharer of a common vision and vocation, was and is especially comforting. Olympias was certainly a soulmate: she shared John's ascetic calling, like him holding to a strict diet and devoting herself to a celibate life defined by chastity. They both had oversight of communities, she over a community of 250 nuns and many philanthropic ventures, as well as vast estates, while he had had spiritual oversight of a great city and a turbulent diocese from which he had been forcibly ejected and exiled. They both struggled against forces that sought to destroy their authority, and to persecute them. John wrote from exile. Olympias wrote after extensive interrogation concerning her role in the riots and the fire in Hagia Sophia, following John's arrest. They relied on each other for comfort: John for information of the city as well as a channel for his messages and instructions;[39] Olympias for her own depression and struggles. It was a correspondence that would stand as an example of Christian encouragement and of remaining steadfast in suffering, which was one of John's chief themes.

John tells Olympias about his trials: his journey from Nicaea to Caesarea and his reception in Caesarea by a hostile bishop. He writes:

> When finally, after a long time, we entered Caesarea, exhausted, withering away, lying there in the highest flame of fever, distraught suffering in the furthest extreme. I came upon an inn, situated at the edge of the city, and I made haste to summon doctors who could tend to the furnace [of the fever], which was now at its height.

He goes on:

> In addition to this there was the exertion of travelling, the weariness, the strain, the dearth of those who could care for us, the lack of necessities, the absence of any physician for us, and the ravaging from fatigue, the heat, and the sleeplessness. So being nearly dead, I thus entered the city.[40]

Such a description would only give Olympias greater grounds for concern. But for John there was great comfort in sharing his trials, the discomfort he experienced, his sickness and dangers. He poured out his troubles to her.

While the correspondence gave John the opportunity of telling his dear friend of his trials, and of stating that the Christian calling was to endure all these things patiently,[41] it also gave him the opportunity of helping her combat her depression. John's advice is a mixture of stoical endurance and Christian perseverance, and often more of the former than the latter. Thus, he writes, "For the immutable laws of nature do not make it impossible for us to force ourselves to make a change. Rather the power to manage our own welfare easily lies *in the free decisions of our will*, and in this our joy resides." He continues. "For it is certainly not in the nature of things but in the will of man, that our happiness naturally resides."[42] However, this appeal to the will comes with a heathy admixture of biblical examples, ranging from Joseph, who overcomes the temptations of Potiphar's wife and the sufferings of imprisonment, to Moses, Job and the Apostle Paul.[43] All these had to deal with adversity; they were examples of faith working through a resolute will.

John's advice seemed unable to shift the pall of depression that had settled on Olympias, however. He acknowledged that

> despondency (*athumia*) is for souls a grievous torture chamber, unspeakably painful, more fierce and bitter than every ferocity and torment. It imitates the poisonous worm that attacks not only the body but also the soul, and not only the bones but also the mind. It is a continual executioner that not only tears in pieces the torso but also mutilates the strength of one's soul. It is a continuous night.[44]

John could not have been more descriptive of this deep depression that had settled on his friend, nor more assiduous in trying to shift it. He praises her as a ship with sails unfurled sailing in the midday sun.[45] He promises her rich rewards for bearing her sufferings faithfully, but amidst all this teaching and encouragement, we get the sense that the depression will not move from Olympias.

Indeed, in his last letter to her, it seems that John has given all he can to her, but it may not have brought a cure. Perhaps there is even a note of exasperation at this point, for he writes:

> If you strive against us, neither healing yourself nor wishing to bring yourself out of the stagnant waters of despair, even though you are enjoying an abundance of advice and exhortation from us, then it will not be easy for us to consent to send you numerous, long letters, as long as you are not about to gain anything from them for your happiness.[46]

There is more than a touch of steel in John's comforting letters. With this in mind, perhaps, John developed one letter into a more general pamphlet about using suffering for God's glory. This he titled, "To prove that no one can harm the man who does not injure himself".

John's intention with this work was to strengthen any Christian facing suffering. It combines Greek philosophy[47] and the Christian doctrine of perseverance. From Greek philosophy comes the subjugation of human passions to the call of virtue; from Christian perseverance the example of Christ who suffered whilst entrusting his cause to the Father (1 Peter 2:21ff.). In the third section of this treatise, John comes to the nub of his argument:

> What then is the virtue of man? Not riches that thou shouldest fear poverty; nor health of body that thou should dread sickness, nor the opinion of the public, that thou shouldest view an evil reputation with alarm, nor life simply for its own sake, that death should be terrible to thee: but carefulness in holding true doctrine, and rectitude in life.[48]

While John's description of the virtue of man is rather understated, i.e., that it is to hold to true doctrine and rectitude of life, as compared, say, with the object of man presented in the Westminster Confession of 1647, which is "to glorify God and enjoy him for ever", nonetheless we get the drift of his argument. Since our "virtue" does not reside in health, wealth, reputation or life itself, we cannot be affected by the loss of any or all of these things. It is only by leaving off true doctrine or rectitude of life that we are able to harm ourselves. John proceeds to show that living for wealth, food and drink, or reputation is a snare, and concludes in the way that he began by reiterating that

> I will now conclude my discourse by repeating what I said at the beginning, that if anyone be harmed and injured he certainly suffers this at his own hands, not at the hands of others even if there be countless multitudes injuring and insulting him; so that if he does not suffer this at his own hands, not all the creatures who inhabit the whole earth and sea, if they combined to attack him, would be able to hurt one who is vigilant and sober in the Lord. Let us then, I beseech you, be sober and vigilant at all times, and let us endure all painful things bravely that we may obtain those everlasting and pure blessings in Christ Jesus our Lord, to whom be glory and power, now and for ever.[49]

The truth was that John would now have plenty of opportunity to apply this to himself, not only during his present exile, but, when it came, during his final more severe banishment to a place where he would not have anything like the communication with visitors or through messages as at Cucusos. An imperial edict was given in the summer of 407 that he should be removed to Pityus (Pisunda) on the Black Sea in present-day Georgia, well beyond the reach of most visitors, and from where communication would be yet more difficult. The reason for this banishment was the continued hostility against John in the East, and the desire to remove him further from the support of the West, and in particular, from Pope Innocent I.

As we shall see, John never reached this destination. Meanwhile events in Constantinople had moved on, and the political situation had changed. In Rome, more voices were raised in John's favour, and Alexandria was looking more isolated.

Notes

1. Theodoret, *Ecclesiastical History* V.34.5 GCS 44.335.
2. Palladius, Dialogue 9, in Palladius, *Dialogues*, in *Dialogue sur la vie de Jean Chrysostome/Palladios*, ed. and tr. Anne-Marie Malingrey with Philippe Leclercq, *SC* 341, Vol. 4 (Paris: Les Éditions du Cerf, 1988), p. 181.
3. Sozomen, *Ecclesiastical History* VIII.18, in *Nicene and Post-Nicene Fathers: Second Series, Vol. II: Socrates, Sozomenus: Church Histories*, ed. Philip Schaff (Grand Rapids, MI: Eerdmans, 1987), p. 411.
4. Socrates, *Ecclesiastical History* XV.16, op. cit., p. 149.
5. Sozomen, *Ecclesiastical History* VIII.17, op. cit., p. 411.
6. Sozomen, *Ecclesiastical History* VIII.17, op. cit., p. 411.
7. Socrates, *Ecclesiastical History* XV and XVI, op. cit., p. 148/9.
8. Sozomen, *Ecclesiastical History* VIII.19, op. cit., p. 412.
9. J. N. D. Kelly, *Golden Mouth: The Story of John Chrysostom, Ascetic, Preacher, Bishop* (Ithaca, NY: Cornell University Press, 1998), pp. 230–1.
10. Kelly, *Golden Mouth*, p. 239.
11. Sozomen, *Ecclesiastical History* VIII.20, op. cit., p. 412.
12. Palladius, Dialogue IX, op. cit., pp. 191–3.
13. Socrates, *Ecclesiastical History* VI.18, op. cit., p. 150, 151.
14. Chrysostom, Ep. I *ad Innocentium SC* 342.82, p. 243–8.
15. Palladius, op. cit., p. 195.
16. Kelly, *Golden Mouth*, p. 244.
17. Sozomen, *Ecclesiastical History* VIII.21, op. cit., p. 412.
18. Sozomen, *Ecclesiastical History* VIII.21, op. cit., p. 413.
19. Sozomen, *Ecclesiastical History* VIII.21, op. cit., p. 413.
20. Palladius, *SC* 342, ed. Anne-Marie Malingrey (Paris, 1988).
21. Palladius, Dialogue 10, op. cit., p. 207.
22. Sozomen, *Ecclesiastical History* VIII.21, op. cit., p. 413.
23. Sozomen, *Ecclesiastical History* VIII.21, op. cit., p. 413.
24. Sozomen, *Ecclesiastical History* VIII.21, op. cit., p. 413.
25. Palladius, Dialogue 11, op. cit., p. 217.
26. Chrysostom, *PG* 52.673, p. 118.
27. Kelly, *Golden Mouth*, p. 253.
28. Chrysostom, Ep. *PG* 52.674–5, p. 120.
29. Chrysostom, Ep. 9 *PG* 52.608.

30. Palladius, Dialogue 9, op. cit., p. 185.
31. Chrysostom, Ep. 14.3 *PG* 52.615; Kelly, *Golden Mouth*, pp. 256ff.
32. Chrysostom, Ep. 61, *PG* 52.642; Kelly, *Golden Mouth*, p. 260.
33. Kelly, *Golden Mouth*, p. 261.
34. Sozomen, *Ecclesiastical History* VIII.27, op. cit., p. 417.
35. Chrysostom, Ep. 94 and 104, *PG* 52.657–9; 663–4.
36. Chrysostom, Ep. 147, *PG* 52.699.
37. Chrysostom, Ep. 14.5, *PG* 52.7267,
38. See Kelly, *Golden Mouth*, p. 262 and p. 264.
39. Chrysostom, Letter 9.5a, in *Letters to Saint Olympias*, tr. David C. Ford (Crestwood, NY: St Vladimir's Press, 2016), p. 94.
40. Chrysostom, Letter 9.2a, op. cit., p. 87.
41. Chrysostom, Letter 10.10a, op. cit., p. 113.
42. Chrysostom, Letter 10.c, op. cit., p. 97.
43. Chrysostom, Letter 10.c, op. cit., pp. 114ff.
44. Chrysostom, Letter 10.2b, op. cit., p. 99, see also Psalm 88.
45. Chrysostom, Letter 12.c, op. cit., p. 133.
46. Chrysostom, Letter 17.bc, op. cit., p. 167.
47. Stoic philosophy and Platonism, especially Book 10 of *The Republic*.
48. John Chrysostom, *None can harm him who does not injure himself*, in *St. Chrysostom: On the Priesthood, Ascetic Treatises, Select Homilies and Letters*, ed. Philip Schaff, NAPNF, First series, Vol. IX (New York: Cosimo, 2007), p. 272–3.
49. Chrysostom, *None can harm him who does not injure himself*, op. cit., p. 284.

13

The final journey

Soon after John's deposition and exile, and certainly by the early autumn of 404, the political and ecclesiastical landscape in Constantinople changed, but not for the better as far as John was concerned. Firstly, and unexpectedly, Empress Eudoxia died in childbirth, aged only 27. And secondly, by September 404 a delegation left Constantinople for Rome to seek support from Pope Innocent I himself.

This delegation may have arrived as early as late September 404, following the decree on 29 August commanding all clergy, whether supporters of John or not, and who were not normally resident in Constantinople, to leave. This delegation made its way to Rome, arriving in mid-September. Palladius, the future biographer of John, led this embassy. The delegation found a warm welcome in Rome, for Innocent himself, and some wealthy ascetic women like Melania, now very old, and her granddaughter Melania the Younger, were eager to help.[1] Melania the Younger gave Palladius generous hospitality. At the same time, some of the anti-John contingent also made tracks for Rome to bend the Pope's ear in the opposite direction, confirming at least the growing authority of Rome in ecclesiastical affairs and diplomacy. The anti-Johnites, who were led by a priest called Paternos, came with a sheaf of abusive letters from Antiochus, one of John's most determined enemies from the outset.[2] But Innocent had already made up his mind who he was backing, and now took his time to construct his response and to gather support from the Western emperor, Honorius.

Meanwhile, in Constantinople the affairs of the palace were also changing. There was a fierce hailstorm, with hailstones of "extraordinary magnitude", the size of walnuts, falling both on the city and in the suburbs.[3] For a population accustomed to looking for divine portents, this was a sure harbinger of divine displeasure. So when, soon after this, Empress Eudoxia died (6 October 404), it seemed clear to the Johnites that John's deposition was being judged. Indeed, Sozomen makes it clear that these occurrences were regarded by many as indications of divine wrath against the political and ecclesiastical powers in Constantinople, on account of the persecution that had been carried on against John.[4] What is clear is that Eudoxia died very soon after the start of John's exile. We do not hear what John thought of Eudoxia's death in either his correspondence or in any other of his writings,[5] but he must have known of it, and may have hoped that, since she was one of his leading opponents, he would quickly be restored.

Eudoxia was only 27 when she died, having married Arcadius in 395 at the age of 18. She most probably died in childbirth, or from a miscarriage. She had five children who survived childbirth, and most probably two further stillbirths or miscarriages. Strikingly beautiful and of mercurial and erratic temperament, she was also highly religious, superstitious, and devoted to the Church, if not to all its leaders. And her relatively short relationship with John, of about six years, appears to have been tempestuous. Although respecting his holiness and his role in baptizing her children, she also contemptuously dismissed and deeply resented any criticism that he made of her. Not quite Herodias of the New Testament, who despised the criticism of John the Baptist, nor as calculating (see Mark 6:14–29), she nonetheless became angry quickly and acted impulsively towards John. Sometimes there was good cause, perhaps, because of his notorious antipathy towards women, his harsh and public words in calling her a Jezebel, and his seemingly implacable opposition to any overt power that she wielded. But Eudoxia was nevertheless orthodox in belief. She fully accepted the Nicene Creed and had been enthusiastically present at the enshrining of the bones of martyrs in the city early in John's episcopacy. She had also lent a welcoming ear to the complaints of the Tall Brothers against Theophilus.

Although she did not live long enough to see her children develop beyond infancy, her family was to become remarkably influential in the East. Her second, and eldest surviving daughter, Pulcheria (399–453), would govern as regent for her brother, Theodosius II, after their father's death in 408. Throughout her life Pulcheria lived as an ascetic and virgin.

Theodosius II (401–50) ruled as one of the most effective Byzantine emperors, along with Justinian (527–65), in the early centuries of the Byzantine Empire. And following the death of Theodosius II, who had no heirs, Pulcheria married Marcian, who then became emperor from 450–7. She chose to live with him as an ascetic and pursued a life of sexual abstinence.

Eudoxia was buried with her husband's ancestors in the Church of the Holy Apostles where Constantine himself had been laid to rest. More than anything else she had left her mark as a mother. But because of the tragic memories of Easter 404 which lingered on, as well as the influence of the clique at court through whom she had involved herself in affairs of the State, a lasting scar would mar the memory of her reign with Arcadius.

Meanwhile, in Rome, Innocent was slowly putting in place his response to the crisis in the Eastern Church, and in particular to the delegation that had arrived from Constantinople as well as to John's earlier letter, written sometime after the Easter violence and before Pentecost, 7 June 404. The Western empire was also in deep jeopardy and in an almost permanent state of political crisis by the end of 404. From 395, there had been a continual threat from the Goths both to the East and the West.[6] This had already led to the threat of Gainas in Constantinople, as we have seen earlier, the murder of the Prefect Rufinus, and the increasing dependence in the West on Stilicho, the main military commander, to disperse the Goths. For his part, Alaric plundered Epirus in northwestern Greece, before being offered a command by Arcadius, which, however, came to nothing.

But by 401, the Goths, led by Alaric, were once more marching westwards where they were checked, but not destroyed, by Stilicho. They appear then to have retreated north of the Alps where they remained until 405. They split into three groups, recrossed the Alps and one army was destroyed by Stilicho's troops in Tuscany in 405.[7] The administration of the Western empire now moved to Ravenna and became deeply preoccupied with the Gothic threat. It was in this atmosphere of political crisis that the delegation from Constantinople arrived in Rome to intercede for the restoration of Chrysostom.

The replies of Innocent and Honorius did not come until 406, meaning that there was well over a year, nearly two in fact, between the delegation's arrival and the response. Eventually, Innocent replied both to John himself and separately to the clergy of Constantinople. His reply arrived through Cyriacus the Deacon and, following the visit to Rome, through Bishops Demetrius, Cyriacus, Eulysius and Palladius.[8]

Innocent's letter to John was written in very general terms: praising him as "the teacher and pastor of so great a people" and warning him that God only tries the best of his servants, "to see whether they will continue in the height of patience".[9] John might have hoped for more from Innocent, and for greater assurance of Innocent's *active support*, but the Pope's counsel was very much in line with John's own thinking: that this exile, and the sufferings that preceded it, were part of the burnishing of his faith (see 1 Peter 1:7). More encouraging was Innocent's more pointed second letter to the clergy of Constantinople. At the outset, Innocent acknowledges the love of those who have written to him and the need for patience in the situation. He then identifies, without naming them, those who are destroying the peace of the Church and recalls that "far from maintaining peace, they [John's opponents] expel guiltless priests from the front seat of their churches. John our brother and fellow-minister and your bishop, had been the first to suffer this unjust treatment without being allowed a hearing. Whatever accusation was brought, none was heard."[10] Innocent writes that priests were simply replaced, although the rightful priest was still living, and that nothing more audacious has been done before.[11] He then says that only the canons of Nicaea should be relevant in this struggle, believing that some extraneous canons had been misapplied in this case. And finally, he calls for a full synodical investigation into the events of John's deposition. The trouble was that there was no intention among the new leadership in the diocese to open an investigation, nor in the palace, and nor were they, in any event, willing to see the restoration of John. The palace remained determinedly opposed to this, even though both Pope Innocent I and the Western emperor Honorius were in favour of his restoration.

Honorius, the Western emperor, wrote to his older brother Arcadius in less diplomatic terms. In his letter, he abhors the bloodshed at the Easter services. He reproves the Eastern government for its intervention in church affairs. He notes that no time was given for negotiation, arbitration or reconciliation. He records that no representatives had been sent to

Rome for Innocent's opinion and help. Furthermore, those bishops who remained in contact with John had been given no real reason for breaking fellowship with him.[12] While the pope is circumspect in his indictment, there is no such reticence in emperor speaking to emperor, although neither letter was to produce any change in the Eastern court or among John's clerical opponents.

The combination of Innocent and Honorius's letters and the empress's death did not lead to the change in attitude of the palace for which John might have hoped. Instead, the imperial administration in the East had gone through a period of consolidation, and Constantinople was more assured of its future and confident in its rule. In succession to the clique that ruled with Eudoxia, there was now a properly formed Roman government. Anthemius held the office of *praefectus praetorio* from 405 to 414. He was a man of considerable experience in government and had "links with the orthodox church establishment and pagan circles".[13] He ruled with a firm Roman hand: the Johnites were brought to heel; the borders of the empire were secured in the East and the threat of Alaric was checked in Epirus by 407. All this meant that there was little hope that there would be a change of heart and John recalled: more than anything else, the Roman government in Constantinople wanted uneventful rule.

After the government in Constantinople rejected Innocent's first request that a synod be summoned to enquire into the circumstances of John's dismissal, Innocent and Honorius redoubled their efforts to secure fair treatment for him. Honorius sent Arcadius a list of all the complaints he had received about John's treatment and embarked on closer co-operation with Innocent. In the summer of 405, a synod had met in Rome to review John's treatment, including leading Western bishops like Chromatius of Aquileia and Palladius from the East. They found that John had been unjustly treated, called for the excommunication of Theophilus, Arsacius and others, and likewise for John's restoration; or at least that a further synod comprising both Eastern bishops and those who had formed the Western synod be held at Thessalonica to re-examine the case.

The lobbying from the West on behalf of John had now passed into a purely political campaign. Arcadius was unlikely to heed his younger brother Honorius and Innocent's letters; and without Arcadius's support, their suggestions were unlikely to succeed. Nevertheless, a substantial delegation of at least nine bishops (five from the West and four that had fled from the East) was sent by ship from Rome and Ravenna to Constantinople,[14] setting out most probably in the spring of 406 following the unsuccessful first round of letters and delegations. In the meantime, the new Bishop of Constantinople, Arsacius, had died, and some hoped this might provide an opportunity for the reappointment of John. But relations between East and West were already tense with Anthemius's consulship in the East not recognized by Stilicho. Stilicho himself was firefighting against the Goths (405–6) in the Western empire, and against a British usurper, Constantine III (406). His inability to snuff out this insurrection in Gaul and along the Rhine, and rumours he had ambitions to place his son on the Eastern throne, led to his downfall in 408. The Western empire was severely weakened by his loss.

The delegation from Rome set sail, but this was soon seen as unwanted interference by the West in the affairs of the East; and this was to prove a regular response from the East right up to and beyond the fourth Crusade of 1204, when the Venetian Catholics virtually sacked Constantinople, which in turn underlined the great schism between the Orthodox and the Catholic Church in 1054. The delegation sent from Rome in 406 was kept under continuous military surveillance after rounding the Peloponnese. The ship was not allowed to harbour at Thessalonica or to deliver a letter from Innocent to the bishop there. It was boarded and the two groups of Western and Eastern bishops were then carried in separate ships. When they arrived in Constantinople, the emperor refused to see them, and they were only allowed to leave their letter. Furthermore, an attempt was made to bribe them to enter into communion with Atticus, the successor to Arsacius, Bishop of Constantinople. The Western bishops were summarily dismissed with only the most desultory transport laid on for them, including initially, until it was changed at the Dardanelles, an unseaworthy ship. They arrived home after three weeks at sea with nothing to show for their efforts except their humiliation and loss of face. Worse befell the Eastern bishops who were sent into exile to remote corners of the empire. The imperial administration was in no mood for relaxing its strictures on John and his followers. Indeed, they were ready to turn the screw, and John would suffer the consequences.

In 406/7, still in exile in Cucusos or Arabissus, John was hopeful. After all, powerful voices had taken up his cause; there was no monolithic antipathy towards him in the East, despite the political gerrymandering emanating from the palace. In correspondence of that period, he thanks the Latin bishops for their support, expresses hope for his future, but also recognizes the odds stacked against him. The style of the letters is secretive, not mentioning the recipient by name, presumably for fear of imperial recriminations.[15] In his last letter to Olympias (no. 17), he exhorts her to be free from her "despondency" or depression, but as far as he is concerned, he says, "we are in good health, that having been encompassed with so many difficulties, we have been delivered from sickness and infirmity—on account of which our enemies, who know this, are in exceeding grief and pain. It follows that this should be your greatest encouragement and your chief consolation."[16]

Later in the year, John wrote a final time to Pope Innocent, thanking him for his efforts, asking him to redouble them, and expressing gratitude for the trust Innocent had placed in him.[17] But neither Innocent's efforts on his behalf, nor Olympias's prayers and support would prevent John facing one last and fatal journey into a more remote exile. Indeed, in the final part of his letter to Innocent he suggests that he has heard rumours that his exile is to become more severe.[18]

Palladius maintains that the bishops of Syria, including Severian and Porphyrius of Antioch, were jealous of the attention that John received, even in exile. Nor did they appreciate the words of Paul, which were becoming so true in John's case, that God's power is "made perfect in weakness" (2 Corinthians 12:9).[19] If we combine the jealous complaints of the Syrian bishops with the hardening policy of the court towards the plea from the West that John's case be heard by a new synod, and the momentary crack in the clouds of Gothic ambitions after their defeat by Stilicho at Fiesole in 406, then it all amounts to a strengthening of the government's determination to finally silence John.

At some point in the summer of 407, an order or rescript came from the government to transfer John to a new place of exile at Pityus on the Black Sea. According to varied sources, the journey took either three months or three weeks. It was, in any event, an arduous journey over mountainous terrain, heading north in both the scorching heat of late August and intermittent heavy hailstorms. John was in a weakened state. He was made to walk. Some of his guards were compassionate towards his fragility; others sought to increase his suffering. Palladius tells us that his guards were under the impression that should John die en route they would be promoted.[20] With this in mind, when they arrived in a village where John might have taken a restorative bath, so important for his health, he was hustled on without respite. North of present-day Tokat they crossed the Yeçil Irmak River at a bridge still visible today. After a further eight kilometres, they reached the hamlet of Bizeri, where stood a chapel to a local martyr, Basiliskos, who was executed in 312 under Maximinius Daia near the end of the Great Persecution. Here they decided to spend the night close by the martyr's tomb. Palladius tells us that the martyr addressed John in a dream with the words, "Courage, brother John, tomorrow we shall be together."[21] The following day, 14 September 407, the party set out again, despite John's protests of extreme weakness and exhaustion. He struggled on for a few kilometres and then collapsed, unable to go any further. He was taken back to the chapel where he asked for clean white garments. He gave away his old clothes and shoes to bystanders. He received the sacrament and then joined with the other believers in a prayer, his last prayer, "Glory to God for everything", uttered his last Amen, drew up his feet and was reunited with his fathers in the fashion of the Patriarchs (Genesis 49:33).[22] He died aged about 58. As Palladius says, he left life like a victorious athlete. He was buried in the chapel, but in death as in life, there was dispute as to where his body should finally rest.

Also in death as in life, John's status remained a source of contention. His supporters back in Constantinople remained steadfast in their loyalty to him, but by the time of his death, moves of reconciliation by the authorities had begun to woo them back. The authorities did not want the sort of permanent schism that had been so debilitating in Antioch during the years following Nicaea. Equally, John's main episcopal opponent, Theophilus, Patriarch of Alexandria, did not wish to maintain the breach with John's supporters after his bête noire, John himself, had died. Nevertheless, the restoration of John's rightful reputation was slow in coming and there were sticking points to overcome.

It would be nearly 30 years after his "illegal" deposition in 404 before John's body would be restored to Constantinople, and to Hagia Sophia. His supporters sought his complete rehabilitation. They lobbied for his name to be included in the formal liturgy of the Church, and in particular in the diptychs, which was the sanctioned list of prayers for significant martyrs, leaders and bishops of the Church. Pope Innocent I gave his full support to this move, making inclusion of John's name in the diptychs the condition for resumption of fellowship with the Eastern churches. Although the authorities in Constantinople resisted, no such resistance was found in Antioch. A new bishop, Alexander, had been appointed in succession to the anti-Johnite, the loathed imperial placeman, Porphyrius, who had himself succeeded the beloved Flavian, John's earlier bishop. Alexander made it his business to reconcile the divisions in Antioch by including the hardline Nicene congregation led by Paulinus and Evagrius, accepting their ordinations, and reinstating John's name in the diptychs, the official prayers of the Church.

What had been achieved in Antioch would in time spread, but progress was still intermittent. Alexander's successor, Theodotus (417–29), tried to overturn John's inclusion in the prayers, but a popular uprising in Antioch prevented that. In Constantinople, John's rehabilitation was more faltering, but a combination of the boycott of services by the Johnites, the example of Antioch, and the stipulation by Innocent I that neither the bishop of Constantinople, Atticus, nor the church in Constantinople, would be in communion with Rome until John's name was included in the prayers, meant that it was only a matter of time before this happened. Admittedly, such an inclusion meant the admission that John had been illegally deposed and had never ceased to be bishop of Constantinople, but that was a pill that Atticus and the authorities would have to swallow. In the end, with the support of the new boy emperor, Theodosius II, under pressure from the populace, and with the encouragement of Alexander of Antioch, Atticus agreed that John could be remembered officially once more, and swallowed the bitter pill of accepting John and remembering him as a former bishop of Constantinople. He explained his action in a letter to Cyril, the yet more despotic and John-hating Patriarch of Alexandria, and the nephew of Theophilus. The letter was received by Cyril with "cold contempt".[23] Nevertheless, despite Cyril's scorn for Atticus's capitulation, and more fundamentally for John himself, ecclesiastical realpolitik meant that some ground must be given to restore relations with Rome and with Theodosius II. By 418, it seems that Alexandria had also agreed to restore John to the prayers of the Church.

But still the Johnites demanded more. Peremptory inclusion of John's name in the lists of prayers was one thing. What they wanted was greater acknowledgement of their faith-hero, namely public acknowledgement in the liturgy of John's exemplary ministry and the return of his body to his rightful resting place in Constantinople. This would take longer. On 26 September 428, John's name was solemnly celebrated in the liturgy of the Church for the first time. The newly appointed Bishop Nestorius who initiated this would soon be in full-on collision with Cyril of Alexandria over the definition of Christ's human and divine nature, and indeed with the whole Church, as a result of which he would be deposed as a heretic and go into exile. But in 434, with the full support of Emperor Theodosius II and his celibate sister Pulcheria, Bishop Proclus (434–6), successor to Nestorius, who was by then exiled for heresy, gave permission for the reburial of John in the Church of the Holy Apostles. A ship conveying his remains arrived at the Bosphorus on the night of 27 January 438. It was surrounded by other boats in a torchlit entrance to the city. Emperor Theodosius II was there to welcome the reliquary of John's remains. Bowing before the coffin he prayed that his parents, Empress Eudoxia and Emperor Arcadius be forgiven by John for any injustices they had done to him in ignorance.[24] John's body would remain in the Church of the Apostles until the destruction of that church in the fourth crusade in 1204. (He would lie near both Arcadius, and Eudoxia, united in death if not in life.) The Venetians then seized John's body and took it to Rome as a precious relic, where it was buried in St Peter's Basilica. In 438, however, the Johnites were satisfied that due honour had been paid, and that their bishop, so beloved of the people, had received his final rehabilitation since his unjust deposition by a conspiracy against him at the Synod of the Oak.

John's near contemporary, Gregory of Nazianzus, also briefly bishop of Constantinople in 380, once wrote that "the guiding of man, the most variable and manifold of creatures, seems to me in very deed to be the art of arts".[25] He went on to say of spiritual care in the same Oration (*On his Flight to Pontus*) that "none of these [medical interventions], laborious and hard as they may seem, is so difficult as the diagnosis and cure of our habits, passions, lives, wills, and whatever else is within us, by banishing from our compound nature everything brutal and fierce, and introducing and establishing in their stead what is gentle and dear to God, and arbitrating fairly between soul and body".[26] If Gregory found it hard ordering the wills of others in his charge, perhaps because of his dislike of faction and rancour, John had no such qualms. He was sure of himself, clear in his understanding of Scripture, aware of his authority as a bishop, and able to submit his own passions to rigorous discipline and asceticism. But for all his genuine qualities of leadership, he had blind spots which stored up trouble for his main objective. If his main project was to establish a city of God, whether in Antioch or Constantinople, then he knew the main tools at his disposal for the task: the consistent preaching of Scripture in a manner expository, attractive and relevant to the populace. Few, if any, had his skills as an orator, able to hold a crowd with his vivid language and willingness to apply the moral teaching of the text without fear or favour. Alongside this, John understood the theatre of an occasion, including the power of the liturgy itself, which would retain an abiding place in Orthodox worship to this day. And indeed, John's liturgy set to music by the greatest composers (e.g., Rachmaninov) would provide literally heavenly moments of worship. John was also able to preach into the dramas of the statues in Antioch or the asylum of Eutropius as he sheltered beneath the altar in Hagia Sophia while John preached. Through his gifts and these opportunities, John became a very significant figure in Constantinople, and on several occasions was used by the emperor to negotiate with others, notably with Gainas, the Gothic leader.

While on the one hand, John's very great combination of gifts and character worked for his vision for the city, in the scales against him was his willingness to make, or to exacerbate, enmity towards himself. Admittedly much of this hostility was malevolent, based on jealousy or suspicion, especially when it came from Theophilus of Alexandria. For some time now, Alexandria had viewed with suspicion the rise of Constantinople following its official founding in 330 as a new imperial and now ecclesiastical centre. There were already signs of Alexandrian interference in the echelons of power in Constantinople in the days of Gregory of Nazianzus. But in the past John had showed his vituperative side against the Jews in Antioch, and now in Constantinople against women in general, who he saw as a snare. And although he had deep respect for Olympias, he still wanted to control her munificent generosity. Finally, when it came to the empress, John saw himself as a latter-day Elijah preaching against a Jezebel, and the only one left who was righteous (1 Kings 18:22; 19:10). The claim that Eudoxia was a Jezebel was an eye-catching, ear-tingling trope, replete with all kinds of rhetorical flourish, but did it further his cause? Eudoxia was emotional and mercurial as a character with too much influence over the emperor for John's good. She did have a silver statue of herself erected near Hagia Sophia on a Sunday, but given all we know about the imperial statues in Antioch, was that so unusual? She was not leading a band of prophets of Baal, and she did respect John as the baptizer of her children. Early on she accompanied John piously to a new shrine. She wanted justice for the Origenist monks, the Tall Brothers, so loathed by Theophilus. Her family was brought up in the strictest of Christian traditions. But in driving a wedge between himself and the empress, John managed to solidify a coalescence of malcontents who pursued him unjustly through the Synod of the Oak, with all its jumped-up charges, into exile. In truth, John had given his opponents a stick to beat him with. The preacher that John was saw an opportunity of preaching against her, while a pastor may have used the arts available to him to establish "what is gentle and near to God". Surely the experienced 56-year-old bishop should have been able to lead the headstrong 20-year-old empress into better ways? But John was what he was, and in his near martyrdom in exile he established his legend and burnished his reputation as a golden-mouthed preacher who sought the salvation of the city with every ounce of his depleted energy and all the determination he possessed. Whether he wanted to or not John did create a legend for himself that would live on powerfully.

In the sixteenth century, John was the go-to preacher for the Reformers. His example of preaching Scripture to a city in an expository verse-by-verse manner, whatever the cost or opposition, was a powerful example to the city preachers of the Swiss Cantons, not least in Geneva and Zurich. If Calvin did not consciously follow John's example in Geneva, much of what he did in preaching Scripture to a city and seeking its reform was surely influenced by Chrysostom's example. And from Geneva the example spread to other cities in Switzerland, Germany, England and Scotland, especially.[27] Elsewhere in England, when a survey of cathedral libraries was conducted by Cranmer, one of the authors he expected to find in Canterbury cathedral library was John Chrysostom.[28] And in the services of morning and evening prayer in the Church of England 1662 Prayer Book, first assembled by Cranmer in 1549, a prayer attributed to John Chrysostom was included in which the worshippers ask that their supplications be answered in a way that "may be most expedient for them: granting [them] in this world knowledge of the truth, and in the world to come life everlasting". Surely John, who ministered sacrificially through preaching and teaching in Antioch and then Constantinople, would have wanted God's people wherever they are to have that prayer fulfilled, that they might have knowledge of the truth.

Notes

1. J. N. D. Kelly, *Golden Mouth: The Story of John Chrysostom, Ascetic, Preacher, Bishop* (Ithaca, NY: Cornell University Press, 1998), p. 275.
2. Kelly, *Golden Mouth*, pp. 202, 275.
3. Sozomen, *Ecclesiastical History* VIII.27, *Nicene and Post-Nicene Fathers: Second Series, Vol. II: Socrates, Sozomenus: Church Histories*, ed. Philip Schaff (Grand Rapids, MI: Eerdmans, 1987), p. 417.
4. Sozomen, *Ecclesiastical History* VIII.27, op. cit., p. 417.
5. Kelly, *Golden Mouth*, p. 272.
6. R. C. Blockley, "The dynasty of Theodosius", in A. Cameron and P. Garnsey (eds), *The Cambridge Ancient History*, Vol. XIII (Cambridge: Cambridge University Press, 1998), pp. 114ff.
7. Blockley, "The Dynasty of Theodosius", p. 121.
8. Sozomen, *Ecclesiastical History* VIII.26, op. cit., pp. 416–17.
9. Sozomen, *Ecclesiastical History* VIII.26, op. cit., p. 416.
10. Sozomen, *Ecclesiastical History* VIII.26, op. cit., p. 416.
11. Sozomen, *Ecclesiastical History* VIII.26, op. cit., p. 416.
12. Kelly, *Golden Mouth*, p. 277.
13. Blockley, "The Dynasty of Theodosius", p. 123.
14. Palladius, Dialogue 4, Palladius, *Dialogues*, in *Dialogue sur la vie de Jean Chrysostome/Palladios*, ed. and tr. Anne-Marie Malingrey with Philippe Leclercq, SC 341 (Paris: Les Éditions du Cerf, 1988), p. 85.
15. Chrysostom, *PG* 52.705, p. 160.
16. Chrysostom, Letter 17, in *Letters to Saint Olympias*, tr. David C. Ford (Crestwood, NY: St Vladimir's Press, 2016), p. 168.
17. *PL* 52.535–6.
18. *PL* 52.535–6.
19. Palladius, Dialogue 11.75ff., op. cit., p. 223.
20. "S'il mourait en route ils accéderaient à un grade supérieur", *SC* 341 XI, p. 225.
21. Palladius, op. cit., p. 227.
22. Palladius, op. cit., pp. 229–30.
23. Kelly, *Golden Mouth*, p. 288; Ep.76. *PG* 77.352–60.
24. Socrates, *Ecclesiastical History* VII:45, op. cit., p. 177, Kelly, *Golden Mouth*, p. 290.

25 Gregory Nazianzen, *Oratio* 1:15: *In Defence of his flight to Pontus*, in *Nicene and Post-Nicene Fathers: Second Series, Vol. VII: Cyril of Jerusalem, Gregory of Nazianzen*, ed. Philip Schaff (New York: Cosimo, 2007), p. 208.
26 Nazianzen, *Oratio* 1, op. cit., pp. 208–9.
27 T. H. L. Parker, *John Calvin* (London: Dent & Sons, 1975) pp. 89ff.
28 Thomas Cranmer, *Articles of Visitation of The Cathedral Church of Canterbury 1550*, Parker Society (Cambridge: Cambridge University Press, 1846), p. 161.

Timeline

306 Constantine proclaimed Emperor of the West in York.
313 Edict of Milan: freedom of worship for Christians in the empire.
324 Empire united by Constantine: the founding of Constantinople.
325 Council of Nicaea.
***c*.349** Birth of John Chrysostom in Antioch.
367 John completes his education under the pagan rhetorician Libanius.
368 John is baptized at Easter and becomes Bishop Meletius's lay assistant while instructed by Diodore of Tarsus.
372 John takes on the life of an ascetic on Mount Silpios and writes *A king and a monk compared* and *To Theodore who fell away*.
379 Gregory of Nazianzus preaches his *Orations on the Trinity* in Constantinople.
381 Opening of the Council of Constantinople and sudden death of Meletius. Flavian succeeds Meletius in Antioch.
379 John serves as deacon in Antioch first to Meletius and then to Flavian, his successor.
380–7 John writes *Contrition of heart*; *To Stageiriu*; *Against the enemies of monasticism*; *Christ's divinity proved against Jews and Pagans*; *Virginity*; *To a young widow*; and *Single marriage*.
386 John is ordained Priest and preaches his first sermon 13 March 387. From 387–97, John becomes the leading preacher in Antioch. During this period, he preaches biblical series on Isaiah, Romans (32 homilies), 1 Timothy (18), 2 Timothy (6), Titus (6), Ephesians (24), The Psalms (52), Matthew (90), John (88), 1 Corinthians (14), 2 Corinthians (30). John also writes *On Priesthood* and *On Educating children*.
397 John becomes Bishop of Constantinople after the death of Nectarius.

397–402 John preaches on Philippians (15), Colossians (5), Acts of the Apostles (55), 1 Thessalonians (11), 2 Thessalonians (5), Philemon (3), Hebrews (34).

399 Fall of Eutropius, his taking sanctuary in Hagia Sophia and John's sermon.

400 John deals with Gainas on behalf of the emperor; his reputation is high.

400 July Uprising in Constantinople against the Goths.

401 Eudoxia gives birth to the future Theodosius II. John calls her "Jezebel" for dispossessing a widow of her vineyard.

October Appeal of Ephesus to John to appoint a new bishop.

Winter Arrival of the Tall Brothers in Constantinople seeking support.

402 January John embarks on a pastoral tour of Asia. Severian of Gabala appointed as stand-in bishop in Constantinople during John's absence.

Herakleides of Cyprus and follower of Evagrios of Pontikos and Origen appointed bishop of Ephesus. Enquiry into the actions of Antoninus and simony.

Eastertide John returns to Constantinople. Attitudes at court have hardened against John. Dispute and reconciliation service with Severian.

Theophilus of Alexandria campaigns against the Tall Brothers and John.

24 June The Tall Brothers request Eudoxia's intervention on their behalf and to hear their case.

Theophilus's presence required by the emperor in Constantinople.

403 Epiphanius of Cyprus enlisted by Theophilus to support him and denounce all Origenist thought, including the Tall Brothers and John.

May John preaches against the weaknesses of women, implicating Eudoxia.

August Theophilus arrives in Constantinople. John is called by the imperial court to hear charges against Theophilus. John refuses to judge a fellow bishop. Instead, Theophilus assembles a charge sheet against John to be heard at the Synod of the Oak outside Chalcedon.

September Synod of the Oak meets to hear trumped-up charges. John refuses to appear.

John is deposed and arrested. He is sent into exile. Riots in support of John break out in the city. John is recalled by Arcadius at Eudoxia's request, following her miscarriage.

October John returns expecting complete exoneration. John condemns a silver statue of Eudoxia.

404 Easter John under house arrest. Hagia Sophia closed to his supporters. Easter baptisms attacked by troops.

20 June John finally leaves Constantinople for exile. A fire ravages Hagia Sophia.

September John arrives at Cucusos in Armenia. He remains there for three years, corresponds with Olympias. He writes *No man can be harmed save by himself.*

6 October Eudoxia dies. Her son Theodosius II will become one of Byzantium's greatest emperors. Arcadius dies in 408.

405 Pope Innocent I supports John.

407 John exiled further into Armenia. He dies en route to Pityus (Pitsundia, Abkhazia) on the Black Sea, dying at Bizeri on 14 September at the shrine of Basiliskos.

438 27 January John's body is returned to Constantinople and buried in the Church of the Holy Apostles. Destroyed in the 4th Crusade 1204, John was finally buried in St Peter's Rome.

Dramatis personae

Arcadius (*c*.377–408)   The eldest son of Theodosius and Aelia Flacilla, born in Italica, Spain before his father became emperor. He was made *co-augustus* by his father in 383 when only five but succeeded fully in 395, aged 17. He married Eudoxia that same year, the daughter of a Frankish general in the Roman army, at the instigation of the court chamberlain, Eutropius. Weak-willed compared to his father, he was strongly influenced by his wife Eudoxia and imperial officials. He survived his wife by only four years, but his son Theodosius II proved one of the most effective rulers of the Eastern empire (408–50).

Arius (*c*.256–336)   Of Berber descent from Libya, he became the spokesman for a widely accepted theology in the East that Jesus was subordinate to the Father, who was alone eternal, thus threatening the Apostolic teaching about the Trinity. Initially opposed by Bishop Alexander of Alexandria and causing consternation there and further afield, the Emperor Constantine called the Council of Nicaea in 325. Arius was condemned, as was his teaching, by the Nicene Creed. Arius made a sham confession of orthodox faith, before Constantine, but died soon afterwards. He was opposed mostly by Athanasius. And in 381 the Nicene-Constantinopolitan Creed was reissued upholding orthodoxy.

Athanasius (*c*.296–373)   Athanasius was the Bishop of Alexandria who strongly opposed Arius and the teaching of the so-called Arian party which was condemned at Nicaea. After Constantine he faced a number of Arian emperors who opposed him. He went into exile five times. He wrote copiously against the Arian movement, in particular his theological treatise *Contra Gentes: De Incarnatione*, about the Incarnation and the divinity of Christ. His *Life of Antony*, the monk/hermit, was the foundation text about Asceticism.

Antiochene Christianity at the time of Chrysostom would be greatly influenced by these writings.

Constantine the Great (*c*.227–337)   First Christian Emperor. Proclaimed *augustus of* the West by his troops in York in 306 after the death of his father, Constantius I, emperor of the West. Defeated his rival Maxentius at the Battle of Milvian Bridge in 312 at which he declared himself a Christian, placing the Labarum on the banners of his soldiers. In 312, at Milan, Constantine and the Eastern Emperor, Licinius declared freedom of worship for Christians, with Christianity becoming a religion of the empire. In 324, he defeated Licinius, becoming emperor of the whole empire, founded Constantinople, and in 325 called the Council of Nicaea at his summer residence in Nicaea.

Epiphanius, Bishop of Salamis, Cyprus *c*.320–403   Trenchant supporter of Nicene orthodoxy and a known heresy hunter. He was bishop for over 40 years. He wrote the *panarion*, a compendium of eighty heresies. He supported Bishop Paulinus of Antioch, the ultra-Nicene bishop who was opposed to the godly Meletius (Bishop of Antioch 360–81). Meletius was an early supporter of Chrysostom. However, Bishop Theophilus of Alexandria used Epiphanius in a campaign against Origen and the Tall Brothers and by implication Chrysostom, who sought to hear their case in Constantinople and who was not himself opposed to Origen's teaching. Epiphanius went to Constantinople to condemn Origen and Chrysostom, but finding little support he returned home, dying on the voyage in 403.

Eudoxia, Aelia (*c*.378–403)   Empress from 395–404, married to Arcadius the older son of Theodosius I. She had five surviving children and may have died shortly after childbirth. Her son Theodosius II proved one of Byzantium's greatest rulers; likewise her eldest daughter, Pulcheria, who took vows of chastity, was briefly empress (450–3). A headstrong woman of great beauty, Eudoxia was accused of being like Jezebel by Chrysostom, with whom she had at times a tempestuous relationship, and ended up as his opponent.

Eustathius of Antioch (*c.*290–360)   The Nicene Bishop of Antioch in the period immediately following the Council of Nicaea, who was deposed by more moderately Arian-leaning bishops. A godly and highly regarded bishop, he was sent into exile, which precipitated a schism in Antioch between the supporters of Eustathius (Eustathians) who chose Paulinus and a number of moderate Arian bishops, culminating in Meletius (360–81), who chaired the Council of Constantinople in 381, until his sudden death, being succeeded briefly by Gregory of Nazianzus until his own resignation.

Eutropius (*c.*330–99)   A eunuch who had been a body-servant to Roman soldiers and officials, who eventually became the Chamberlain at the court of Arcadius, and the first eunuch to be a Consul. Mocked by the court poet Claudian, he was resented by many in the hierarchy for his interference and unmanliness, and in particular by Gainas the army commander. He was instrumental in the appointment of Chrysostom to Constantinople, but a court plot orchestrated by Eudoxia and Gainas toppled him. He sought sanctuary in Hagia Sophia, where Chrysostom preached with him cowering beneath the altar. He was later executed.

Evagrius of Antioch (*c.*320–92)   He succeeded the ultra-Nicene Paulinus as bishop in 388. He perpetuated the division in Antioch and wrote in harsh terms to Basil of Caesarea. He opposed Flavian, Chrysostom's godly and much-respected bishop. He was supported in the West by the contentious Bishop of Rome, Damasus I.

Flavian, Bishop of Antioch (381–404)   Flavian succeeded Meletius as the orthodox Bishop of Antioch appointed by the emperor. But the Church was still in schism with the ultra-Nicene Church led by Paulinus and then Evagrius, who in turn followed Eustathius. John Chrysostom was wholly in support of him, and John acted as his close associate as Presbyter and main spokesman.

Gainas (*c.*350–400)   A Gothic commander in the Roman army. Gainas, like Stilicho in the West, was typical of a number of Roman army commanders in the late Roman Empire used by the emperors in their struggle with encroaching, non-Roman barbarians. Gainas rose from being a foot soldier to *magister militum*, assassinated the *Prefect* in the East, Rufinus, at the behest of Stilicho, and found in Eutropius, until his fall, a rival to further power. He rebelled against the emperor Arcadius. Chrysostom negotiated with him in 400 but in the same year Gainas overreached himself and was defeated and killed by the Huns under Uldin, who sent his head to Arcadius.

Gregory of Nazianzus (*c*.329–90)   One of the three Cappadocian Fathers, along with Basil of Caesarea and Gregory of Nyssa. Ordained in 361 by his father and made a bishop by Basil, he became renowned for his Orations on the Trinity at the Chapel of Anastasia in Constantinople in 379. He was briefly Bishop of Constantinople and chaired the Council of Constantinople in 381 but resigned that office, retreating to Nazianzus to write up his Orations. Often bruised by events, he nonetheless was an elegant writer of Trinitarian theology. He was succeeded by Nectarius, the predecessor of Chrysostom.

Honorius (384–423)   Emperor of the West and the second son of Theodosius I. His brother Arcadius was Augustus in the East. Initially the Western empire was held together by Honorius's army commander Stilicho until 408 when he was executed. However, under increasing numbers of invasions from the east and from Britain, the empire began to disintegrate. Honorius's court was based in Ravenna after the sack of Rome in 410 by Alaric. The empire in the west struggled on until 478. Honorius supported Chrysostom with the support of Pope Innocent I.

Innocent I (pope 401–17)   He used his pontificate to extend the power of Rome in resolving church disputes. He defended Chrysostom against Theophilus of Alexandria, and likewise defended Augustine of Hippo against the Pelagians, upholding the Council of Carthage of 416. He survived the sack of Rome by Alaric in 410.

Libanius (*c*.314–93)   He was a teacher of Rhetoric in the Second Sophist school. He was born in Antioch and one of the greatest teachers of history and rhetoric in the fourth century. He remained a pagan throughout his life and taught in Antioch and Constantinople. Among his pupils were John Chrysostom, whom he regarded as a worthy successor to himself had he been available, and Theodore of Mopsuestia. Libanius credited Chrysostom as being the finest orator in his school. He wrote extensive works on history including an account of the crisis of the statues in Antioch in 387, and over 1500 letters.

Meletius (Bishop of Antioch 360–81) Although he was opposed by the ultra-Nicene Paulinus, after being initially mildly Arian as a bishop he was later exiled twice in 365 and 371/2 for his pro-Nicene views and was regarded by Theodosius I as orthodox. He chaired the opening sessions of the Council of Constantinople in 381 but died suddenly, being replaced by Gregory of Nazianzus. He supported Chrysostom in his early vocation, and John became a close aide of him before his ordination. He was succeeded by Flavian, also much beloved by Chrysostom.

Olympias (c.362–408) A member of the elite aristocracy of the Eastern empire. Her father, Seleucus, was a Count of the empire and her grandfather a Praetorian Prefect. She inherited vast estates and wealth. After the early death of her parents, she was raised by Christians: her governess, Theodosia, was the sister of St Amphilocus, the protégé of Basil of Caesarea. Aged 17 she supported Gregory of Nazianzus and his preaching the Trinity at the Anastasia Chapel in Constantinople in 379. Gregory of Nyssa dedicated his work on *The Song of Songs* to her. After the early death of her husband, her assets were put in trust until she was 30 by Emperor Theodosius. In *c.*395, she began life as an austere ascetic and formed a monastic order which grew to 250 "nuns". After 398, she formed a close bond with John Chrysostom, who lived nearby in Constantinople. During his exile, John corresponded with Olympias, who wrote him 17 letters in which she focuses on her growing depression. John found consolation in her friendship. And as a "Johnite" she was later tried in Constantinople for starting a fire in Hagia Sophia, and acquitted.

Origen (c.185–253) Theological teacher in Alexandria and Caesarea. He was an ascetic, possibly having castrated himself. He was a theologian teaching at the Alexandrian theological school and later in Caesarea and writing a theological work entitled *On*

First Principles. He was an exegete, producing a text of the Hebrew scriptures in eight translations called the *Hexapla* and numerous commentaries on John, the Pauline Epistles and Old Testament books, including favouring the allegorical method of interpretation, especially *The Song of Songs*. He was an apologist, writing *Contra Celsum* against a pagan critic of Christianity. He was controversial because he was heavily influenced by Platonism and the neo-Platonism of Plotinus. He believed in the pre-existence of the soul, the reconciliation of all things and God using pre-existent matter in creation. For these things he was criticised and condemned. His teaching was condemned by the Fifth Ecumenical Council in 555 in Constantinople. He remains a brilliant but controversial figure.

Palladius (364–*c*.430) Bishop of Helenopolis and later Aspuna in Galatia and biographer of John, in his book called the *Dialogues*. He gave an eyewitness account of John's final years. He was intensely loyal to John and may have airbrushed legitimate concerns about John's style. He met the Tall Brothers and Isidore in Egypt. He wrote a book about Egyptian monastic life and the Desert Fathers entitled the *Lausiac History*. He travelled to Rome to lobby Innocent I and gain support for John in 405.

Paulinus Bishop of Antioch (362–388) He was the leader of the ultra-Nicene party in succession to the exiled Eustathius. A schism was caused between the saintly Meletius, Bishop of Antioch, ordained by Arians, and himself. He was supported by the See of Rome, Epiphanius of Salamis in Cyprus. He ordained Jerome.

Severian, Bishop of Gabala, Syria (*c*.355–408) Severian was a popular preacher in Constantinople in the period 400–404, and of the court party supported by Eudoxia. He opposed John Chrysostom and took on preaching responsibilities while John was out of the city. An attempt at reconciliation by Eudoxia did nothing to heal the rift and Severian opposed John at the Council of the Oak, seeking his dismissal.

Socrates (*c*.380–*c*.450) A barrister who was born and spent his life in Constantinople. His church history was written between 438–43 and covered the period of the Church's life from 306–439. As a careful historian, he drew on a wide range of sources. He was wide-ranging in his views, tolerating Origen and supporting the Novatians. He supported John and "was impressed by his character and eloquence but puzzled by his severity and aloofness". Unlike the contemporary historians Zosimus, a convinced pagan, and Philostorgios, an unreformed Arian, he was thoroughly orthodox.

Sozomen (*c*.400–*c*.460)   Also practised as a barrister in Constantinople where he lived from 425. He was born in a village near Gaza. He wrote a church history covering the period 324–439 and dedicated it to Theodosius II. He used Socrates's account liberally and wrote for the elite. He was an uncritical supporter of John.

Theodosius I (347–95, Emperor 379–95)   The last emperor of East and West. A Roman general who was appointed emperor by Gratian after the defeat of Valens and Roman arms at Adrianople in 378. He was the first emperor in the East since Constantine to hold to Nicene orthodoxy. He called the Council of Constantinople, which endorsed and expanded the Nicene Creed, in 381. He stabilized the empire and temporarily dealt with the Gothic threat, which later re-emerged. He defeated the usurper Maximus in 388 at Poetovio (Croatia). He carried forward legislation intended to dismantle paganism. He was buried in the Church of the Apostles in Constantinople. His sons, Arcadius and Honorius, failed to rule with anything like his strength.

Theodore of Mopsuestia (*c*.350–428)   An early associate of Chrysostom who was persuaded by John in a passionate piece *To Theodore upon his Fall* to forego a relationship with Hermione for an ascetic life. Of the Antiochian school of biblical preaching, he became Bishop of Mopsuestia, not far from Tarsus, and became known for his biblical commentaries and ascetic studies. However, brief association with Julian of Eclanum, a Pelagian, and Nestorius, the heretic denounced for his teaching about the dual nature of Christ, clouded his reputation.

Theophilus (Bishop of Alexandria 384–412 and 23rd Pope of the Coptic Church)   Typified the Pharaonic power of the Bishops of Alexandria from the time of Athanasius to Cyril, his nephew and successor (the period 328–451), and the Coptic split from the Orthodox and Roman Catholic Church. Theophilus led the assault on the Pagan Temple of the Serapeum in Alexandria. The Alexandrian See resented the emergence of a new ecclesiastical centre at Constantinople under Chrysostom and his seeming support of Origen and his views. Theophilus orchestrated the attack on Chrysostom at the Council of the Oak, and with others brought about John's exile and untimely death. He purged Alexandria of Origenism and Paganism and for some time was at odds with both Constantinople and Rome.

The Tall Brothers (*c*.360–410)   The Brothers, known for their height, were a group of four Egyptian monks from Wadi el Natrun. They comprised Dioskorus, also Bishop of Hermopolis (Damanshur) about 60 kilometres southeast of Alexandria, Ammonius, Eusebius and Euthymius. Known for their following of Origen and for leading a further 50 monks, they were driven from their homeland by the Origenist purge led by Theophilus of Alexandria. Chrysostom gave them hospitality and promised to hear their case, for which he too was opposed by Theophilus, who called the Council of the Oak against him. They followed Evagrius Ponticus, a notable ascetic and Origenist teacher known to the Cappadocian Fathers as well as to Rufinus and Melania the Elder.

Glossary of terms

anthropomorphism conceiving of God in human terms of description.

Arian a follower of the heresiarch Arius (c.256–366) from Libya who did not believe in the divinity of Jesus, writing against it. He represented a movement of church members who did not accept the doctrine of the Trinity, principally opposed by Athanasius and the Council of Nicaea.

asceticism a movement of self-denial popular in the Church from the fourth century.

diptychs the formal list of intercessions in a two-sided folder, kept for worship and prayer in the church.

encomium an address in praise of a deceased person, like a eulogy or tribute.

epinoia the discipline of reflection on the person and qualities of God in order to understand them.

foederati tribes bound by treaty to come to the defence of the Roman Empire.

Goths a people group which invaded Roman territory from the east eventually threatening the stability of the empire. In 410, the Visigoths sacked Rome.

Hagia Sophia the name of the great church in Constantinople, meaning Holy Wisdom.

homoiousios the Greek word describing the Son as being like the Father.

homoousios the Greek word used in the Nicene Creed to describe the Son as being of the same substance as the Father.

Manichaeism those who followed the Mani (216–c.274), a mystic religious leader from Persia, not unlike other Gnostic sects that preached dualism and sought an ascetic response.

Nicene Creed   produced by the Council of Nicaea called by the emperor Constantine in 325 to deal principally with the Arian heresy, which sought to subordinate the Son to the Father, as not being eternally God.

Novatian   followers of the Roman priest Novatian (c.200–58), made a counter pope in Rome, who sought to enforce a strict rejection in the Church of those who had lapsed, i.e., who had succumbed to persecution.

oarrhesia   bold speech often used by bishops or church leaders in calling out immoral or unchristian behaviour.

Pneumatomachi   those who spoke against the Spirit being divine, mostly in the late fourth century.

psogos   a diatribe or speech designed to attack a person or group.

Quartodecimans   those who celebrated Easter on 14 Nisan regardless of whether it was a Sunday.

stasis   the ascetic practice of not lying down to sleep but keeping standing.

Abbreviations

NAPNF   Nicene and Post Nicene Fathers
PG   *Patrologia Graeca*
PL   *Patrologia Latina*
SC   *Sources Chrétiennes*
TCAH   The Cambridge Ancient History

Primary sources

Ammianus Marcellinus

The Later Roman Empire (A.D. 354–378)/Ammianus Marcellinus, selected and translated by Walter Hamilton with an introduction and notes by Andrew Wallace-Hadrill (Harmondsworth: Penguin, 1986).

The Apostolic Fathers

The Apostolic Fathers Vols I & II, ed. Bart D. Ehrman, Loeb Classical Library Vols 24 and 25 (Cambridge, MA: Harvard University Press, 2003).

Basil of Caesarea

Letters in Five Volumes, ed. and tr. Bart D. Ehrman, Loeb Classical Library Vols 24–8 (Cambridge, MA: Harvard University Press, 2003).
St Basil's Ascetical Works, tr. Sister Monica Wagner, The Fathers of the Church Vol. 9 (Washington D.C.: Catholic University of America Press, 2000).

Benedict

The Rule of St Benedict, tr. Leonard J. Doyle (Collegeville, MN: The Liturgical Press, 1982).

Clement of Alexandria

The Instructor (Savage, MI: Lighthouse Christian Publishing, 2014).

Cyril of Jerusalem

Catechetical Lectures, NAPNF Second Series Vol. VII (New York: Cosimo, 2007).

Desert Fathers

Sayings of The Early Christian Monks: The Desert Fathers, ed. Benedicta Ward (Harmondsworth: Penguin, 2003).

Eusebius of Caesarea

The Life of Constantine (Limovia Net, 2013).

Gregory of Nazianzus

In Defence of his Flight to Pontus, NAPNF Second Series Vol. VII (New York: Cosimo, 2007).
The Five Theological Orations, NAPNF Second Series Vol. VII (New York: Cosimo, 2007).
On the Arrival of the Egyptians, NAPNF Second Series Vol. VII (New York: Cosimo, 2007).
The Last Farewell, NAPNF Second Series Vol. VII (New York: Cosimo, 2007).

Gregory of Nyssa

On Virginity, NAPNF Second Series Vol. VII (New York: Cosimo, 2007).
On the Making of Man, NAPNF Second Series Vol. VII (New York: Cosimo, 2007).

Jerome

Select Letters, Loeb Classical Library Vol. 262 (Cambridge, MA: Harvard University Press, 1975).

John Chrysostom

Homilies on Genesis 1–17, ed. Robert C. Hill, The Fathers of the Church Vol. 74 (Washington D.C.: The Catholic University of America Press, 1985).
Homilies on St John's Gospel, ed. Sr Thomas Aquinas Goggin, Fathers of the Church (Washington D.C.: Catholic University of America Press, 1957).
Homilies on Acts and Romans, NAPNF First Series Vol. XI (Grand Rapids, MI: Eerdmans, 1975).
Homilies on Paul's Epistles to the Corinthians, NAPNF First Series Vol. XII (New York: Cosimo, 2007).
Homilies on Galatians, Ephesians, Philippians, Colossians, Thessalonians, Timothy, Titus and Philemon, NAPNF First Series Vol. XIII (Whitefish, MO: Kessinger Publishing, 2011).
De Virginitate, PG 48.
On the Incomprehensible Nature of God, The Fathers of the Church Vol. 72, ed. Paul W. Harkins (Washington D.C.: The Catholic University of America Press, 1984).
On Marriage and Family Life, ed. Catherine P. Roth (Crestwood, NY: St Vladimir's Seminary Press, 1986).

On Poverty and Wealth, ed. Catherine P. Roth (Crestwood, NY: St Vladimir's Seminary Press, 1981).
Sur L'Égalité du Père et du Fils, SC 396 ed. Anne-Marie Malingrey (Paris: Les Éditions du Cerf, 1994).
Sermons of John and Severian, PG 52.
On the Priesthood, NAPNF Series 1 Vol. IX (Grand Rapids, MI: Eerdmans, 1975).
Letters to the Fallen Theodore, NAPNF Series 1 Vol. IX (Grand Rapids, MI: Eerdmans, 1975).
Letter to a Young Widow, NAPNF Series 1 Vol. IX (Grand Rapids, MI: Eerdmans, 1975).
Two Homilies on St Babylas and on St Ignatius; *Homily on Lowliness of mind*, NAPNF Series 1 Vol. IX (Grand Rapids, MI: Eerdmans, 1975).
Two Homilies on Eutropius, NAPNF Series 1 Vol. IX (Grand Rapids, MI: Eerdmans, 1975).
Treatise from Exile to prove that no one can harm the man who does not injure himself; Correspondence with Olympias, NAPNF Series 1 Vol. IX (Grand Rapids, MI: Eerdmans, 1975).
Correspondence with Innocent Bishop of Rome (NAPNF Series 1 Vol. IX (Grand Rapids, MI: Eerdmans, 1975).
Palladius, *Dialogue sur La Vie de Jean Chrysostome Vol. I & II*, ed. and tr. Anne-Marie Malingrey with Philippe Leclercq, SC 341 and 342 (Paris: Les Éditions du Cerf, 1988).
Letters to St Olympias tr. David C. Ford (Crestwood, NY: St Vladimir's Seminary Press, 2016).

Origen

On First Principles, tr. G. W. Butterworth (Notre Dame, IN: Christian Classics, 2013).

Socrates

Ecclesiastical History, NAPNF Second Series Vol. VII (New York: Cosimo, 2007).

Sozomen

Ecclesiastical History, NAPNF Second Series Vol. VII (New York: Cosimo, 2007).

Tertullian

On the Apparel of Women, TANF Vol. IV (New York: Cosimo, 2007).
On the Veiling of Virgins, TANF Vol. IV (New York: Cosimo, 2007).
On Modesty, TANF Vol. IV (New York: Cosimo, 2007).
An Answer to the Jews, TANF Vol. III (New York: Cosimo, 2007).

Zosimus

Historia Nova, ed. I. Bekker, *Corpus Scriptorum Historiae Byzantinae* (Bonn, 1837).

Bibliography

Ayres, Lewis, *Nicaea and its Legacy* (Oxford: Oxford University Press, 2009).

Baker, G. P., *Justinian: The Last Roman Emperor* (New York: Cooper Square Press, 2002).

Bardill, Jonathan, *Constantine: Divine Emperor of the Christian Golden Age* (Cambridge: Cambridge University Press, 2015).

Barnes, Timothy D., *Constantine and Eusebius* (Cambridge, MA: Harvard University Press, 1981).

Behr, John, *Irenaeus of Lyons: Identifying Christianity* (Oxford: Oxford University Press, 2015).

Brakke, David, *The Gnostics: Myth, Ritual and Diversity in Early Christianity* (Cambridge, MA: Harvard University Press, 2010).

Brown, Peter, *The World of Late Antiquity* (London: Thames & Hudson, 1971).

Brown, Peter, *The Body and Society: Men, Women and Sexual Renunciation in Early Christianity* (London: Faber and Faber, 1988).

Brown, Peter, *Through the Eye of a Needle: Wealth, the Fall of Rome, and the Making of Christianity in the West, 350–550 AD* (Princeton, NJ: Princeton University Press, 2012).

Cameron, Averil and Peter Garnsey (eds), *The Cambridge Ancient History, Vol. XIII, The Late Empire, AD 337–425* (Cambridge: Cambridge University Press, 1998).

Chadwick, Henry, *The Early Church* (Harmondsworth: Penguin, 1993).

Chitty, Derwas, *The Desert a City: An Introduction to the Study of Egyptian and Palestinian Monasticism under the Christian Empire* (Crestwood, NY: St Vladimir's Press, 1999).

Davis, Stephen J., *The Early Coptic Papacy: The Egyptian Church and its Leadership in Late Antiquity* (Cairo: American University in Cairo Press, 2004).

De Wet, Chris L., *Preaching Bondage: John Chrysostom and the Discourse of Slavery in Early Christianity* (Berkeley, CA: University of California Press, 2015).

Hale Williams, Megan, *The Monk and the Book: Jerome and the Making of Christian Scholarship* (Chicago, IL: University of Chicago Press, 2006).

Hanson, R. P. C., *The Search for the Christian Doctrine of God: The Arian Controversy 318–381* (London: T&T Clark, 1988).

Heine, Ronald E., *Origen: Scholarship in the Service of the Church* (Oxford: Oxford University Press, 2009).

Herrin, Judith, *Byzantium: The Surprising Life of a Medieval Empire* (Harmondsworth: Penguin, 2008).

Hughes, Bettany, *Istanbul: A Tale of Three Cities* (London: Weidenfeld & Nicolson, 2017).

Kelly, Christopher, *Ruling the Later Roman Empire* (Cambridge, MA: Harvard University Press/The Belknap Press, 2004).

Kelly, J. N. D., *Golden Mouth: The Story of John Chrysostom—Ascetic, Preacher, Bishop* (Ithaca, NY: Cornell University Press, 1998).

Ludlow, Morwenna, *The Early Church* (London: I. B. Tauris, 2009).

Mayer, Wendy and Pauline Allen, *John Chrysostom* (London: Routledge, 2000).

McGuckin, John A., *Saint Gregory of Nazianzus: An Intellectual Biography* (Crestwood, NY: St Vladimir's Seminary Press, 2001).

McLynn, Neil B., *Ambrose of Milan: Church and Court in a Christian Capital* (Berkeley, CA: University of California, 1994).

Osborn, Eric, *Clement of Alexandria* (Cambridge: Cambridge University Press, 2008).

Potter, David, *Constantine the Emperor* (Oxford: Oxford University Press, 2013).

Potter, David, *Theodora: Actress, Empress, Saint* (Oxford: Oxford University Press, 2015).

Ramsey, Boniface, *Ambrose* (London: Routledge, 1997).

Rousseau, Philip, *Basil of Caesarea* (Berkeley, CA: University of California Press, 1998).

Shaw, Teresa M., *The Burden of the Flesh: Fasting and Sexuality in Early Christianity* (Minneapolis, MN: Fortress Press, 1998).

Sivan, Hagith, *Galla Placidia: The Last Roman Empress* (Oxford: Oxford University Press, 2011).

Stark, Andrea, *Renouncing the World yet Leading the Church* (Cambridge, MA: Harvard University Press, 2004).

Sunberg, Carla D., *The Cappadocian Mothers: Deification Exemplified in the Writings of Basil, Gregory, and Gregory* (Cambridge: James Clarke & Co, 2018).

Trenham, Josiah B., *Marriage and Virginity according to St. John Chrysostom*, Durham University, 2003. Available at Durham E-Theses Online: <http://etheses.dur.ac.uk/1259/>.

Trigg, Joseph, *Origen* (London: Routledge, 2005).

White, Caroline, *Gregory Nazianzus: Autobiographical Poems* (Cambridge: Cambridge University Press, 1996).

Whitworth, Patrick J., *Three Wise Men from the East: The Cappadocian Fathers and The Struggle for Orthodoxy* (Durham: Sacristy Press, 2015).

Whitworth, Patrick J., *Constantinople to Chalcedon: Shaping the World to Come* (Durham: Sacristy Press, 2017).

Whitworth Patrick J., *Suffering and Glory: The Church from the Apostles to Constantine* (Durham: Sacristy Press, 2018).

Whitworth, Patrick J., *Defining God: Athanasius, Nicaea and the Fourth Century Trinitarian Controversy* (Durham: Sacristy Press, 2023).

Williams, Rowan, *Arius: Heresy and Tradition* (London: SCM Press, 2001).

Williams, Rowan, *Silence and Honey Cakes: The Wisdom of the Desert* (Oxford: Lion Hudson, 2003).

Williams, Stephen and Gerard Friell, *Theodosius: The Empire at Bay* (London: Routledge, 1998).

Index

Acacius of Haleb (Aleppo) 127, 217
Actium, battle of (31 BC) 49
Adrianople, battle of (378) 7, 13–14, 33, 77, 81
Aelia Eudoxia, Empress *see* Eudoxia, Empress
Aelia Flacilla (wife of Theodosius I) 117, 122
Aetius 32, 83
Agelius (Novatianist) 127–8
Alaric the Visigoth 83, 128–9, 233
Alexander, Bishop of Alexandria 27–8, 29
Alexander, Bishop of Antioch 239
Alexander, Bishop of Byzantium 28
Alexander the Great 49
Alexandria
    and the Arian controversy 24–8
    Athanasius in 14, 33
    and ecclesiastical politics 185
    history and intellectual prominence 49–52
    library of 50, 53, 116
Ambrose of Milan 70, 104, 117, 139, 190
    On Virginity 86
Ammianus (chronicler) 6, 8, 11, 81
Ammonius (Tall Brother) 197, 208
Ammonius Saccas 51
Anatolius, Bishop of Constantinople 186
Anthemius (prefect of Constantinople) 223, 235, 236
Anthemius of Tralles 118
Antioch
    and the Arian controversy 26–7, 31, 64
    Church in 42–5
    Council of (341) 31, 64
    Great Church in 31, 42, 64, 65, 83, 90, 92
    John Chrysostom's ministry in 133
    Luke's Gospel written in 19
    resistance to Julian the Apostate 11–12
    riot in (387) 103–4
    synod (351/2) 7
Antiochus of Ptolomeias 208, 217, 231
Antoninus of Ephesus 186–8, 190
Antony the Great 35, 36, 52, 139, 196
Apollinarians 58
Arabissos 222
Arcadius, Emperor
    and Eutropius 167, 170
    and the Goths 173, 175–6
    and John's deposition 209, 217, 218
    made *augustus* in Constantinople (383) 16, 54
    marriage to Eudoxia 177
    summons John to be Bishop of Constantinople 111–12, 117
    and the Tall Brothers 207
Arian controversy 4–7, 12–16, 19, 23–34, 43–4, 46–8, 52, 55–8, 64, 81–2, 82–3, 120–1
Ariminum, Council of 9
Arius 26–8, 30, 43
Arles, Council of
    (314) 29
    (353) 8, 32
Arsacius, Bishop of Constantinople 219–20, 236
Asceticism 21, 34–7, 66–9
Asia Minor, John's intervention in 181

267

Athanaric (leader of the Thervingian Goths) 128–9
Athanasius
   and the Arian controversy 3, 4, 6–7, 12–13, 27, 30–3, 43, 47, 52, 56–7
   Bishop of Alexandria 14
   defence of Dionysius of Alexandria 25
   Life of Antony 35, 36, 66, 139
Atticus, Bishop of Constantinople 236, 239–40
Augustine of Hippo 70, 95, 125
Aurelian, Emperor 26
Aurelianus (Roman Prefect) 172, 173, 176

Babylas, St 11, 42, 97–8
Barnabas 43
Basil of Ancyra 6, 32, 139–40
Basil of Caesarea 10, 34, 37, 63, 66, 86, 88, 139, 140–1, 221
Basil the Great 139
Baxter, Richard 70
Bede, The Venerable 125
Benedict of Nursia 37, 124
Bible
   Vulgate 58
   Septuagint 50
Brison (eunuch) 213
Brown, Peter 87–8, 145, 168
Byzantion/Byzantium *see* Constantinople

Caesar, Julius 49, 50
Caesarius (Roman Prefect) 173, 176
Caligula, Emperor 51
Callistus, Bishop of Rome 24, 55
Calvin, John 112, 243
Candidianus (Roman general) 224
Cappadocian Fathers 32, 33, 37, 43, 189
Catholic Christianity 53
Cave, William, *Ecclesiastici* 26
cenobitism 35
Chadwick, Henry 168

Chalcedon, Council of (451) 47, 48, 186
Chalmers, Dr 112
Christmas, designated by Pope Julius as celebration of the Incarnation 94
Chromatius of Aquileia 235
Church, early Christian communities 19–20
Claudian the poet 168–9
Clement of Alexandria 22, 24, 51, 85–6, 137–8
Constans, Emperor 2, 3–5
Constantine II, Emperor 2
Constantine III 236
Constantine the Great 1–3, 29, 45–7, 53–4, 54, 151
Constantinople
   and the Arian controversy 120–1
   Church in 41, 45–9
   Constantius completes Hagia Sophia 9
   Council of (381) 15–16, 44, 47, 84
   delegation to Pope Innocent (*c*.404) 231, 233–4
   ecclesiastical politics 185–6
   John becomes Bishop of 118–19
   and the Tall Brothers 195, 200–2
   uprising against the Goths 174–6
Constantius II, Emperor 2, 3, 4–9, 30–3, 46, 57
Coptic Christianity 53
Coptic Egyptian Monophysite Church 49
Coptic monasticism 36
Cornelius, Pope 127–8
Cranmer, Thomas 243
Crispus (son of Constantine) 2
Cucusos, Armenia 219, 220–1, 222
Cyprian, Pope 128
Cyriacus the Deacon 234
Cyril, Patriarch of Alexandria 239–40
Cyril, Pope 49
Cyrinus, Bishop of Chalcedon 179, 189, 206, 208, 217

Damasus, Pope 56, 57–8, 82

De Wet, Chris L. 157
Decius, Emperor 20
Dedication Council (Antioch, 341) 31, 64, 216
Delphi temple of Apollo, destruction of 116
Demetrius I of Alexandria 51
Demophilus, Bishop of Constantinople 15, 120
Desert Fathers 35–6, 67
Didache (Church handbook) 123
Diocletian, Emperor 7, 20, 52
Diodore 44
Dionysius of Rome 25
Dionysius the Great (of Alexandria) 25
Dioskorus (Tall Brother) 197, 202, 208
Donatist schism 4, 20

Egyptian monasticism 195–6
Ephesus 19, 186–91
Epictetus 134
Epiphanius of Salamis 201, 203–5
eremitism 35
Eudoxia, Empress
  baptism of Theodosius II 188
  and Bishop Severian 178–81
  Christian devotion 126
  and Eutropius 167, 169
  influence of 117, 176, 177–8
  John's criticism of 200, 215–16, 242
  sides with Theophilus against John 206–7
  and the Tall Brothers 202, 205
  death 231–3
Eudoxius, Bishop of Antioch (*later* Constantinople) 44, 64
Eugenius, Emperor 116
Eunomius 32, 94, 120
eunuchs 168
Eusebia (wife of Constantius) 8
Eusebius (Tall Brother) 197
Eusebius, Bishop of Caesarea 1, 28, 29
Eusebius, Bishop of Valentinopolis 186–8, 190–1
Eusebius of Nicomedia (*later* Constantinople) 28, 29, 31, 120

Eustathius, Bishop of Antioch 44, 64
Euthymius (Tall Brother) 197
Eutropius (eunuch) 117, 167–72, 177, 185
Euzoius, Bishop of Antioch 44
Evagrius Ponticus 36, 69, 189, 196

Fausta (wife of Constantine) 2
Fiesole, battle of (406) 237
Flacilla (daughter of Eudoxia) 213
Flavian, Bishop of Antioch 44, 45, 58, 84, 92, 104, 109–10, 127, 219

Gainas (Gothic military commander) 169, 172–6
Galerius, Emperor 52
Galla (wife of Theodosius I) 117
Galla Placidia 83, 117, 178
Gallus (*caesar* to Constantius) 5, 7, 10
George of Laodicea 33
Gerontius, Bishop of Nicodemia 190, 192
Gibbon, Edward, *Decline and Fall* 3
Gilbey, Monsignor 128
Gnosticism 21–2, 51
Goths 13–15, 46, 54, 81, 83, 128–30, 151, 174–5, 233
Gratian, Emperor 13, 14–15, 16, 77, 82, 115–16
Gregory of Cappadocia 30
Gregory of Nazianzus 10, 15–16, 34, 37, 44, 46, 47–8, 58, 64, 70, 83, 84, 120, 241
Gregory of Nyssa 34, 37, 72, 121, 140, 196
  On Virginity 86
Gregory the Great 70

Hadrian, Emperor 158
Hagia Sophia, Constantinople 9, 46, 118, 169–70, 214, 217–18, 219
Hebrew scriptures, translated into Greek 50
Helena (wife of Julian) 8
Heracles, Bishop of Alexandria 51–2

Herakleides, Bishop of Ephesus
  189–90
heresy and false teaching 21–2, 57–8
hermits 35–6
Hesychius of the Hellespont 187–8
Hilary (theologian) 32
Hippolytus 24–5, 55, 56
homoiousios 6, 14, 32, 33
homoousios 4, 6, 14, 25, 29–34, 43
Honorius, Emperor 116–17, 172, 178, 231, 233–5
hypostasis 56, 57

Iamblichus of Apamea 26, 43
Ignatius of Antioch 20, 35, 43, 97
Innocent I, Pope 206, 207, 224, 231, 233–5, 237, 239
Irenaeus 22
Isaac (monk) 124–5, 207–9
Isaurians 222
Isidore (Alexandrian Guest Master) 127, 185, 198, 199
Isidore of Miletus 118

Jerome 36, 58, 63, 69, 86–7, 139
Jewish Diaspora 158
Jews, and the Church 158–61
John, Gospel of 19
John, Count (favourite of Empress Eudoxia) 173–4, 220
John Chrysostom, St
  birth and education 61–5
  baptism 65
  ascetic life 66–9
  ascetic writings 69–77
  ministry in Antioch 83–5, 92–3
  ordination 92
  preaching 92–9, 104–11, 243
  chosen to be Bishop of Constantinople 111–12, 117–18
  reforms in Constantinople 120–6
  relations with Alexandria and Rome 126–8
  ministry to the Goths 128–30
  promotion of sexual abstinence 139
  on Christian marriage 141–5
  chastisement of the wealthy 146–50
  on slavery 152–8
  on Jews 159–60
  and the fall of Eutropius 170–2
  negotiation with Gothic leaders 173–5
  conflict with Bishop Severian 178–81, 200
  departs from Constantinople for Ephesus and Asia 188–91
  support for the Tall Brothers 199–202
  preaching against female vice 205–6
  refuses to conduct trial against Theophilus 207
  deposition and departure from the city 208–10
  returns to Constantinople 213–14
  breach with the imperial family 215–17
  writes to Pope Innocent I 218
  forced to leave Constantinople 219–20
  in exile 220–4
  correspondence while in exile 223–4, 237
  correspondence with Olympia 224–8, 237
  death on journey to Pityus 237–8
  body restored to Constantinople 239–40
  On Contrition 90
  De non iterando contiguo 88
  Against the Enemies of Monasticism 69, 77, 91–2
  How Parents should Educate Children 92
  Against the Jews 159–60
  A King and a Monk Compared 77
  Letter to Stageirius 90
  Letters to Theodore 74–6
  On the Priesthood 61–2, 67, 69–74, 85
  On Vainglory 92
  On Virginity 66, 69, 87–8

To a Young Widow 88–9
Johnites 219, 239–40
Jovian, Emperor 12, 33
Judaism, sexual mores 134–5
Julian, Emperor ("the Apostate") 2–3, 9–12, 33, 98
Juliana (wife of a Roman consul) 224
Julius I, Pope 30, 31, 56, 94
Julius Nepotianus 5
Justin Martyr 22, 23
Justinian, Emperor 46, 233

Kelly, J. N. D. 57, 109
kontakion liturgy 145

Leontius, Bishop of Ankara 221
Libanius 3, 10, 63, 103–4, 109
Liberius, Pope 8, 32, 56, 57
Logos theology 24–5
Lucian of Antioch 26, 43
Luke, Gospel of 19

Macarius 36
Macedonius, Bishop of Constantinople 120, 122
Magnentius, Flavius Magnus 5–6
Mamertinus 10
Manicheism 95, 97
Marcellus of Ancyra 5, 31
Marcian, Emperor 233
Marcion of Sinope 22, 55, 95, 97
Mark the Evangelist 19, 51
Martyrius (biographer of John) 209
martyrs, cult of 125
Matthew, Gospel of 19–20
Maximus, Bishop of Constantinople 48, 53, 185
Maximus, Emperor 115–16
Melania the Elder 36, 119, 231
Melania the Younger 231
Meletian schism 20, 30, 52
Meletius of Antioch 15, 44, 58, 64–5, 83, 84, 98
Milan, Council of (353) 32
Milan, Edict of (313) 56, 144–5
Milvian Bridge, battle of (312) 53, 54

Monarchian controversy 23–5, 26, 55
Monasticism 35–7, 123–4, 139, 140–1, 195–6
Mons Seleuchus, battle of (353) 6
Mount Silpios 67
Muratorian Canon 20
Mursa, battle of (351) 6

Nag Hammadi, Egypt, Gnostic Gospels found at 22
Nectarius, Archbishop of Constantinople 16, 117, 118, 121, 185
neo-Platonism 26, 51
Nestorianism 48–9
Nestorius, Bishop of Constantinople 48–9, 118, 240
New Testament, completion of 20
Nicaea, Council of (325) 19, 29–34, 43–4, 168 *see also* Arian controversy
Nicene Creed 4, 12, 15–16, 34, 43, 186
Novatianists 20, 127–8, 191–2

Oak, Council of the (403) 48, 207–9
Olympias 119–20, 123, 224–8, 237
Orietris, Bishop of Arabissos 222
Origen 24–5, 51, 51–2, 56, 137, 138, 168, 189, 192–3, 196–9, 201, 203–4
Orontes river 42
Orthodox Christianity 53
Ossia, Bishop of Cordoba 28
Ossius, Bishop 57

Pachomius (ascetic) 35–6, 66
Palladius (John's biographer) 64, 66, 92, 119, 122, 124, 186–7, 187–8, 189, 189–90, 198, 202, 203, 216, 220, 221, 231, 235, 237–8
Pannonia 8
Pansophius, Bishop of Nicodemia 192
Pantaenus 51
Paternos (anti-Johnite priest) 231
Patrikios (lawyer) 219
Paul, Bishop of Heraklea 187, 189, 208
Paul, St 43, 55, 135–6, 143
Paul of Samosata 26, 55
Paulinus 44, 44–5, 64, 65, 83

Pentadia (deaconess)   223
Perpetua, St   35
persecution, of early Christians   20, 35, 52, 55, 125
Peter, Bishop of Alexandria   27, 47–8, 52, 53, 82
Pharetrius, Bishop of Caesarea   221
Philo of Alexandria   50
Phokas (martyr)   126
Photinus of Sirmium   5–6, 31–2
Pityus (Pisunda)   228, 237
Plato/Platonism   26, 50, 192–3, 196
Plotinus   51, 195–6
Porphyrius, Bishop of Antioch   219, 237
Praxeas   23
Prayer Book (1662)   243
Proba (widow of S. Claudius Probus)   224
Proclus, Bishop of Constantinople   240
Procopius   12
Ptolemies   49–50
Pulcheria (daughter of Eudoxia)   178, 232–3, 240

Quartodecimans   191–2

Ramsey, Michael   70
Ravenna   233, 236
relics   125–6
Rimini, Council of (359)   32–3, 57
Roman Catholicism   58
Romanos the Melodist   145
Rome
  authority of the popes   56
  Constantine consolidates Christianity in   54
  delegation to Constantinople   236
  diminished importance of   53–4
  doctrinal disputes in   55–8
Rufinus   36, 63, 177, 233

Sabellianism   23–4, 31, 44, 64
Sapor (Persian leader)   9, 14
Saturninus (military general)   173
Seleucia, Council of (359)   9, 33, 57
Seleukos I Nikator   42

Septimus Severus, Emperor   45
Serapion, Archdeacon   178–9, 188, 204
Serdica, Council of (343)   31, 56–7
Severian, Bishop   178–81, 188, 193, 200, 208, 210, 214, 217, 219, 237
Severus, Emperor   20
sexual abstinence   135–41
sexuality, early Church teaching on   134–45
Shepherd of Hermas (book)   136–7
Simon Stylites   77
simony   190–2
Simplicius (prefect)   215
Siricus, Pope   127
Sirmium (or "Dated") Creed (359)   32–3
Sirmium, Council of
  (351)   5–6, 13, 31–2
  (357)   57
Sisinnius, Bishop (Novatianist)   127–8, 192
slavery   150–8
Socrates (church historian)   10, 179, 180–1, 190, 191, 197, 205
Sozomen (church historian)   6, 103, 117–18, 122, 124, 129, 205, 209, 210, 214, 215, 217, 232
Spirit-fighters   57–8, 95
Spurgeon, Charles Haddon   112
Stilicho (Gothic military commander)   169, 172, 233, 236, 237
Symmachus (senator)   152
Synkletius of Thrace   187

Tall Brothers (Egyptian monks)   195–202, 207–8
Tertullian   22, 23, 55–6, 86, 95, 137, 141–5
Thecla of Iconium   139
Theodore, Bishop of Mopsuestia   63, 74–6
Theodoret of Kyrrhos   67–8, 130
Theodosian Code   4, 133
Theodosius I, Emperor   15–16, 34, 44, 65, 82–3, 104, 108–9, 115–17, 215

Theodosius II, Emperor   4, 116, 118,
    178, 188, 205, 233, 239, 240
Theodotus, Bishop of Antioch   239
Theophilus, Bishop of Alexandria
    and the appointment of John as
        Bishop of Constantinople   117,
        127, 185–6
    campaign against John Chrysostom
        205–8, 216–17
    destruction of the library of
        Alexandria   53, 201
    presides at the Council of the Oak
        208
    returns to Alexandria   214
    and the Tall Brothers   195–203
Theotimus, Bishop of Scythia   203–4
Toledo, Council of (589)   129
Tribigild (Gothic leader)   173
Trinity, and the Arian controversy   23–5
Tyre, Council of (335)   30, 47

Ulfilas, Bishop   81, 129, 174

Valens, Emperor   13, 13–14, 46, 81–2
Valentinian I, Emperor   5, 13
Valentinian II, Emperor   16, 116
Valentinus   22, 55
Vasianalla (wife of Roman general)   224
Vetranio   5
Visigoths   128

Wadi Qumran documents (Dead Sea
    Scrolls)   135
Williams, Rowan   24, 29

Zenobia, Queen of Palmyra   26
Zephyrinus   24
Zosimus (historian)   175, 177

PATRICK WHITWORTH, *having completed an MA in History at Oxford and in Reformation Studies at Durham, has served for nearly 50 years in Anglican ministry. He has written five books on Early Church history, including* Three Wise Men from the East: The Cappadocian Fathers and the Struggle for Orthodoxy, *and* Defining God: Athanasius, Nicaea and The Trinitarian Controversy of the Fourth Century *(all published by Sacristy Press). He is married to Olivia, and they have four married children and nine grandchildren.*

EU GPSR Authorized Representative:

LOGOS EUROPE, 9 rue Nicolas Poussin, 17000 La Rochelle, France

contact@logoseurope.eu